An author of walking and travel books, Peter Caton has walked on Dartmoor for almost sixty years. He has an extensive knowledge of the moors, their history, legends and many places of interest.

Cover photo – Looking to Great Mis Tor from the slopes of North Hessary Tor

Vixen Tor, Dartmoor

DARTMOOR

ENGLAND'S LAST WILDERNESS?

Peter Caton

Copyright © 2024 Peter Caton

The moral right of the author has been asserted.

Apart from any fair dealing for the purposes of research or private study, or criticism or review, as permitted under the Copyright, Designs and Patents Act 1988, this publication may only be reproduced, stored or transmitted, in any form or by any means, with the prior permission in writing of the publishers, or in the case of reprographic reproduction in accordance with the terms of licences issued by the Copyright Licensing Agency. Enquiries concerning reproduction outside those terms should be sent to the publishers.

Troubador Publishing Ltd
Unit E2 Airfield Business Park
Harrison Road, Market Harborough
Leicestershire LE16 7UL
Tel: 0116 279 2299
Email: books@troubador.co.uk
Web: www.troubador.co.uk

Maps produced by Location Maps Ltd

ISBN 978 1 80514 521 9

British Library Cataloguing in Publication Data.
A catalogue record for this book is available from the British Library.

Printed and bound by CPI Group (UK) Ltd, Croydon, CR0 4YY
Typeset in 10.5pt Sabon by Troubador Publishing Ltd, Leicester, UK

TO DAD – MICHAEL CATON

It was my father who introduced me to Dartmoor and to whom I owe my love of the moor. For more than sixty years he walked all over Dartmoor, recording each walk in notebooks, which I'm honoured to have in my possession.

Dad was a great campaigner for Dartmoor with the Dartmoor Preservation Association (DPA), for whom he set up a London Group in the late 1960s. He was very much involved in the battle to save the iconic Fox Tor Mire from a reservoir that would have ruined much of the moor. He led walks and took groups from London for day trips or weekends.

Dad often referred to Dartmoor as *'England's Last Wilderness'* and it was these words that were the inspiration for this book.

In 2018 Dad published a book, *Walks on Dartmoor Paths and Trackways*, which describes routes on paths and tracks, some of which may not have been recorded elsewhere. He considered it an important achievement to have documented these for current and future generations.

Dad died peacefully on 25th March 2023, a day after we'd celebrated his 88th birthday with him. He was pleased that I was travelling to Devon and planning a walk from Okehampton station the next day, railways being another of his great loves. When I heard the next morning that he'd died in the night it seemed appropriate that I should still go to Dartmoor, but I changed my plans and repeated a walk to Spurrell's Cross that I'd first visited with Dad in 1969. It was a sad day but the right place to remember the person who enthused me about the most wonderful place that is Dartmoor.

The author is always pleased to hear from readers through his website:

www.petercatonbooks.co.uk
Facebook   Peter Caton Books

CONTENTS

Introduction			xi
PART 1	MISHAPS ON THE MOOR		1
	1	Enroute to Wild Tor	3
	2	The Butter Brook	7
	3	Minor Mishaps & Near Misses	12
PART 2	DEFINING WILDERNESS		19
	4	Defining Wilderness	21
PART 3	THREE WALKS FROM RAILWAY STATIONS		29
	5	Okehampton	31
	6	Buckfastleigh	38
	7	Ivybridge	45
PART 4	FOUR PREHISTORIC REMAINS		51
	8	Stalldown Stone Row	53
	9	The Grey Wethers	62
	10	Corringdon Ball Burial Chamber	67
	11	Black Pool	73
PART 5	DARTMOOR TORS		79
	12	Great Mis Tor	81
	13	Leighon Tors	88
	14	Vixen Tor	93
PART 6	THREE DARTMOOR WOODS		103
	15	Piles Copse	105
	16	Bellever Forest	111
	17	Fatherford Wood	117

PART 7	THREE REMOTE HOUSES	125
18	Nun's Cross Farm	127
19	Brown's House	133
20	Bleak House	140

PART 8	FOUR BATTLES TO SAVE THE MOOR	147
21	Swincombe	149
22	Meldon	155
23	High House Waste	162
24	Area Y	170

PART 9	TWO DARTMOOR VILLAGES	177
25	Grimspound	179
26	Hound Tor Medieval Village	183

PART 10	TWO DARTMOOR CHURCHES	189
27	St Leonard's Church Sheepstor	191
28	Huntingdon Chapel	197

PART 11	TWO WALKS EXPLORING INDUSTRIAL ARCHAEOLOGY	205
29	Sourton Tors Ice Works	207
30	Powdermills	213

PART 12	THREE DARTMOOR RAILWAYS	217
31	Haytor Granite Tramway	219
32	Rowtor Target Railway	225
33	The Princetown Railway	230

PART 13	DARTMOOR GORGES & WATERFALLS	237
34	Steeperton Gorge	239
35	Lydford Gorge	245
36	Shavercombe Waterfall	248
37	Becky Falls	252

PART 14	IN SEARCH OF WILDERNESS	257
38	Black Lane & Crane Hill	259

39	Knattabarrow Pool	265
40	North Hessary Tor	268
41	Eylesbarrow & Plym Ford	272
42	Cut Hill	276
43	Ryder's Hill, Great Mis Tor, East Mill Tor & Ugborough Beacon	286
PART 15	**WILDERNESS**	**291**
44	Rewilding	293
45	Wilderness?	301
46	England's Last Wilderness?	316
47	Reflections	320
Postscript		327
Bibliography		329

Thank you to my sister Sally and brother David for their help
and advice with the writing of this book.

INTRODUCTION

'England's Last Wilderness' – that's what Dad called Dartmoor, a phrase that's remained in the family for sixty years, along with *'Dartmoor pace'* and *'Food, drink, map, compass'*, his checklist that I still recite before every walk.

There seems little doubt that Dartmoor is a wild place, or at least that parts of it are, but is it a wilderness?

A visitor who only sees Haytor and Widecombe, as many do, might see it as a place of beauty and majesty, but perhaps not as wild as they'd imagined. Those who venture into the remote central core of the southern and northern moor will however discover what some describe as a barren, featureless, wilderness.

Dartmoor is however far from barren. It is rich in history and all across the moor are remains left by prehistoric settlers, industrial archaeology, remote dwellings and evidence of farming past and present. Natural beauty, both 'pretty' and 'raw', is provided by Dartmoor's hills and tors, its rivers, waterfalls and woodlands. Many legends are associated with the moor, some with maybe a grain of truth and others rather hard to believe. Dartmoor, a unique and truly magical place, is somewhere I have come to know and love in almost sixty years of walking.

In this book I have used a series of themed walks to explore Dartmoor's beauty, history, conflicts, stories and legends. I have discussed some of the many controversies resulting from conflicting demands on a moor where people live, work and farm, with natural resources that some wish to harvest but with so many antiquities to preserve and a unique environment to visit and enjoy. Four chapters focus on battles to save parts of Dartmoor. I've referred back to childhood walks which were recorded in my father's notebooks and repeated a few of these as part of my explorations for this book.

The book is quite varied, starting with stories of mishaps on the moor, then narratives of walks, some of which look for wilderness, and concluding with more technical chapters considering the question, is Dartmoor really, as many people claim, 'England's Last Wilderness'?

I have included both colour and monochrome photos which I hope provide further insight into the beauty, features and potential wilderness of Dartmoor. A few weren't taken at the time of the walks described but all record the moor as I saw it, so not always in the best weather for photography. Other than cropping, I don't believe in digitally altering photographs. Three photos were taken by my wife Debbie and one historic picture purchased online and reproduced with permission. A map on the centre pages shows the National Park with many of the places I visited marked.

A word about units. I have given distances in miles as these are still preferred by most walkers, hence to avoid mixing units I've used the traditional yards not metres. Otherwise I've stayed with whatever units my source stated, so as with the general usage of language, there is a mix of metric and imperial.

Names too are a bit of a mixture. Many places on Dartmoor have two or more versions of their name and the Ordnance Survey maps often don't show traditional or local names. Generally I have used the map versions but sometimes have preferred to stick to the old names which I've always used, such as Broadafalls (Broad Falls on OS maps).

Before moving on to the walks I should first introduce myself. My parents come from near Torquay and we've always visited Devon regularly, particularly in more recent years. My father first took me to Dartmoor at the age of six and on walks several times a year until my late teens. Since then I've walked widely on the moors, sometimes with my wife Deb, sometimes with our two boys, but mostly alone.

After selling my business in 2018 I took advice to invest the proceeds in property, buying a flat in Torquay which provides a base to visit Dartmoor. In 2022 I published my own walking guide, *Walks Discovering Lesser Known Dartmoor,* describing routes of varied length, and assisting walkers to discover the beauty, history and hidden places of what I described as, *'the wildest, most remote and arguably the most beautiful area in Southern England'*.

I've walked extensively on the coasts of Devon, Cornwall, Essex and Suffolk, visited forty-three tidal islands, forty of our most remote railway stations, climbed hills and mountains, but it is to Dartmoor where I most wish to return. It is in this wonderful and varied landscape that I feel most inspired. The fresh air, the solitude, the remoteness, the numerous antiquities and the beauty all add up to make Dartmoor, in my opinion, the most wonderful place in the whole of the country. But is it really England's Last Wilderness?

Wild Tor

PART I

MISHAPS ON THE MOOR

Having enjoyed many hundreds of Dartmoor walks it could only be expected that occasionally something would go wrong. Walking books often start with the standard safety advice but I have instead chosen to commence with some examples of days when mishaps were or could have been encountered.

Generally I've been fortunate. I've stepped in many a bog but never sunk below a knee. There have been a few incidents with cows but either I've managed to skirt round them, or found that the hard stares and threatening moos weren't backed up by aggressive action. I've got very wet and sometimes cold, but never to the point of risking hypothermia. It would be untrue to claim that I've never made a navigational error, especially in thick mist but whilst I've occasionally found myself to be not quite where expected, I've never got seriously lost. There have however been two walks where I was fortunate to be able to get off the moor under my own steam and quite a few minor mishaps along the way.

Chapter One

ENROUTE TO WILD TOR

The plan was for a simple walk to Wild Tor. Deb dropped me by the moor gate at Scorhill Farm, then returned down the narrow winding lanes to Chagford. She was to swim in the lovely outdoor pool by the River Teign, then look round the village and pick me up after my walk. I nearly didn't return.

I followed the path through the strole, then headed right towards Sandy Ford. The route of the walk arced ahead in a magnificent panorama of Northern Dartmoor – Buttern Hill, Kennon Hill, Wild Tor, Watern Tor, with the unmistakeable Steeperton Tor behind them, all surrounding marshy valleys of the North Teign, Walla Brook and Gallaven Brook. This was wild Dartmoor and potentially wilderness.

At Sandy Ford I branched right to Buttern Hill Stone Circle, possibly the least visited of the arc of stone circles in this corner of Dartmoor. Although only five of the twenty-three stones are standing, some showing marks indicating that they have been worked by stone cutters, it is well worth seeing and a very quiet spot between the low hills of Buttern and Kennon.

Buttern Hill Stone Circle

The stone circle made a suitable stop for lunch but keen to get on I gobbled down my sandwich, then returning to Sandy Ford, picked up the main path once more. Climbing gently on the slopes of Kennon Hill I suddenly felt a slight ache in my chest. For a while I thought nothing of it, then decided it might be indigestion from rapid consumption of the sandwich. Continuing, I started to feel unwell and a bit short of breath. I sat down by the path. Was this a cause for alarm? What should I do?

There was no phone signal. I walked on a few yards, hoping there might be a signal as I climbed and that maybe I'd feel better. I didn't. I felt worse. I really wanted advice and the reassurance of company but few people walk on this bit of Dartmoor. I'd heard two men pass when I was eating lunch. Would they come back? I lay down for a while, the objections I'd made to new mobile phone masts on the moor crossing my mind. I've since registered my phone to allow 999 messages by text which might just have got through.

I had plenty of clothes and a survival blanket in my rucksack but on the one occasion it might have been needed, had forgotten to pack a whistle. It was three hours before Deb was due to pick me up and longer before her concern at my non-arrival would merit calling for help. Here I was, alone on the moors, maybe in need of help but with no way of letting anyone know.

After an hour I felt no better and brooding clouds suggested that the forecast rain might be on its way. I decided I had to walk back.

Slowly, stopping regularly, I returned to Sandy Ford. This was downhill and I managed it without too much difficulty. The next section was uphill. I felt quite ill now but with still no phone signal or other walkers, had to carry on. Slower, with more frequent stops, and considering dumping my rucksack, I climbed what is only really a gentle slope on Gidleigh Common. The slight ache became a pain as I ascended but I made it to the top and at last a phone signal. Fortunately Deb was out of the pool and answered the call. She would come back to pick me up. I messaged my sister who told me to go to A&E. It seemed that a heart problem was a real possibility but now close to the edge of the moor, rather than call 999, I felt it would be as quick to get Deb to collect me. Maybe not the best decision in retrospect but in a stressful situation we don't always make the correct call.

By the top of the strole I was really struggling but it was only a couple of hundred yards to the gate. A family walking towards Scorhill Circle saw me standing hands on knees, but they didn't come to me and I didn't call them. I reached the gate first and lay on the grass. A lady walked by, we said hello, but I didn't let on that I might be having a heart attack. Deb had been parked by the medical centre in Chagford and we decided to go there for help. The lanes are so slow and winding that if an ambulance was needed I'd get it sooner by driving down to the village. Several times we had to back to pass cars but eventually reached the car park and considering it a possible emergency, parked in the only free space, one marked reserved.

Deb went inside and the receptionist explained that both doctors were out on calls. Call 999 she said, so we did. Soon a man came along and told us we were in his reserved doctor's space. He looked a bit cross but seemed to understand when the circumstances were explained. After looking at me he must have realised that I was quite ill and told me to wait while he got a wheelchair. Despite walking 1½ miles off the moor he didn't want me to walk the few yards into the surgery.

The doctor quickly decided that I was probably having a heart attack. I was given a magic spray under my tongue and a soluble aspirin, which promptly caused me to vomit on the surgery floor. Not only had I stolen the doctor's parking place, usurped his waiting patients but now he had to clear up sick. Fortunately he was a kindly man and a serious Dartmoor walker, so we chatted quietly until the ambulance arrived.

Once on board I was wired up to an ECG and we followed Deb along the lanes. On the A30 the paramedic calmly advised that the hospital had examined the ECG, that I was having a heart attack and they were to take me straight to the Cardiac Unit at Royal Devon & Exeter Hospital. The ambulance accelerated, blue lights now flashing and overtook my now even more concerned wife. Covid rules meant that she couldn't come with me, so could just drive back to Torquay and wait for news.

The time saved by blue lights and sirens through Exeter's rush hour traffic was lost by the paramedics taking me to the wrong part of the hospital (apparently the Cardiac Unit had moved) but within minutes I was in the

Cath Lab, surrounded by medical staff. A stent was fitted and I was told that as a reasonably fit man of 59 I was unfortunate to have had a heart attack (family history seemed to be the problem), but very fortunate not to have been incapacitated and unable to walk off the moor. I'm extremely grateful to all those who looked after me and that I'm still able to walk on the moors. Now I carry an emergency satellite beacon.

Chapter Two

THE BUTTER BROOK

It should have been a straightforward walk. It wasn't! Not long before completing *Walks Discovering Lesser Known Dartmoor* it had become apparent that Harford Moor car park was likely to remain closed for some time. An alternative route was required and the nearest good-sized parking area is Ivybridge, from where there are various routes onto the moor. I chose the picturesque path alongside the River Erme.

Arriving by train, I followed the road into Ivybridge, soon passing Stowford Mills, a paper mill from 1787 to 2013 and now being transformed into homes, offices, retail units and restaurants. It's tempting to take a short cut through the site and use their private bridge over the Erme but choosing not to trespass I crossed on the humpback bridge downstream – the original Ivy Bridge.

The wooded path on the west bank of the Erme makes a delightful walk at all times of the year. Summer sunlight enlivens the river's cascades, winter torrents show us the water's power and autumn brings spectacular colours.

The path soon passes far below the eight-span Ivybridge Railway Viaduct, built in 1893 to the design of Sir James Inglis. It replaced Brunel's original 1848 viaduct when the line was converted from broad gauge. Six piers from Brunel's bridge remain but the timber decking is long gone.

Not far beyond here are the remains of a reservoir which was built in 1874 to supply clean water to Ivybridge. It was constructed inside the ancient stone walls of a pound once used to enclose sheep being taken to and from the high moor. No longer required when Butter Brook Reservoir was established in 1914, it was converted to a swimming pool in the 1920s. Changing facilities and a diving board were constructed and many children learnt to swim here.

The pool was used by the people of Ivybridge until the 1960s and has now been partly filled in, however the old plug mechanism can still be seen.

After stopping to eat lunch on a rock beside the river, saving a cake for later, I followed the path as it becomes steeper, moves away from the river and eventually comes out on the lane opposite Hall Farm. At Harford village I considered options for my return route then set off up the lane to Harford Moor, not expecting to see the village again that day.

I stopped at the car park for a while, confirming train times and my choice of route and speaking to a couple who I'd met earlier by Harford Bridge. They were heading for the Redlake Tramway and planned to wild camp. I corrected their choice of path then set off down the hill to the Butter Brook. After a quick walk around the well-preserved hut circles just below the now disused reservoir, I looked for the best place to cross. It's usually easy in summer when the water is low but can be more difficult in winter. In late September I hadn't anticipated problems but the stepping stones at the ford were covered. Wary of slipping on wet rocks I walked downstream, soon selecting a place to jump the stream. It wasn't a big leap and I thought little of it as I took off. Well, 'took off' is perhaps an exaggeration. Seconds later I was descending - horizontally, my legs above the stream and my face rapidly approaching a rock. A simple error – I hadn't checked the ground and was pushing off from a boggy section of bank. My foot slipped and with no purchase I simply fell flat.

Oh bother, I thought as I landed. This wasn't one of the occasional trips on the moor from which one gets up without another thought. There were consequences. My leg hurt. It was still in the stream. My nose hurt – a lot. It had landed with force on the rock. Somewhat dazed I extracted myself from the water. Then I realised that not only did my thumb also hurt but that it wouldn't move at all. A hanky revealed copious amounts of blood emanating from both the outside and inside of my nose. This was going to require a trip to hospital.

Still rather shocked I considered the options. No one was about. Should I take the direct route across the moor or return to Harford and back to Ivybridge down the lane? I don't think I was really able really to think it

The Butter Brook

through thoroughly but perhaps conscious that walking alone on the moor after a bang on the head, with a hurt leg and a bleeding nose, wasn't the best idea, I headed back to Harford. First the Butter Brook had to be crossed – easily done on the stepping stones. Why didn't I do that first time? Wet feet was a small price to pay.

I sat down on a log opposite Harford church to review the situation. My nose was still bleeding, both my hankies were blood-soaked, my leg was bleeding and my thumb probably broken. My 'first aid kit' consisted of a couple of small plasters. I was still two miles from Ivybridge station.

Then a car pulled up and two young ladies got out. They stopped at the bleeding man sitting on the log. Ella and Katie, my rescuers, had arrived. I asked if they could tell me how bad my nose looked. Katie took a photo to show me. It had a hole in it! Ella knocked at a house and a kind lady came back with her carrying first aid supplies. Ice was applied to my thumb and dressings on my nose and leg. A ride to the station was offered. What a relief.

We chatted in the car, although I hope that in my slightly shocked state I made sense. They were both dancers with a Christian dance company. So friendly, kind and such characters. There was an hour to wait for the train and it was cold. I was still a bit shaky. After a couple of minutes a train came the other way and on an impulse I told the guard I'd had an accident so could I could stay warm by riding to Plymouth and catching the train back from there? He was happy, as was the guard on the train back to Newton Abbot. It was only on seeing my face in the toilet mirror that I realised the accident was obvious. Blood was still seeping through the bandage on my nose. After eating the cake saved from earlier I felt a bit better. Cake is good for shock I decided.

With a long queue for taxis I walked the mile to Newton Abbot Hospital. By now my thumb was very painful but still wouldn't move. I was sure it was broken. The nurse said no. An X-ray said yes. With a splint on my thumb, dressing on my leg and sutures holding my nose together, I was sent on my way.

A few days later the orthopaedic doctor told me it wasn't a bad break and should be better in four to six weeks. Six weeks later he admitted that was optimistic. A V-shaped crack was healing but a piece of bone had been

Hut Circle near Butter Brook

chipped off and hadn't re-joined. Three months later it still hadn't. With physiotherapy the thumb would move but that soon wore off. Now he said it would take a year. Physio continued and after six months, if warm and with a bit of massage, it would move about 45 degrees. After a year it still wouldn't move any further. An operation was possible but advice was that scar tissue may well make it worse. I had been permanently injured by a Dartmoor stream.

I've kept in touch with Ella and Katie. 'Dartmoor Rescuers' is how they head their emails and very grateful to them I am. Lessons have been learned. I now carry a first aid kit and am far more cautious. No longer do I leap before I look. In fact I try not to leap at all.

A few weeks after the incident I met a couple of Dartmoor Rescue volunteers on the slopes of Ger Tor and when I skipped over a bog as we walked was told that they advise against jumping anywhere. I'd never thought of this before but it's good advice. Once leaping through the air all control is lost and as I found, it's very easy to slip or fall. I had been fortunate that all my previous little falls had avoided rocks. Now when I cross a stream I plan where each footstep will be placed. No longer do I bound across the moor. I take it gently, often having to tell myself to slow down, remembering that I'm in my sixties not twenties. That split second error at the Butter Brook has certainly made me think. It could so easily have been a broken leg not just a thumb and I could have been lying in the stream for hours. It could have happened not at the edge of the moor but in a remote spot with no phone signal. Perhaps we all need a warning to slow down. This was my second.

Chapter Three

MINOR MISHAPS & NEAR MISSES

In almost sixty years of Dartmoor walking the odd little mishap is to be expected. Fortunately most walkers manage to avoid heart attacks and broken bones but we've probably all experienced more minor problems or near misses. Lessons can be learned nearly every time.

I'll start with a foolish action that could have had serious consequences. In sub-zero temperatures on a January morning I set out from Princetown to the Crock of Gold burial chamber on Royal Hill, with the intention to make a circular walk, returning via South Hessary Tor. Turning right beyond the end of the Conchie Way, a track built by First World War conscientious objectors, I followed the path towards Whiteworks above the River Swincombe. With the sun shining and the ground frozen it made for good walking and all was well until I reached the bogs around the Strane River. Here the icy ground wasn't so helpful. There was no way of knowing whether on each step my foot would stay above the frozen surface, or break through the solid crust, immersing it in freezing bog. Seeking better ground I veered to the right, a poor decision. The 1:50,000 Ordnance Survey map shows the area as marsh but my larger scale version doesn't – one of many OS anomalies. The going was rough and every time my feet couldn't balance on the tufts of grass they slipped into the freezing mire between. It wasn't pleasant walking but I reached the stream.

The path crosses at a ford but having made my own way a suitable place to jump had to be found. I paced up and down. The water was fast-flowing, quite deep and very cold. I didn't fancy falling in. After perhaps fifteen minutes consideration of possible spots a decision had to be made. Go for the leap or turn back. I really didn't want to trudge back through all those bogs, so took my rucksack off, thinking that if I threw this over first the jump would be easier. But I didn't throw it. I'd be committed then – plus it might fall in itself. Then I found a spot with a large rock on the far bank. I'd have to land on this and make sure I fell forward and not back into the icy water. I still wasn't sure. The consequence of falling into such cold water with no one nearby didn't bear thinking about. But I did, and so I didn't jump.

As I stood on the bank two lads, probably in their late teens, approached on the path the other side. A path that runs close to the stream but doesn't cross it here I might add. They could see my predicament and offered a solution. Throw the rucksack then jump and one of them would give me a hand. I could hardly say no to their kindness. The rucksack made it safely over. Now I was committed. I jumped, grabbing the lad's outstretched hand but with my weight pulling me back towards the icy water. I was helpless, entirely in the hands (or more precisely hand) of this young stranger. It took a few seconds for him to steady, then he pulled me up. Such relief. It had probably been harder than we'd both envisaged and in retrospect foolhardy would seem to be an appropriate adjective.

As well as the Butter Brook and heart attack, Dartmoor has sent me to hospital on one other occasion. I'd walked from Cross Furzes to Broadafalls on the River Avon and was wandering around the falls when my foot disappeared into a hole, resulting in a sharp pain in my knee. I'd already

Broadafalls

established that there was no phone signal, so it was with some relief that I extricated the leg and found I could still walk on it. In fact it barely hurt so I set off back down the river thinking little more of the incident.

Walking over Lambs Down I became aware of a bit of an ache, then moderate pain but it didn't seem much to be concerned about. Deb met me at Cross Furzes but an hour later, on exiting the car in Torquay I could no longer walk. My leg wouldn't take any weight and I needed a stick to get back into the hotel. A trip to hospital would be required but not until dinner had been consumed, lest there be a long wait and hunger ensued. An X-Ray showed that all the bones were OK but I'd damaged my cruciate ligament, just like footballers do but they tend to suffer the injury on the pitch not down a rabbit hole in a National Park. Recovery with physio took a few weeks but I was soon fit, if not for the World Cup, at least back to Dartmoor walking, now with a little more care.

Anyone who walks regularly on Dartmoor will have encountered mist. I try to avoid the more remote parts of the moor if the weather forecast suggests poor visibility but of course the forecast isn't always right. Nevertheless, I can only recall a few instances where Dartmoor's notorious mist has caused to me to make what I'll call 'a navigational error'. One I will include as an example of how easy it is to go the wrong way in Dartmoor mist.

I walked from Ivybridge to a ford on the Lud Brook below Creber's Rock, before considering that it was too wet to continue and deciding to return by the same route. On the way I'd found Butterdon Hill Long Barrow, a Neolithic burial chamber, which isn't easy to locate. It was only discovered in fairly recent years and there's not a great deal to see but I managed to find it again on the way back. By now the mist was very thick but I knew that a path downhill led to a wall by Cuckoo Ball Burial Chamber and all I had to do was hit the wall and turn right. The wall is due south and a quick check of the compass would have ensured I was heading the right way. But I didn't. I followed a path downhill and after a while wondered why I hadn't reached the wall. This was my second mistake. If in doubt stop. Don't plough on in hope. I was on a path heading downhill, could see maybe 25 yards ahead, so surely at any moment out of the mist would appear a stone wall. No - instead out of the gloom appeared a pool – Black Pool. A place I know well so fortunately I immediately identified where it was. I should have walked 300 yards due south. I'd actually gone 840 yards south-west. Even though I had a compass and had a feeling something was wrong, I still made the error. In this case I could continue to the Redlake tramway and follow this off the moor so all was well, but what if I'd been out in the wilderness? With no points of reference one can easily walk in completely the wrong direction and become lost on the moor.

I am shall we say, a little apprehensive about cows. Twice being chased by herds on the Essex coast and having to vault fences to escape is I think quite a reasonable justification. Watching too many episodes of air ambulance programmes where stoical Yorkshire farmers stagger home with broken bones after being crushed by their animals might be another. Reading of incidents where people have been badly hurt on Dartmoor would seem to further justify any concern (OK fear) but perhaps worrying about the way they moo and look at us is less rational.

Some years ago I was walking along the path beside the stone wall east of Fox Tor Mire, on my way to Childe's Tomb and Duck's Pool when ahead of me appeared a herd of cows. Normally I would divert around them but one

Huntingdon Clapper

side was the wall and the other very rough, boggy ground. I carried on and as they do, the cows stopped whatever they were doing (eating of course – do they do anything else?) and stared. Some people find their big stary eyes endearing. I view them as threatening. Then they started to move, closing in on me and just in case I was thinking of curtailing my walk to get away, two stood right behind me to cut off my escape. I was left with three choices. Stay still and hope they'd get bored, carry on and hope they chose not to savage me, or climb over the wall.

Conscious that Dartmoor walkers have been seriously injured by cows and having recently read of a 'troublesome' herd near Nun's Cross Farm, I chose the last, finding a way up the drystone wall. This is not something that is recommended, either for the safety of the wall or climber, but nor is getting squashed by cows. Once on the top I found that the drop the other side was greater and it wasn't going to be easy to descend. The cows were still watching very closely, no doubt looking for any opportunity to pounce. Hence anyone watching from afar would have seen the strange site of a man walking along on top of a drystone wall, observed by a herd of vicious cows, their moos almost certainly a conversation as to whether they should try to butt him off.

There's a fine line between over-ambition, unpreparedness and recklessness. Let's put the next tale down to over-ambition.

My first visit to the iconic Fur Tor, Dartmoor's most remote tor, was on 25th August 1972. I was eleven. Dad's notebook records the walk:

Fur Tor with Peter. Weather sunny rather hot, some breeze.
Bus to Rundlestone. Walked to Fur Tor via Fitz Well (clapper nearby) along track to where track petered out. Crossed Blackbrook, Cocks Hill direct to Sandy Ford. (A better route would perhaps have been to follow the Prison Leat.) Then across Walkham, over Sandy Ford and along right bank of Walkham to bend below Walkham Head & on to Tavy Hole. (Did not find Phillpotts Peat Pass). Then direct to Fur Tor. Back to Tavy Hole then to Phillpotts Peat Pass – stone marking entrance to pass to right above head of gulley. Through peat pass then above Walkham to Cocks Hill. Kept well above river & on to Longstone (tea). Then along

leat to Roos & Staple Tors to main road. Walked towards Tavistock – got lift at top of Pork Hill to Tavistock.
Total time from leaving bus to lift 6½ hours.

What Dad didn't put in his notebook was that the walk had been too ambitious. On a hot day we walked about 14 miles, much of it across rough and hilly ground. Part way back he realised there was no hope of getting the last bus from Princetown, so we'd have to walk to Tavistock. Hence the westerly diversion via Roos and Staple Tors. Nor did he mention that the lift wasn't part of the plan. As I trailed behind, Dad resorted to waving his thumb at passing cars and a kindly couple soon stopped. They dropped us in Tavistock and we caught a bus to Plymouth for the eight thirty train to Newton Abbot. The next one left at midnight so without the lift we'd have had a very late night. Mum wouldn't have been happy!

I took Deb, my then wife to be, to Dartmoor for the first time in 1981. We were ill-prepared. We hadn't planned to go walking but on finding that the steam train from Paignton wasn't running decided to go to the moors. We bought a map in Buckfastleigh, parked at Cross Furzes and walked past Huntingdon Warren to the River Avon. Our objective was Broadafalls but as we walked a large dark cloud approached down the valley. We continued to Huntingdon Clapper at which point the heavens opened. Dressed for a steam train ride and day in Dartmouth, we didn't even have waterproofs. Fortunately the cloud remained reasonably high (I didn't have a compass) but we were soaked to the skin after the three mile walk back to the car. We hadn't been going out together for long and Deb was a little shocked when I took off my wet trousers, driving back to Torquay in underpants.

Deb came to the moor again, unlike Mum, who said she'd never go back to Dartmoor after she and Dad missed the train at Shaugh Bridge Halt and had to call out my grandfather to pick them up from Newton Abbot at one in the morning. Dad hadn't helped the situation by saying what a wonderful sight the little train made as it puffed down the valley, leaving them stranded on the moor and it wasn't for about twenty years that Mum relented.

Only in one other place has a walking mishap sent me to hospital (although a couple of tumbles down Essex sea walls might easily have done so). That necessitated a trip to Broadford Hospital on Skye, thanks to a kind castle owner, a tale that's told in *Remote Stations*. I'm definitely more careful now, probably partly as a result of advancing years and partly lessons learned from mishaps. When I updated *No Boat Required* I decided that some of the tidal islands I'd visited twelve years earlier were no longer safe to walk to. The islands hadn't changed but my perception of the risk of walking near quicksand or climbing down cliffs had altered.

I'm now much more cautious on Dartmoor, trying to avoid bad weather, going over-equipped rather than under, staying well within my limitations and assessing risks. My advice to fellow walkers, should they want it, is to start taking care before rather than after you've an accident. A sign at Reading railway station sums this up – *'Don't Learn Safety by Accident'*. Unfortunately I did!

PART 2

DEFINING WILDERNESS

Chapter Four

DEFINING WILDERNESS

This is quite a technical chapter considering definitions. It is important if we are to decide whether Dartmoor is wilderness but I won't be offended if anyone chooses to skip the chapter and move on to the walks. It will however be helpful to read the definition in bold at the end of the chapter.

So is Dartmoor *'England's Last Wilderness'*? In order to decide it will first be necessary to consider the definitions of wilderness. Here are just a few:

Collins Dictionary: *A wilderness is a desert or other area of natural land which is not used by people.*

Cambridge Dictionary: *An area of land that has not been used to grow crops or had towns and roads built on it, especially because it is difficult to live in as a result of its extremely cold or hot weather or bad earth.*

Wikipedia: *Wilderness or wildlands are natural environments on Earth that have not been significantly modified by human activity or any nonurbanized land not under extensive agricultural cultivation.*

Oxford Languages: *An uncultivated, uninhabited, and inhospitable region.*

Oxford Reference: *An area which has generally been affected more by natural forces than by human agency; a region little affected by people. An area devoid of human habitation, cultivation, or significant use.*

Macmillan Dictionary: *An area of land where people do not live or grow crops and where there are no buildings.*

To consider it further, I found four more dictionary definitions and listed the key words in all ten. Six words or phrases (or their similes) were included in at least 20% of the definitions:

Uncultivated (or not extensively cultivated)	70%
Undeveloped (or largely undeveloped)	60%
Uninhabited (or sparsely inhabited)	40%
Natural	30%
Not used by people	20%
Wild	20%

Our Essex home is two minutes' walk from the countryside. Most of this is used for arable farming but closest to home is a well-managed nature reserve that was once a brickworks. A strip of land between this and houses is privately owned and has been abandoned for probably seventy years. Inevitably there have been proposals to build on it but so far these have been fought off. When not in Devon I walk through it several times a week and one night it struck me that this small piece of land, roughly 330 by 130 metres, meets many of the criteria for wilderness. In fact it meets almost all the main dictionary definitions: natural, uncultivated, undeveloped, not used by humans (other than to walk through) and no one lives on it. The land was last cultivated in World War Two and after being left to nature most of it is now dense scrub, with some well-established trees, a marshy area, a path and a few open glades. It is arguable whether historical cultivation rules it out but other than this according to the definitions the land could easily be described as wilderness.

If this small piece of land adjacent to houses is wilderness, then I may as well stop now as the question has been answered. There are countless similar areas across the country, so Dartmoor could not be England's last wilderness. On the assumption that most people would not consider this little patch of Essex to be a wilderness we need a broader definition.

Hence I sought further opinions. An eclectic mix of people in my address book were sent an email asking them to give three words which they would use to describe what is meant by wilderness. The 51 replies gave 72 different words, shown here in order of frequency with very similar words grouped together.

13	Nature, Natural, Nature in charge
12	Wild, Untamed
11	Remote, Far from civilisation, Isolated
7	Few residents, Unpopulated, Uninhabited, No humans nearby
6	Barren, Empty
6	Untouched, Limited trace of human hand, Minimal human impact
6	Peaceful, Peace, Quiet
5	Large, Big, Huge, Vast
5	Uncultivated, Agriculture-free
4	Solitude, Solitary
4	Spiritual, Holiness, Genesis 28.16
3	Desolate, Desolation
2	Savage / Fierce, Undeveloped / Unmanaged, Freedom, Raw, Open, Lonely, Wildlife, Uncharted
1	Ecosystem undisturbed, Pre-human, Escape, Biota, Outdoors, Discernment, Bewildering, Abandoned, Forest, Precious, Dry, Unspoilt, Primaeval, Lifeless, Wildflowers, Inspiring, Desert, Beautiful, Full-sky, Challenging, Abundant, Windswept, Beyond, Boundless, Rugged

Whilst, as one would expect, there is significant overlap, there are also some major differences between the two sets of words. Most notably:

70% of dictionary definitions included 'uncultivated' but only 10% of email respondents, although some of the other words given would imply that the land was not cultivated.

Whilst neither size nor remoteness were included in the dictionary definitions, remote or its synonyms was one of the most common words given by my respondents and size was stated by 10%.

Military intrusion on the slopes of Great Mis Tor

As perhaps would be expected, more evocative words such as peaceful, spiritual, solitude and desolate featured in the email responses but not dictionaries.

Untamed could be linked with untouched, undeveloped, undisturbed and uncultivated, and if these are all added together more than half the respondents gave words that include in the definition of wilderness that it is a place that has not been altered by humans. The top two words in dictionary definitions give this same characteristic, so it seems it is going to be a key element in our definition.

Returning to my little patch of Essex, it is questionable whether it can be described as wild, barren or lonely, it certainly isn't remote and is far from large. The land meets much of the dictionary definition but falls well short of the 'common' definition, suggesting that both need to be incorporated.

Finally, I looked at three wilderness organisations:

Wild Europe is a foundation which, *'promotes a coordinated strategy for protection and restoration of large natural ecosystem areas (wilderness and wetlands), addressing the threats and opportunities facing them'*. They build on the definition from IUCN (International Union for Conservation of Nature) and conclude:

'A wilderness is an area governed by natural processes. It is composed of native habitats and species, and large enough for the effective ecological functioning of natural processes. It is unmodified or only slightly modified and without intrusive or extractive human activity, settlements, infrastructure or visual disturbance.'

The Wilderness Society give virtually the same definition which they say that means:

'No human extraction e.g. hunting, logging, mineral extraction, mining, deadwood collection.
No human intervention e.g. disease or alien species control, restoration measures, permanent human infrastructure.
Open ended undefined natural dynamic processes.'

Keeping it simple, in their notes for school visits to the Grand Teton National Park, USA National Park Services say:

'A good definition of wilderness for young children is that of a place influenced by the forces of nature, where people visit, but do not live.'

Before settling on a definition it is worth considering what others have written:

Ray Bryant, a student at Virginia Commonwealth University, writing for *International Journal of Wilderness* adds some analysis:

'The wilderness is described as "an uncultivated, uninhabited, and inhospitable region." Uncultivated? Yes. Uninhabited? No. In fact, many Indigenous tribes and peoples live in harmony with the wilderness. Inhospitable? Absolutely wrong. Wilderness is everywhere. It is all the land with little to no human activity or modifications.'

A succinct definition came from Shahrar Ali, former Deputy Leader of the Green Party:

'Wilderness pertains to the wild, with limited trace of human hand or intervention.'

Alyssa Swartz, writing for the Wild Rockies Field Institute, gives her definition of wilderness, which she says draws on perspectives from both science and philosophy:

'A home to plants and animals that did not earn our respect, but simply deserve our respect through their existence. A natural area that allows humans to escape, find solitude, and practice mindfulness. A home and refuge that must be protected and fought for by the naturalists and passionate advocates, few in number, but strong in heart.'

It seems that the definition of wilderness is fluid, perhaps illustrated by the spread of answers and none of my fifty-one respondents giving the same three words. It will be hard to nail down a firm definition but something appropriate is needed to consider whether Dartmoor meets it. We could have two definitions, one from dictionaries and one from ordinary people but I'd prefer to keep it simple and talk round the edges as needs arise. The most common elements from the various sources can be built into a definition but I was left with one query – size. If there is no minimum size could any patch of undisturbed land be wilderness? On this basis I used the same wording that I'd included in *No Boat Required* for my definition of tidal islands – 'significant size'.

A wilderness is an area that is natural, uncultivated, undeveloped, little used or modified by human activity, and uninhabited or sparsely populated. It is commonly considered to be wild, remote, untamed and of significant size.

There is still plenty of room for delving further into the definition, and our question is not going to be easy to answer. A supplementary question also arises; is only part of Dartmoor wilderness?

The walks described in the following chapters took me all across Dartmoor, giving the opportunity to discuss, along with other issues, the various aspects as to whether the places I visited can be described as wilderness. In my final chapters I consider in more depth whether Dartmoor is indeed a wilderness and if so is it England's last?

PART 3

THREE WALKS FROM RAILWAY STATIONS

Encircled by two main lines and with various branches, Dartmoor was once well served by railways. Then a series of closures, starting with the Princetown branch in 1956 and ending with the Okehampton line in 1972, left just the main route to Plymouth skirting the National Park but even this lost all its local stations. No longer could one alight for a walk on the moor from the likes of Ingra Tor Halt, Lydford or South Brent and for many years Dartmoor was not served by rail at all but then the tide began to turn.

Ivybridge station reopened in 1994, providing a park and ride link to Plymouth, a train service for the much expanded town and access to Dartmoor. Although further from the town the new station is better placed to reach the moor. In 1997 a summer 'Sunday Rover' started to Okehampton, then in 2021 the line at last fully reopened, so walkers now had rail access to both sides of the moor.

Consideration is being given to reopening the whole of the old Southern Railway route beyond Okehampton through Lydford and Tavistock to Plymouth and with new stations opening across the country we may one day have other opportunities to access Dartmoor by train. For the moment we can be grateful to those who campaigned long and hard for Ivybridge and Okehampton and of course the South Devon Railway, which links Buckfastleigh with the main railway at Totnes.

Chapter Five

OKEHAMPTON

'The completion of the railway to Okehampton gives to tourists and excursionists the opportunity of visiting a most picturesque neighbourhood, and the valetudinarian may now easily reach the breezy heights of Dartmoor.'

Perhaps the word valetudinarian (I had to look it up – it means a person who is unduly anxious about their health) gives away that this quote refers not to the railway's reopening in 2021 but dates from its original construction in 1871. *Trueman's Exeter Flying Post* writer may have been surprised to know that 150 years later the station would have been closed, then reopened and that travellers would use it to walk on the moors regardless of their health concerns.

My first walk from Okehampton station was in August 1969 when aged eight my father took me to the Island of Rocks in the West Okement Valley. Two years later we walked to Cranmere Pool in the centre of Northern Dartmoor but that was my last walk from the station until Summer Sunday Specials started running in 1997. With regular trains recommencing in 2021 it was good to have another point of access to the moor that didn't require use of a car.

On an April Sunday morning the train from Exeter was busy and arriving at Okehampton quite a crowd were waiting to board for the return. The well-preserved station is painted in Southern Railway green commensurate with its history, as trains once arrived here from Waterloo. This part of Devon was Southern territory not Great Western.

Crossing the footbridge I turned up the lane, then took a permissive footpath through Station Wood, which was once part of Okehampton Castle deer park and contains a small reservoir that provided water for steam locomotives. Emerging from the wood the path crosses the A30 on a very high footbridge. This section of the road forms the National Park boundary but a few yards to the west it enters the Park. The road was built amidst great controversy, opening in 1988. My brother studied this as a student project and sat through all six hours of the parliamentary debate.

The issue wasn't so much should the road be built but whether it went through farmland north of the town, or into the National Park to the south. Farmers wanted to protect their land, whilst conservationists and walkers strongly opposed the incursion of a busy dual carriageway into the moor. Cornish MPs supported the southern route as it would improve road access to their county sooner, whilst others sought to protect the National Park. Conservationists suggested that to allow this incursion would act as a precedent, leading to more road building in other National Parks.

Most locals and holiday travellers wanted the annual traffic jams in Okehampton to be relieved as soon as possible and it was the shorter time required to build the road on Dartmoor that swayed the decision. What however was never explained was why only the southern route had been surveyed, meaning that this could be completed sooner and arguably pre-determining the outcome. Would it be controversial to suggest that this is a fine example of how 'the establishment' goes through the 'democratic process' but ensures that more often than not it gets its own way?

There were angry exchanges in the House of Commons when Nicholas Ridley, the Conservative Government's Secretary of State for Transport, made the announcement in July 1985. Labour MP Dr David Clark's words summed up the feelings of those who had fought to protect the moor:

> *'Does the Minister appreciate that, while we recognise the importance of jobs and the need for a bypass at Okehampton, his statement will be seen as shameful? He has come to the House on the last day of this term to make it and, for the sake of two years, he is prepared to desecrate one of our national parks. This is final proof of the Government's complete disregard of things environmental.'*

Bearing left to a gate, I then turned right along a track running beside a wall along East Hill, which in spring is a spectacular mass of bluebells. The track comes out on the road to Okehampton Camp which passes Fitz's Well, a natural spring beside the road. A low cross stands by the well which may have been moved here from St Michael's Chapel at nearby Halstock after it was destroyed during the Reformation.

It's said that a girl drinking from Fitz's Well on Easter Day will be married within a year, a story originating from a couple who became lost when pixies brought down mist on the moor. They knew that to drink from a clear spring would break their spell and on finding what was to become Fitz's Well quickly drank some of its fresh water. Immediately the mist lifted and they could see their way home. The grateful man erected a cross by the well, the waters of which were deemed to hold magical properties to determine a young lady's future.

Okehampton Camp is the army's main base on Dartmoor. It was built in 1893 but military activity on the moor goes back to the early 1800s when volunteers were recruited to train for defending England against Napoleon and guarding prisoners of war in Dartmoor Prison. Three ranges on the north and west of the moor are used for live firing and closed to the public on up to 120 days a year. Heavy artillery is no longer used, most activities being on foot, sometimes with parachute jumps, and it is ideal terrain to train for yomping across inhospitable countryside. Nevertheless, the military's use of the moor, which denies public access to a National Park, remains highly controversial. The army have to train somewhere and Dartmoor provides ideal terrain but should National Parks have unfettered access? The current compromise of live firing in three areas with dates advertised well in advance seems likely to continue for many years.

I am inclined to agree with the renowned Dartmoor author F.H. Starkey, who writes in *Dartmoor Then and Now* (1986):

'*I cannot understand how anyone, even a politician, can hope to reconcile the idea of a National Park, established with the purpose of caring for and making accessible to the public an area of outstanding natural beauty with the use of the area for battle training with live ammunition and explosives. The thing is a ridiculous anomaly; it has already lasted a hundred years too long and the sooner it ceases altogether the better'.*

Writing in Dartmoor News (March/April 2005) environmental campaigner Kate Ashbrook gave similar views:

'Dartmoor is a national park, and the military's activities conflict with the two purposes of national parks of conserving natural beauty and promoting understanding and enjoyment of their special properties. Northern Dartmoor which should be the wildest place in southern England, is besmirched with lookout huts, flagpoles and garishly coloured posts and notices, with tarmac roads carrying civilian vehicles far into the moor.'

The military roads on the moor are a further area of controversy. The public highway stops at a cattle grid by the Camp but roads continue ahead and to the right. When I was young these were tarmacked and extended almost to the centre of the northern moor. Then a policy of 'benign neglect' was agreed and most of the roads reverted to unmetalled tracks but more recently those closer to Okehampton have been resurfaced. Whilst the loop road that ran far into Dartmoor closed to cars in 2009, the roads still allow vehicles to drive some distance, park on the moor, add noise and visual pollution and detract from 'wilderness'. There is a slight frustration in walking an hour from the station only to find cars parked but on the other hand the roads allow people easy access to the National Park. I'm not the only person who won't use them on principle and before Okehampton station reopened always parked by the Camp, however for some visitors they may provide the only way to get onto this side of Dartmoor. As we will see in later chapters, the balance between access and wilderness is fraught with controversy.

I took the right fork, which runs close to the Moor Brook, then where the road bends left towards High Willhays went straight on along a stony track ascending Black Down. After half a mile a low straight bank crosses the track. This is the Black Down Military Target Railway, which runs directly in a line towards Yes Tor and is marked as a waterway on the OS Explorer map. The 960 metre straight north – south alignment was constructed in the late 19th century and its earthworks are well preserved. The earthworks of

West Mill Tor & Yes Tor

another later curved target railway can also be seen. The railways operated on a pulley system, with men-shaped silhouette targets on sledges hauled by stationary engines or horses. They closed around 1960.

Following the railway, a shallow pond is soon passed on the right. After a while it changes from a bank to a channel which once held a pipe taking water from the Red-a-ven Brook and leads to the little gem of Red-a-ven Dip. A small pool formed by damming the infant Red-a-ven Brook as it descends the valley between Yes Tor and West Mill Tor, this was once a reservoir for Okehampton Corporation Water Works. At no more than ten yards square the pool cannot have acted as more than a small supplement to the town's supply and may have been merely an extraction point, but it is marked on the 1940 OS map as a reservoir. Water was taken through a pipe running along the course of the railway to a filtration plant at Anthony Stile on the Okehampton Camp boundary. With a lone hawthorn tree standing above and water cascading over rocks, the tiny pool is a most attractive Dartmoor feature and arguably an example of human activity adding to the moor's beauty, whilst perhaps detracting from its wilderness characteristics.

My walk continued along a path on the right bank of the Red-a-ven Valley. Much care is needed here as the path is narrow and a slip could easily result in a fall to the river down the steep valley sides. In several places winter erosion had made the path more difficult but it's a route well worth following, looking down on the babbling brook (the Red-a-ven being officially a brook such an opportunity for alliteration cannot be allowed to pass). The stream flows over a series of cascades as the valley opens out into a grassy area with mountain ash trees by the water. This is another of Dartmoor's hidden gems and just as I was thinking that I'd rarely seen anyone walking through the gorge a couple with a dog appeared. We chatted for a while expressing our mutual appreciation of this little-known valley.

After half a mile of delightful walking a small stream comes in on the left through a dip beside Longstone Hill, after which the valley narrows again. Staying by the river, after stepping over the Mether Brook I reached a fenced, gorse-covered mound, a spoil heap around a shaft of Meldon Mine. The mine, which is also known as Devon Copper Mine and Okehampton Wheal Maria, was originally prospected for tin but found to contain worthwhile deposits of copper. It was last worked in the 1920s. Closer to the river is a rubble-filled wheel pit which today was clearly visible but on my last visit had been largely obscured by bracken.

Red-a-ven Dip

Turning right onto a grassy path I ascended Black Down, then walked beside a wall with a good view of Yes Tor, a superb panorama over North Devon and Cornwall and finally of Okehampton Camp. A last point of interest just before meeting the military road is a boundary stone inscribed 'L'. It's one of five in the area and 'L' denotes 'Lydford'.

With time to spare before my train back to Exeter I visited the small museum and shop on Okehampton station. The chap in the shop said that GWR were very pleased with the initial usage of the reopened line and confirmed that an hourly service would soon be starting. The buffet on the main platform would soon be open and it was hoped that heritage trains would be able to start running to Meldon once more, opening up another station serving Dartmoor. A minibus to the edge of the moor would assist those unable to ascend the hill but Okehampton station still offers many options for Dartmoor walks without the need for a car.

Chapter Six

BUCKFASTLEIGH

Just one railway station remains actually in the National Park – Buckfastleigh, terminus of the South Devon heritage railway from Totnes. Whilst basically a tourist railway that doesn't run all year, it does provide a rail link to Buckfastleigh, enabling visitors to explore the historic town. The combination of a steam train and a walk promised an interesting, and as someone who enjoys both trains and Dartmoor, dare I say exciting day out.

Originally a busy 9½ mile branch linking the towns of Buckfastleigh and Ashburton with the main line at Totnes, carrying wool from their mills, coal to power them, plus of course passengers, after traffic declined following World War Two its days seemed numbered. What everyone thought was the last passenger train ran on 3rd November 1958, however this line didn't die. Local businessmen and preservationists considered that a scenic steam-operated railway in a popular tourist area could be a potentially profitable enterprise and seeing the success of the Bluebell Railway in Sussex, plans were made to reopen the line.

The first trains ran in 1969, sadly only to Buckfastleigh as the final 2½ miles to Ashburton had been earmarked for widening of the A38 road. With no bay platform at Totnes it wasn't practical for trains to run into the mainline station but eventually a new station, Totnes Riverside, was constructed, linked to the town by a footbridge over the Dart. The steam railway now provided a real service, carrying tourists and maybe an occasional Dartmoor walker between Totnes and Buckfastleigh.

My connecting train having arrived some time before the first Buckfastleigh service of the day, I spent a pleasant half hour sitting in the sunshine on the peaceful Totnes Riverside station. An elderly man sold me my ticket and a couple more looked after matters on the platform. A group of young schoolchildren passed excitedly through, making use of the toilet facilities but not the train, as they crossed the track to the rare breeds farm, an attraction like the butterfly and otter centres at Buckfastleigh, that exists symbiotically with the railway.

Peace returned until distant whistles became closer, then the immaculately turned out GWR tank engine 5526 arrived with our train. Built at Swindon in 1928, the locomotive spent most of its working life in the West Country and after being rescued from Barry scrapyard is happily back at home on a Devon branch line. Smuts from the engine blew in through the window as we chugged along beside the River Dart. Then came a grasshopper who'd decided to hop in for a ride. I released him (or her) hoping she (or he) knew the way back home. I spoke to a couple in the next seats, showing them my map and suggesting walks, then another chap who advised that the vintage bus I'd previously seen meeting the train only runs for special events. What a shame there isn't a minibus up to the moors. An even more elderly man came round to check my ticket and another sold me a guidebook. There's a lovely atmosphere on the railway, which seems to be largely operated by kindly old men but like many such organisations, who will keep it going in twenty years' time?

Several of my childhood walks had started at Buckfastleigh, necessitating a 2¾ mile walk from the bus station to Cross Furzes, or 4 miles to Lud Gate, to reach the open moor. It's half a mile further from the railway station, so even if I'd had the inclination, the 4 hour interval until the last train departed meant there wasn't time to walk to the moors. There was however time to enjoy some rural countryside and explore three historic sites above the town.

Leaving the station after stopping in the refreshment room to pick up a pasty, I turned left into the town, then up the 196 steps which ascend Church Hill. A narrow path in a tunnel under low trees then took me to what the Ordnance Survey describes as '*Chapel (rems. of)*'. The spire of Holy Trinity Church can be seen from far around but on approaching one soon sees that all is not well with what was once the parish church of Buckfastleigh. Whilst the tower still stands proud, most of the 13th century church is just a shell, destroyed by fire in the early hours of 21st July 1992.

The fire was no accident. The lock on the door had been broken and the fire started beneath the altar. In the preceding few weeks there had been three arson attacks on Devon churches. Break-ins and vandalism had occurred at the church and intruders discovered carrying out satanic rituals. There was no proof but most people blamed the fire on devil worshippers.

The tower and spire were saved and restored along with the porch. Bells are still rung and the burial ground used for internments but partly due to its inconvenient location, rather than restore the building a new modern

Trinity Church Buckfastleigh

church was built in the town centre. The outer walls still stand and carrying out my own risk assessment, into which I factored that if the hazards were considered that great the entrances would be blocked, I ignored the 'Danger' signs and ventured in. It was strange to stand in a roofless building that had been a ruin for just thirty years and not a long-standing consequence of neglect, war or Henry the Eighth's disagreement with the Pope. No one could write about such a building without using the word 'atmospheric', so that will suffice for me too.

I took a wander round the churchyard, stopping at a most extraordinary grave, which perhaps provides a clue to the apparent interest of Satanists in Holy Trinity. It is the resting place for Squire Richard Cabell, described as a 'monstrously evil man' who it is said had killed his wife and sold his soul to the Devil. Cabell however didn't seem to do much resting here. After his death in 1677 he apparently could be found leading a phantom pack of baying hounds across the moor and riding in a coach pulled by headless horses driven by a headless coachman, so to keep Cabell in his grave a stone building was constructed around it. A large stone slab was lain above his body and iron bars fitted cross the entrance. This seemed to halt the squire's excursions onto the moor but the phantom hounds still came to visit him, howling at the tomb. It is said that if one runs round the tomb seven times then put your hands through the iron bars, they will be bitten either by Squire Cabell or the Devil himself. After my good fortune avoiding injury despite so blatantly ignoring the danger sign I didn't feel I should chance my luck with the Devil, so continued on my way.

Holy Trinity Church could be described as a mixture of beautiful, intriguing and of course atmospheric, but turning right into a path just up the lane I was happy to be in a place where I could settle for just beauty. With views to distant Dartmoor hills, wildflowers in abundance and saplings in what a plaque told me was *'The Queen's Green Canopy'*, recently planted for the 2022 Platinum Jubilee, the path took me though a lovely meadow, then down to Buckfast Abbey.

Founded by King Canute in 1018 (excavations after the fire suggested that the original abbey may have been on the site of Holy Trinity Church), Buckfast Abbey is home to a working community of Benedictine monks and

Buckfast Abbey

one of Devon's top tourist attractions. After it was dissolved by Henry the Eighth in 1539 and its treasures taken to the Tower of London, the abbey buildings were stripped and left to decay. More than three hundred years later monks exiled from France constructed a temporary church here and in 1907 work started on rebuilding the abbey. It was constructed by the monks themselves, using wooden scaffolding, manual hoists and block and tackle. With no more than six monks carrying out the building work and funds limited, it took until 1938 to complete but what now stands is a beautiful building, a testament to their faith and tenacity.

Having been inside many times I took just a quick walk around the abbey, admiring as always the striking stained glass window in the east wall with Christ standing arms outstretched in a purple robe and appreciating the peaceful atmosphere within the building. On emerging and passing a monk I bode him '*good morning*'. After he responded '*good afternoon*' we agreed that the monk was correct and deciding that this meant it must be lunchtime, I found a bench in the shade upon which to consume my pasty.

One could easily spend half a day at the abbey and no one should really leave without sampling their treacle tart, but I had a train to catch. Looking at the OS map I'd planned a route through North Wood using a track marked on the north side of the Holy Brook, a tributary of the Dart but a 'Private' sign halted me a short distance down the lane from Buckfast. Access was only to Northwood Farm. It was however a pleasant walk along Grange Road, part of the Dartmoor Way, a 108 mile circular route around the moor, then turning right towards Hembury Woods, my next point of call. A locked gate just beyond a bridge over the Holy Brook confirmed that my decision not to trespass had been correct. The track marked on the map didn't seem to exist.

On what was now a hot day, walking became more strenuous as the lane climbed steeply into the woods. Taking the third track on the right, almost at the road's high point, I walked around a locked gate and into Hembury Woods. Owned by the National Trust, the 224 acres of oak are typical of the many wooded areas on the fringes of Dartmoor. It is a Site of Special Scientific Interest and considered an ancient wood, meaning that it has been continuously forested since at least 1600. The trees provide homes for birds and bats, a large population of dormice thrive amongst the carpet of leaf fall, whilst the more open areas attract butterflies, including rare fritillaries of which five species flourish here.

In common with practice on much of Dartmoor, the National Trust have chosen not to waymark paths so careful map reading was required to reach Hembury Castle, the final objective for my walk. On the basis that this is a hill fort I took a left fork that ascended through the trees and soon brought me into a clearing in the wood. The castle I have to say was somewhat underwhelming – a few earthworks and with tall trees all around, not even the amazing view I'd expected. Yet this is not one castle but two - an Iron Age fort dating from between 500 BC and 50 AD and a Norman motte (earth mound). The former consisted of earth banks and ditches, enclosing an area 300 metres wide and probably contained timber round houses. Finds of sling stones suggest that it was once subject to attack, possibly by Romans who are known to have lived nearby. A thousand years later the Normans chose the site with its views in all directions to build a motte and bailey castle in a corner of the abandoned Iron Age compound. A wooden tower would have stood on the earth mound.

Hembury Woods

According to legend Hembury was once subject to attack by Viking warriors who sailed up the Dart, drove off defenders and took over the castle. As was their custom, the Vikings captured and raped the women but on this occasion it led to their demise, as once the warriors were asleep the women slit their throats. Opening the gates, they let their menfolk back in who quickly slew the remaining Vikings. The plausibility of this tale is somewhat reduced if historians are correct and the castle was abandoned in the 1st century AD, long before Viking raiders came to England.

It was an easy walk along quiet lanes back to Holy Trinity Church, then descending the 196 steps, arriving at Buckfastleigh station in plenty of time for the 15.45 to Totnes. I headed for the buffet car, securing their penultimate scone and with a fitting end to a very enjoyable day enjoyed a cream tea as the train ambled along beside the picturesque Dart.

Chapter Seven

IVYBRIDGE

When Ivybridge station closed to passengers in 1959 few people would have thought that one day trains would be calling here again but on 15th July 1994 my father was aboard the first train to stop at the new station. The only passenger going walking, he was the first person for thirty-five years to use the train to access Dartmoor from Ivybridge.

The service and usage have never been as hoped, partly as the number of trains stopping was never adequate for the advertised role as a Park & Ride station. Amongst my father's papers I found a leaflet announcing reopening of the station which showed that an average of just ten trains a day stopped in each direction. The same number called in 2023, with the occasional service running to or from London, but some two hour gaps are not ideal for either walkers or those leaving their car to travel to Plymouth.

Hence on a sunny March morning I was one of just three passengers alighting and the only Dartmoor walker. Following the footpath then road beside the railway, I soon turned right into Harford Lane and on crossing Stowford Bridge entered the National Park. This stretch of railway forms the boundary.

In a field on the right is a standing stone. The gate is locked but I once sneaked in when the hay was being cut to take a closer look and found no inscription on the granite. This would tend to confirm what I'd read, that it is probably a scratching post for cattle rather than a boundary stone like those on the moor above.

From Stowford Farm a steady climb up a track took me to the open moor. This is part of the Two Moors Way, a 117 mile route crossing the moorlands of Dartmoor and Exmoor and the gentler countryside between them. Opened in 1976, it waymarked existing paths running for 102 miles from Ivybridge to Lynmouth but has more recently been linked with the Erme - Plym Trail to Wembury, making a coast to coast walk.

On passing through the moor gate there is a grassed-over quarry to the left and a popular path ascending Western Beacon to the right. I took the path left of this reaching the Redlake Tramway after half a mile. Completed in 1910 this 3 foot gauge tramway ran for 8 miles across wild Dartmoor, serving the china clay extraction works at Red Lake and Left Lake. Steam locomotives pulled trucks and coaches, taking workers and goods to and from the works. The line was engineered by Richard Hansford Worth, an authority on Dartmoor and prolific author, who routed it away from prehistoric remains. Known locally as the Puffing Billy, it roughly follows contours with a gradual ascent, making it an easy if not direct walk into the centre of Southern Dartmoor. After the best clay had been exhausted the China Clay Corporation was liquidated in 1933 and the tramway track lifted the following year.

The china clay works were named after Red Lake, a small tributary of the River Erme (streams on Dartmoor are often called 'lake') but the tramway tends to be referred to as 'Redlake', although even the most knowledgeable authors can't agree. Eric Hemery's *Walking The Dartmoor Railroads* says 'Red Lake', whereas E.A. Wade titled his book *The Redlake Tramway and China Clay Works*. I shall perpetuate the anomaly, using one word for the tramway and two for the works.

A Two Moors Way marker stone directs walkers to follow the tramway and I stopped here for lunch, taking in fine views. Greetings were exchanged with a cyclist, who I didn't envy as he pedalled hard on the constantly ascending stony track. Resuming my walk I paused to look at some of the eighty inspection points to the china clay pipeline which can be seen adjacent to the tramway and to enjoy the views to Tristis Rock and Stalldown. A lady who'd walked up from Wrangaton passed me and we chatted until, bored with our conversation, her collie dog decided it was time they moved on.

I'd set out with the intention of walking to Spurrell's Cross and back along the Lud Brook but with such fine weather opted to change my plans and

Hangershell Rock

return over the hills. At Hangershell Rock, a small tor on the hillside, I left the tramway, walked past the rocks and picked up a path ascending Butterdon Hill. Six white horses watched me from a distance. A magnificent view from the summit extended across Southern Dartmoor, to the Tamar, Plymouth Sound and into Cornwall. Two huge Bronze Age cairns and a trig point stand on top of the hill.

The descent follows a line of boundary stones, marked 'U' one side and 'H' the other, denoting the boundary between Harford and Ugborough. Black Pool lies in the dip between Butterdon Hill and Western Beacon. Today there was water in the pool but in summer it's often just mud or completely dry. Whatever the time of year horses tend to congregate here and three kept an eye on me as I negotiated a boggy area then climbed towards Western Beacon.

I'd first walked this path in April 1969, my father's notebook describing our route from Davey's Cross, over Western Beacon and Butterdon Hill, with

Western Beacon looking to The South Hams

lunch at Hangershell Rock, before we went on the view Bronze Age remains on Piles Hill, returning to Wrangaton via Spurrell's Cross. I distinctly recall finding a sheep stuck in a bog and Dad eventually pulling it out with much difficulty. His notes record the incident adding, *'not sure whether would live on not'*. My grandfather used to be a farmer and when we got home Dad asked his advice on lifting sheep, lest he should find another in a similar predicament.

More cairns and boundary stones stand on the summit but it is the breathtaking vista across a mosaic of fields to the coast for which most people climb. I stopped for a while, taking in the view and feeling as if with another step forward I'd fall off the moor. A steep descent took me back to the tramway, passing a quarry just below the beacon's summit, from which stone was extracted for building Bittaford Viaduct on the main railway line. Near the start of the tramway the top of a rope-hauled incline railway which took dried clay to the GWR mainline can be seen and in an area cut into the hillside are the bases of buildings that held the winding gear.

The final point of interest as I left the moor was a stone trough, marked on the OS map as a reservoir. It was built in 1866 and like many Victorian constructions seems unnecessarily ornate for its purpose. The inscription is not easy to decipher but reads: '*As made by Mr John Widdecombe of Torhill with the consent of Sir W.P Carew.Bart (Lord of the Manor). For the use of stock depastured on the moor. May the spring never fail. October Xll MDCCCLXVI*'.

After passing through a gate a track leads between trees to a lane, which crosses the railway and meets the main road at Davey's Cross. From here it was half a mile along roads to Ivybridge station, where I arrived in time to eat a cake before boarding the train. This walk had been 5½ miles but with more time there are many options for walks from Ivybridge on a part of the moor that affords magnificent views and is well covered with paths and artefacts of historical interest.

Whilst some walkers alight at the station as a starting point for the Two Moors Way it's a pity that more people don't use it to access Dartmoor. There is useful information posted on the platform but the railway company and National Park Authority could do more to promote it. Stopping more trains here would be a good start. Much could be learned from the provision and promotion of public transport in Snowdonia and the Lake Distract. A minibus service to Harford for those unable to manage or preferring to avoid the climb to the moor would help but as I've found many times, Ivybridge station provides an excellent access point to this part of Southern Dartmoor.

PART 4

FOUR PREHISTORIC REMAINS

Humans have come to Dartmoor for more than ten thousand years and the many granite structures left by prehistoric people are one of the moor's great attractions.

In the Mesolithic Period (10,000 – 4000 BC), small groups of hunter-gatherers used Dartmoor in a limited way, searching the forests for food but leaving little trace other than their stone tools. Neolithic people lived around Dartmoor, from about 4000 – 2500 BC and started limited farming, beginning the process of tree clearance and leaving their large burial chambers. It is however the largest concentration of Bronze Age remains in Britain for which Dartmoor is most notable.

Hut circles, also known as round houses, are low circular stone walls that were the base for conical wood or thatched roofs and used by Bronze Age people as homes and animal housing. There are several thousand on Dartmoor, some of which are contained in walled enclosures known as pounds. Reaves are boundaries of stone and earth, forming field and land boundaries.

Stone circles, circles of stones typically 20 – 40 metres in diameter, are one of Dartmoor's mysteries. Their exact purpose is unknown but it is thought that they acted as ritual centres and maybe places of gathering. They may also have had astronomical uses, perhaps as a calendar mapping movement of the sun, moon and stars.

Also of unknown purpose and amongst the least understood monument types to be found in north-west Europe, are stone rows, roughly straight lines of standing stones (sometimes two or more parallel lines) extending from a few yards to a mile or more. The approximately-seventy five stone rows on Dartmoor is more than half the total found in the whole UK. Menhirs (standing stones), large upright stones either standing alone or forming the terminal stone of a stone row, are thought to be memorials, or to mark graves and may also have been way markers.

Kistvaens (cists / kists) are stone burial chambers consisting of four sides, a capstone and occasionally a paved floor. Most were originally covered with earth or stone and nearly all are oriented in a NW / SE direction, maybe so that the deceased were laid facing the sun. There are around two hundred on Dartmoor. Other burial sites are cairns, mounds of earth or stones, often found on hilltops.

Some of these remains stand alone whilst others are concentrated in particular areas of the moor. There are several major complexes of Bronze Age remains, Drizzlecombe and Merrivale being the best known.

Most Dartmoor walks will pass relics from prehistory, even if the walker doesn't notice, and I have mentioned many in other chapters, but for this section I set out to visit two of the most impressive Bronze Age remains, to repeat a childhood walk to the largest Neolithic burial chamber on the open moor and to investigate one of Dartmoor's 'sacred pools'.

Chapter Eight

STALLDOWN STONE ROW

It's rare to see another person at Dartmoor's tallest stone row, perhaps the most impressive of all its prehistoric remains. The reason isn't remoteness, as whilst it stands in a quiet corner of the moor, the row is less than a mile from the nearest road. The difficulty is that since New Waste car park was shut by the landowner Alexander Darwall in 2014, followed by the Howell family's Harford Moor car park on neighbouring land in 2021, unless one is fortunate to bag one of the very few parking spots in the lanes, a significant walk is required to reach the moor from Ivybridge or Cornwood.

I shall return to the controversial Alexander Darwell later but first commence my walk. My first visit to Stalldown (also known as Staldon), which I recall feeling was very wild and slightly scary, is recorded in my father's notebook:

12th August 1970
Stalldon with Peter
Weather warm, some mist, long fine spells

Bus to Ivybridge. Walked to Harford. Via Hall Farm to Burford Down. Ascended Stalldon direct to stone row. Ground wet in places. (Saw damaged stone about half way along row). Walked along row to N end, back along row to S end then down to track & back to Burford Down Stone Row. Then to Hall Farm & back to Ivybridge. Bus to Totnes, train to N. Abbot. 4½ hour walk.

This time I started with a taxi from Ivybridge to Harford, then descended to Harford Bridge from where there is a pretty view up the River Erme. Passing a few houses, I reached a gate from which a permissive path leads to Burford Down. This was the subject of controversy in 2021 when padlocks appeared on the gate and another by Harford Bridge. Land beyond the latter

Stalldown Stone Row

is designated as Access Land under the Countryside and Rights of Way Act 2000 (CRoW), so the gate should not have been locked, although the path which initially appears to offer a route to the open moor soon disappears in bogs and undergrowth. Strangely a small area beyond the second gate is not Access Land, so walkers rely on the goodwill of the landowner to cover the initial 150 metres towards Tristis Rocks. Fortunately, after an outcry from walkers both locks were soon removed.

Once on Burford Down I followed the stone row from a cairn circle where it starts, then walked through a gateway into an enclosure, part of Yardsworthy Waste. Circular Bronze Age settlements could be seen on Stalldown ahead, which I reached through a gate in the right-hand corner of the field, as going through the obvious gate way on the left soon meets a fence. Whilst one can walk anywhere on Access Land, it is reasonable that gates or stiles should generally be used rather than risking damage by climbing over fences or walls.

There is no path to the stone row, perhaps a consequence of the lack of parking that restricts visitors, but it was an easy walk gently ascending to the left of Stalldown's summit. Soon the remarkable stones came into view.

Also known as the Cornwood Maidens, Dartmoor's finest stone row runs for almost a third of a mile, north – south across the western crown of Stalldown. Much of the row was restored in 1897 by the Dartmoor Exploration Committee, who raised most of the fallen stones but may have slightly altered their alignment as the row is no longer quite straight.

As we did when I was nine, I walked along the row to the northern end where the most impressive stones stand, some up to 8 feet high, with perhaps half as much again below the surface. It would have been a huge job (one could almost say monumental) for the Bronze Age people to erect them without modern machinery, yet we don't know why the rows were built. It is from this end, looking into the remote moor, that the stone row's mystique and majesty are best experienced.

I sat by the final stone looking up the winding Erme Valley, one of the most beautiful on the moor. Mottled patches of sun and shade on the green summer moorland added to the beauty and not one person could be seen. By limiting visitors to only those willing and able to walk a significant distance the controversial closure of the parking areas has effectively increased the monument's isolation. The long-abandoned, conical china clay spoil heap peeping over the hill at Red Lake was the only obvious sign of human activity. I was looking to Green Hill in the centre of Southern Dartmoor, but whilst many of the criteria seemed to be met, the view appeared too pretty and peaceful to be wilderness.

The going beyond the stone row is rough, with tussocky Molinia grass making walking difficult. Increasing dominance of this invasive purple moor grass on Dartmoor's blanket bogs results mainly from reduced grazing and is a growing threat to diversity and carbon storage, an issue we will return to later.

I retraced my steps along the stone row, pausing at a cairn circle, a burial site unusually positioned adjacent to the row. From here I branched off to

Hillson's House

the summit of Stalldown and Hillson's House, subject of one of Dartmoor's intriguing legends.

A small baby was once found on the hill and taken off the moor to safety. Efforts to locate his parents failed and he was eventually brought up by an elderly childless couple who named him Hillson, presumably son of the hill. When he grew up Hillson returned to Stalldown and built himself a small house with stones from the cairn. Here he lived for many years, earning a living from making eight-day clocks.

It is of course debatable as to how much, if any, of the story is true. One could imagine the stones forming a shelter but it seems hard to believe that someone could have lived in a small room on top of the hill and carried out the intricate craft of clock making. The highly respected Dartmoor writers William Crossing and Eric Hemery however both suggest that there is evidence that the house did belong to a man called Hillson who made watches or clocks.

If Hillson did indeed live on the summit of Stalldown he would have enjoyed a fine view into the moor. From this higher viewpoint I could see Left Lake china clay works on the far side of the Erme and the track of the Redlake railway running along the hillside. There was more sign of human activity than could be seen from the stone row but the sun having disappeared the darker moor looked wilder. I was already finding that aesthetic factors influenced my view on wilderness.

Descending Stalldown provided a good view to Plymouth Sound and into Cornwall but just to the right was one of Dartmoor's eyesores - the white china clay spoil heaps of Lee Moor. The Redlake heap, which I had been looking towards in the centre of the moor, was once similarly white and stark but after almost a hundred years is now heather-covered and were it not for the clearly artificial shape could be considered almost natural. Some of the Lee Moor heaps have been grassed over and no doubt in time all will be returned to a more natural state but the moor will have been defiled for many decades and will never be the same again.

I returned to Ivybridge along the lanes, cutting off a corner by taking the pretty path that runs from Harford Bridge to where the lane crosses the Butter Brook and arriving at the station a good twenty minutes before my train. But the train wasn't arriving. For the first time in many journeys they had let me down. The two hourly service meant a long wait, particularly frustrating after timing my walk around the trains. If only more stopped here. Fortune however improved when a café in Ivybridge told me they shut at 3pm. Their clock said 2.59, my phone 3.01. The two minute inaccuracy permitted purchase of toasted tea cakes. Perusal of the excellent Ivybridge Bookshop, where mine and my father's walking guides sat adjacent on the shelf, purchase of a book and a sit by the river occupied the remainder of the wait.

So to return to the controversial Alexander Darwall, who along with his wife bought the 4,000 acre Blanchford Estate in 2011 for a rumoured £8 million. Dartmoor's sixth largest landowner, Darwell, a hedge fund manager, is a very rich man. He has used some of his massive wealth to influence politics, donating significant sums to UKIP, the Brexit Leave Campaign and the Conservative Party and owns a 16,000 acre estate in Scotland. One wonders why such a busy man would choose to buy part of Dartmoor. It would be nice to think that it was for philanthropic reasons, to protect the land and facilitate access for others, but Mr Darwell's actions suggest that this is not the case.

Part of the Blanchford Estate is included in the Cornwood Shoot, which charges a not inconsiderable sum (it's hard to find the current price – their website has been made private) for people to shoot pheasants. Apparently a screenshot taken before access was restricted boasted of shooting 250 pheasants in a day. To ensure that there are plenty of birds for clients to enjoy killing, estates release huge numbers of captive bred pheasants - 50 million a year in the UK. These hungry pheasants have a major environmental impact, competing with wild birds for food. Natural England have expressed concern that the very rare blue ground beetle, that is found in only fifteen sites in the UK, is threatened in Dendles Wood by released pheasants. It has been suggested that Mr Darwill is more interested in facilitating shooting parties on his land than he is access for walkers.

In 1999 Dartmoor National Park Authority (DNPA) made an agreement with the previous landowner to allow car parking and access on foot or horseback to the common land at Stalldown Barrow. After the land was designated as open country (Access Land) under CRoW the agreement was modified to provide permissive access for parking and horse riding (access on foot being automatically permitted under CRoW). The new landowner Mr Darwall however gave notice to terminate the agreement and despite DNPA's efforts to persuade him to allow parking, the car park was closed. One can still walk (although not ride a horse) but closing New Waste car park has made it harder for people to access this part of the moor.

Dartmoor is the last area in England where there is right to 'wild camp' without seeking permission. Also known as 'backpack camping', the term is commonly used to describe sleeping overnight in a tent or bivouac on open land, not in a designated site. It is an activity enjoyed by many people, the vast majority of whom behave responsibly and leave 'no trace'. A few however light fires, leave litter and sometimes even human waste on the moor. In 2022 Mr Darwall went to court, challenging the assumed right to wild camp in the whole National Park. Darwell claimed that he was unable to order individual campers off his land and sought a declaration from the judge that this right did not exist.

On 13th January 2023 the High Court ruled in favour of Darwall that a byelaw in the Dartmoor Commons Act (1985) enshrined a historic custom of open access, *'to all the commons on foot and on horseback for the purposes of open-air recreation'*, excluded wild camping.

The judge, Sir Julian Flaux, said the act did not, *'confer on the public any right to pitch tents or otherwise make camp overnight on Dartmoor Commons. Any such camping requires the consent of the landowner'*, adding that if there were such a right, it would mean *'the landowner would have suffered a loss of control or a usurpation of his rights over his own land'*.

A draft agreement was hastily arranged between DNPA and landowners whereby camping would be permitted in designated areas and the owners paid a fee from public funds. Eight days after the court announcement three thousand people gathered in Cornwood to protest, marching up the lanes to Darwall's land on the moor. There was considerable anger at wealthy landowners imposing restrictions on ordinary people, a view summarised by local man Duncan Hutchinson who was quoted in *The Guardian*:

> 'We are not accepting favours from our masters. We are not their serfs. It isn't the 19th century. Dartmoor is not a private gentlemen's shooting estate.'

Campaigners, many of whom made donations towards costs, urged DNPA to appeal the court ruling, which they agreed to do in April with the case going to the Royal Courts of Justice in July 2023. The outcome hinged on whether wild camping counts as 'open-air recreation' as allowed in a 1985 Act.

Timothy Morshead KC, acting for Darwall, said that the Dartmoor Commons Act only confers the right to *'wander around'*, *'not to linger there'*. He argued if those drafting the law had wanted people to camp, they would have made provision for it and that wild camping cannot count as recreation or enjoyment because, *'sleeping overnight on the commons is not recreation, open-air or otherwise, because you are just asleep'*.

Acting for the DNPA, Timothy Straker KC argued that: *'recreation can

Burford Down Stone Row

embrace sleep – for instance the recreation of taking 16 hours on Dartmoor to include sleeping overnight so one can observe the sunset in the evening or sunrise in the morning. It is not a sensible proposition to suggest that sleeping takes one outside the scope of recreation'.

Arguments continued as to whether camping itself was enjoyable recreation (and the hike perhaps a chore to reach this form of recreation), whether camping can be recreation as one is not in the open air and that sleep is not necessarily enjoyable being just maintaining human capabilities, not recreating.

The court of appeal panel, consisting of Sir Geoffrey Vos, Lord Justice Underhill and Lord Justice Newey, ruled that wild camping counted as open-air recreation and should therefore be allowed on the commons. Giving judgment on 31st July 2023 Voss stated:

'I start by asking whether a walker who lies down for a rest without pitching a tent would be present for the purpose of open-air recreation. It seems to me obvious that they would. The resting is obviously a necessary part of the recreation. If that walker keeps his eyes open and remains awake, the pastime he is enjoying may include simply resting in the open-air in the peace of the countryside. I have then asked myself whether it makes any difference if the putative walker falls off to sleep. The only argument suggesting it might is that recreation is something one does when one is awake and sentient. It seems to me that that argument proves too much. A walker resting by sleeping is merely undertaking an essential part of the recreation of a lengthy walk.

The next question, as it seems to me, is whether it affects the conclusions in the previous paragraph if the walker rests or sleeps on a plastic sheet to prevent the damp, or in a sleeping bag to protect from the cold, or under a tarpaulin or in an open tent or in a closed tent to protect from the rain. The fact that a tent is closed rather than open cannot convert the wild camping from being an open-air recreation into not being one. In my judgment, that walker is still resting by sleeping and undertaking an essential part of the recreation. Nor, in my judgment, does it matter if the walker has not walked far when he rests or sleeps in the manner I have mentioned.'

A victory for Dartmoor walkers and indeed for common sense. This however was not the end of the story as within a month Darwall had lodged an application with the Supreme Court seeking to appeal the judgment, for which he was given permission in January 2024. We still awaited the outcome as this book went to print.

Chapter Nine

THE GREY WETHERS

This was one of the few walks I didn't do alone. Every year my brother and I spend a weekend walking on Dartmoor and today he accompanied me to the Grey Wethers, a double stone circle that is unique on the moor. We walked up the East Dart from Postbridge, leaving behind tourists taking selfies on the clapper bridge and following the path below Hartland Tor. There were good views up the valley but on a sunny morning it seemed to be a place of beauty but not wilderness. Again I was struggling not to equate wilderness with starkness, although none of the definitions suggest an aesthetic element such that it cannot be a place of beauty.

We stopped where the Dart bends sharp left and is joined by the Lade Hill Brook, intending to inspect one of the moor's best preserved beehive huts, which was constructed by tinners a short distance up the tributary. As we stood close to the river four men descended from the direction of Stannon Tor, one of whom immediately divested himself of clothes and entered the Dart. Adjusting our gaze from naked man to Dartmoor valley, we looked back towards Postbridge, seeing a large black cloud approaching. Pre-empting the downpour waterproofs were donned and within seconds rain was falling. We set off up the stream, not bothering to stop at the beehive hut, me glad to be well attired but my brother wishing he had ignored the weather forecast of a dry day and had brought waterproof trousers.

The next part of the walk wasn't the most pleasant. In our haste to get going we hadn't ascended to the main path, instead following a much narrower one close to the river. This soon entered a flat marshy area where the barely discernible path threaded between tufts of tall, wet grass. The ground below was hard to see and it was only as our feet touched the peat that we found whether they would sink into dark bog. It was hard going in pouring rain on rough Dartmoor ground and on seeing a chap running along the hillside

The Grey Wethers

above we gave up the slog and climbed to the proper path. We were fortunate that there was an alternative, unlike some of the central moor where walking through such going is the only way to proceed.

Now out of the Dart Valley, with Winney's Down to the left and Sittaford Tor ahead, the moor seemed wilder. Only earth disturbed by tinning in the valley and the dry Vittaford Mine Leat on the hillside opposite indicated that humans had changed the landscape – other than some cows, the effect of grazing and long-gone trees of course. As we climbed higher the extensive conifer plantation around Fernworthy Reservoir came into view, a more recent human interference that we both felt detracted from the moor's wilderness characteristics.

Suddenly, almost as if in a film, looming over the horizon appeared the granite stones of the Grey Wethers. The highest altitude stone circles on Dartmoor, the Grey Wethers are magnificent yet mysterious Bronze Age monuments. We don't know the purpose of prehistoric stone circles but this double ring suggests even more hypothesis. Could they have been a meeting place for two tribes, or perhaps for men and women, maybe as part of some kind of wedding ceremony? Excavations have shown a thick layer of charcoal inside the circles, suggesting that fire was part of the rituals that took place here. The circles, which consist of between 20 and 30 upright stones (sources vary and I forgot to count), were restored in 1909 by the Dartmoor Exploration Committee. A survey by Barry and Tania Welch (*Dartmoor News Sept/Oct 2013*), showed that the northern circle measures 31.5 metres in diameter and the southern 33 metres, the difference they suggest may be a result of their restoration. The monument is particularly unusual as the rare double stone circles elsewhere tend to be concentric rather than adjacent. The Grey Wethers are one of Dartmoor's great mysteries.

A couple sat quietly leaning on one of the stones. Between the circles sat a man, eyes closed in deep thought, meditation, or prayer, perhaps picking up energy from the ancient stones. We walked past in respectful silence, giving him a reasonable berth as we took in the magic and mystery of one of Dartmoor's greatest monuments.

One respondent gave '*spiritual*' in their three wilderness words. Whilst few would include it in a definition, there is no doubt that some people find a spiritual experience from wild or remote places. Some, perhaps like the man at the Grey Wethers, find ancient stones to be spiritual. Others might gain a similar experience from the moor's beauty, remoteness, ruggedness or atmosphere.

There are of course many legends concerning the stones, one of which explains their name. A farmer had recently moved to the area and rode to Tavistock market to purchase a flock of sheep but decided that none met his

Sittaford Tor looking to Whitehorse & Hangingstone Hills

high standards. Stopping on his way home for a cider or two at the Warren House Inn, he complained to the locals about the poor quality of Dartmoor sheep. Hearing this one drinker told him that he had a fine flock which he was selling and offered them to the farmer. They rode in the mist over Water Hill and the sheep were pointed out in the distance. On seeing the flock the farmer agreed to buy them and only the next day when he went back to collect the sheep did he discover that he'd been sold two circles of stones.

We climbed part way up the nearby Sittaford Tor to gain a better overall view of the stone circles. The arrangement with a gap between the circles is clearer from above but to experience the atmosphere of this mystical place one needs to be amongst them. Sadly the Fernworthy plantation less than half a mile away has reduced the sense of remoteness that comes with being surrounded by miles of open moor but it still needs a significant walk to reach the stone circles.

We ate our lunch on Sittaford Tor, looking across the Teign Valley into the wilds of Northern Dartmoor. The trees by the abandoned Teign Head Farm could just be seen to our right but other than some ancient stone walls and the distant military observation post on Hangingstone Hill there was little else in the way of human interference to detract from wilderness characteristics.

Walking back to Postbridge, this time taking an easier higher path, we discussed the definition of wilderness and the influence of aesthetics on our judgement. My brother rightly held the view that green grass and pretty streams shouldn't determine wilderness characteristics but I still felt that it equated with a rugged, even desolate environment. Barren, rugged, raw, wild and desolate had all featured in my email responses, but only one person had said beautiful and I was finding it hard to equate prettiness with wilderness. I was finding more questions than answers.

Chapter Ten

CORRINGDON BALL BURIAL CHAMBER

It was Easter 1970 when I first visited what we knew as the 'Mutilated Cromlech', a name that came from Dr Marjorie Fielden, my father's next door neighbour in Torquay, who in the 1950s introduced him to Dartmoor. On a cold April day, with a light covering of snow on the moor, we took the bus to South Brent. Dad's notebook records the walk:

1 April 1970 Ball Gate, Diamond Lane
With Peter & Sally.
Weather cold wind, snow showers, sunny spells

Walked Brent (bus stop) via Aish Ridge to Ball Gate. Saw Mutilated Cromlech & stone row, then went E between newtake walls & down Diamond Lane (old bridle path Ashburton – Plympton). Very bad going, large boulders & wet & slippery. Back above Didworthy to S. Brent

This time in late November, as we did when I was nine and my sister seven, I took the bus to South Brent, walked through the village, then followed a path beside the River Avon to the pretty Lydia Bridge. After a couple of months of high rainfall water was pouring down the waterfall, a spectacular sight but not one that's well known to tourists.

At the hamlet of Aish, by a 17th century cottage (the former Post Office) I turned left down a narrow lane towards the charmingly named Gribblesdown. This leads to a track to Aish Ridge, which is accessed by a gate. Two cars were parked on the moorland despite a sign to the contrary. With parking places so limited on the south side of Dartmoor some people are inevitably leaving their cars in unsuitable or illegal places.

There are fine views into the moor from the grassy path across the ridge

Corringdon Ball Burial Chamber

which made for easy walking. It was good to be on open moor and I stopped for lunch, a mountain biker flying past me with a cheery hello as he descended at speed.

An almost straight track took me between the moorland of Corringdon Ball on the left and fields on the right. I say track but the first part was more like a stream than a path. It even had tiny waterfalls in it. A short descent then led to one of the grandest gateways onto Dartmoor.

Once the gate to Brent Manor Estate, Corringdon Ball Gate is an imposing entrance to the moor with stone balls on the head of each post. These were not in place when my father first walked this way but I recall them from our childhood walk. The track through here is known as the Jobbers' Path, the name coming from men trading in wool and cloth who carried their goods over the moor.

Marked on OS maps as a long barrow, the Neolithic chambered tomb is one of the largest burial monuments on Dartmoor. Although badly damaged it is still an impressive monument, formed from huge stones, even more so when one considers it was erected here in the region of 6,000 years ago. The stone chamber, placed within the wider end of a long barrow earth mound, consists of five large slabs. Only one of these is still in the erect position and another lying on the edge of the remains of the mound may be the capstone. There are no side ditches as often seen around such burial sites but these may have been filled by soil washed down from Brent Fore Hill above.

John Earle in *Walking on Dartmoor* casts doubt as to its Neolithic origin but most commentators agree that whilst Neolithic people didn't live on the moor, this tomb along with the burial chambers at nearby Cuckoo Ball and Butterdon Hill, suggests that they came up here to bury some of their dead. George Thurlow, in *Thurlow's Dartmoor Companion* mentions several other possible tombs and it would seem likely that there were more on the moor but that after six millennia little or nothing discernible remains.

As we did in 1970, I sought out the nearby double stone row and followed the stones down to the East Glaze Brook, a pretty little stream in a shallow

Corringdon Ball Gate

gorge. On the slope opposite is a further complex of stone rows, consisting of seven parallel lines, an unusual arrangement but one that is hard to pick out amongst the vegetation. This may be a unique seven-fold stone row, or two adjacent rows of three and four stones wide.

Next I deviated from my childhood walk, following the Jobbers' Path for a mile towards Glaze Head to the point where the path divides. The Jobbers' Path heads right to the Red Brook Valley and the left fork to Three Barrows. I stopped for a while, looking into the wilder moor but with limited winter daylight hours, opted for safety and started my return to South Brent.

Retracing my steps almost to the burial chamber, I then turned left, following a path above Merrifield Plantation. Like the route I'd taken from Lydia Bridge, this is part of the Dartmoor Way. Here I met my first walker of the day, a chap who had also walked up from South Brent, but taking a longer route via Shipley Bridge and was returning by Lady's Wood. We agreed that the ground was particularly wet, which he explained was why he was wearing gaiters so had dry feet, unlike mine which weren't helped by them residing in standing water as we talked.

The path took me to Diamond Lane, an ancient route to the moor and once part of the monastic track from Buckfast Abbey to Plympton Priory. Passing under trees and between moss-covered walls, it makes a most romantic and historic approach to Dartmoor. Diamond Lane was used for taking ponies to and from the moor and is still designated as a bridleway, although a sign at the top advises riders to dismount.

Centuries of water running off the moor have eroded the track, although in recent years the lower part has been restored to a good surface, work that was essential as the ancient walls had been undermined and threatened to collapse. On the upper section it is necessary to pick one's way over often slippery rocks, so great care is needed especially when descending. I made slow progress, keen to avoid a slip, and on meeting three ladies commented that it was easier going up than down. I don't think they agreed.

It is said that a coach and four was once driven up the lane, although that may be another Dartmoor tale that is not entirely true. Also that the militia

Diamond Lane

marched through here on their way from Exeter to Plymouth. On the lower part of the track, just before a gate on the right (if descending), is an abandoned moss-covered granite trough. Its origin is unknown but with no water source, does not appear to have been placed here for watering horses.

A path from nearby Shipley Bridge makes an attractive return on the edge of woods and through farmland to the east of the River Avon, but I stuck to our childhood route along lanes, passing Didworthy on the opposite side of the river. The lane affords good views as it runs close to the water, then after crossing Badworthy Brook climbs to Binnamore Cross. Before reaching Aish a path on the left cuts off the corner, running through the edge of the Woodland Trust's Penstave Copse. The soft ground made a welcome change from tarmac underfoot. A few drops of rain came to nothing but brought with them a splendid rainbow across the hillside opposite.

The final section of path is straight and narrow, running under trees between two ancient moss-covered walls. It's known locally as Fat Man's Alley or

Fatman's Trouble and joins the road a little before Lydia Bridge. Just before the bridge emerges another path, the next section of the Dartmoor Way. As I reached it out popped the chap who I'd met earlier above Diamond Lane. We were equally surprised to see each other again but he didn't stop, disappearing off at a great pace.

Having greatly enjoyed my walk I arrived at the bus stop in plenty of time for the Gold Bus to Totnes. The bus however failed to rendezvous at the appointed hour then got stuck in an enormous traffic jam. Having missed two trains I got out and walked the last mile into the town, calling into Morrison's whose half-price all day breakfast provided reasonably adequate compensation.

Chapter Eleven

BLACK POOL

Taking the train to Ivybridge, I followed the Two Moors Way to the Redlake Tramway as I had in Chapter Seven, this time stopping for a quick lunch at the quarry by the moor gate. Since my last visit two wooden posts, protected by a triangular wooden fence, had appeared either side of the tramway. So what were these mysterious posts? They were too low for a gate, superfluous as footpath marker and didn't appear to be part of a larger structure.

A few weeks later I read in *Dartmoor News* that they were counters and went back to take a look. Close inspection found four tiny holes in each post, presumably to send and receive a light beam but what I couldn't find out was why the counters were there and how they registered people but not wandering livestock. Being a rebellious type I walked round the outside to avoid being counted.

Crossing the tramway, I took a path between Butterdon Hill and Western Beacon, reaching Black Pool after 400 yards. The pool attracts livestock, usually horses but a today a group of cows with calves eyed me suspiciously as I approached. I've walked past here many times, the first with Dad in 1969 which I still recall. Today there was water in the pool, sometimes it's just mud and in a dry summer this bakes hard with nothing for the animals to drink.

There is plenty of water on Dartmoor but most of it is soaked up into the mires and peat, eventually to run off the moor along its many streams and rivers. Unlike some National Parks where glaciers gouged out valleys then deposited material that blocked the flow of water, there are few natural pools or lakes on Dartmoor. The only large bodies of water are reservoirs, the biggest being Burrator, Fernworthy, Avon and Meldon. There are however pools of varying sizes dotted across the moor, many of which were made by humans, either deliberately or as a result of mineral extraction.

Black Pool lies at the low point between the two hills which would seem a natural place for water to gather, however it may have been formed by man as one of many ancient sacred pools on the moor. As with the long barrows, experts are divided in their opinions, Dartmoor's controversies extending to its prehistory as well as more modern conflicts. Not everyone accepts that

Black Pool – Winter

Black Pool – Summer

some of the small, shallow pools to be found on Dartmoor are not natural features but date from prehistoric times when they may have had religious as well as practical use.

In his paper *Dartmoor's Sacred Pools* (2019) which was published in *Dartmoor Magazine,* the cultural environmentalist Dr Tom Greeves lists forty-three pools as candidates for having prehistoric origin. Black Pool, which is recorded as 31 x 21 metres, is included. Many of the pools are in elevated positions with fine views and the majority are close to Bronze Age remains. Whilst Black Pool lies in a dip, it is situated between the cairns on Butterdon Hill and Western Beacon, and not far from Butterdon Stone Row,

Boundary stone, Western Beacon

the second longest on the moor. Like most of the pools listed, Black Pool is roughly oval (others are round), shapes that is considered not to be naturally formed, although there does not appear to be any sign of the low banks that surround a few of the pools.

Greeves suggests that these sacred pools would have been used for watering animals, as gathering places and for religious activity. He notes that there are records throughout Britain and Europe of prehistoric artifacts and human bones being found in rivers, bogs and lakes, although in only one example, Bloody Pool near South Brent, have such objects been discovered in Dartmoor pools. Reflection of the sky in water is suggested by Greeves to have divinatory or other powers and he pontificates that the pools may have been considered entry points to other worlds.

Opinion is divided but I am inclined to agree that the shape, location and proximity to Bronze Age remains of some of these pools does suggest that they are man-made and prehistoric. Black Pool meets only some of these criteria but I like to think that it was formed by Dartmoor dwellers four thousand years ago.

Turning right at the pool I made the easy climb to the summit of Western Beacon. On an overcast day which had threatened rain since I set out, the view from the beacon was more atmospheric than spectacular, with mist covering the tops of Stalldown and Piles Hill and clouds heading my way.

Rather than the direct route with a steep descent, I headed east, meeting up with the path from Cuckoo Ball and passing the engine and carriage sheds of the tramway, which still stand abandoned in a field the other side of a wall. After almost a century out of use, both are deteriorating, although the carriage shed remains the more sturdy, having once been modified to house pigs.

My walk was completed turning left off the tramway, passing the water troughs and reaching the main road at Davey's Cross. I arrived at the station ten minutes before the train. As it pulled into the platform the rain commenced, a downpour that continued for most of the evening. I had been fortunate to have avoided it.

Vixen Tor

PART 5

DARTMOOR TORS

Probably the feature Dartmoor is best known for is its tors – huge outcrops of granite often on the tops of hills. These magnificent rocks were formed around 300 million years ago when magma forced up through the Earth's crust cooled to create granite. This was gradually exposed by millions of years' weathering leaving the massive rocks with which we are so familiar.

How many tors there are on Dartmoor is a matter of much debate. DNPA website *dartmoor.gov.uk* says *'more than 160'*, as does *visitdartmoor.co.uk*, whilst *www.treksandtors.co* list 500 and the excellent *torsofdartmoor.co.uk* displays a database of 922, some of which it describes as *'significant rocks'*.

Emily Woodhouse in *All The Tors*, which describes her walk to visit them all (by her definition) chose just 119. As I did in selecting tidal islands when writing *No Boat Required*, she needed a clear definition but a manageable number. Emily decided that the tors had to be marked on the OS map, to include 'tor' separately in the name (so Haytor did not count) and excluded those in the area east of Widecombe as they couldn't be reached in one walk without leaving designated Access Land.

With so many to choose from it was hard to select just four to visit for this book. After considering many for my first I opted for Great Mis Tor, one of Dartmoor's largest tors, with views into the 'central wilderness' and inevitable legends. The second and third were selected from Max Piper's *East Dartmoor's Lesser-Known Tors and Rocks*. Finally, one of the most controversial places on Dartmoor, Vixen Tor, which I first visited with my father in February 1972.

Chapter Twelve

GREAT MIS TOR

The weather forecast warned of sub-zero temperatures and there was a rare heavy frost in Torquay. Even the pier had ice on it. I met a neighbour on the way out. He'd just come back home, deciding it was too cold to work outdoors at Bovey Tracey. I'm not sure what he thought of me venturing out to High Dartmoor in such weather.

Whilst warning of low temperatures, the forecaster had said that the cold air from the north was clean and the sun would be shining, so visibility would be excellent. Hence today I chose a walk with one of Dartmoor's great views.

By the time I'd stopped for an early lunch at the Old Police Station Café in Princetown most of the moorland frost had melted, although it was still bitterly cold. The sun was shining but banks of cloud were starting to build up on the southern horizon.

I drove the short distance towards Tavistock to the Four Winds car park, an excellent starting point for walks in all directions. Behind the car park is a walled area surrounded by trees. This was once Foggintor School which opened in 1915 to educate children from nearby quarry workers' cottages. The building was centrally heated and children used the pipes for warming their pasties. It had two classrooms and there were initially fifty-five pupils, but numbers dwindled as quarrying declined and the school closed in 1936. It only ever had one head teacher, Fred Stoyle, who was the youngest in the country. The school was demolished by ten teenagers from Northbrook Approved School in 1964, after the National Park Authority had described it as '*a major disfigurement*'. The adjacent house, which had accommodated the teachers, was demolished a year later.

The large fir tree behind the car park dates back to the school but there are several stories as to its origin. According to Fred Stoyle, it was the family's Christmas tree which his son Ivan planted in the school garden in 1924, whilst Eric Green from Princetown, a former pupil, recalled that it was a gift from quarrymen to the school in its final year of operation. Paul Rendell in *Dartmoor News* adds to the first explanation, saying that each Christmas the prison authorities sent a tree to the school and whilst usually they were cut at the stem, the 1924 tree had a full set of roots and in the new year was planted in the garden.

Well wrapped up and with spare clothing in my rucksack, I crossed the road and set off up the track heading north towards Great Mis Tor, the view south expanding as I climbed. After a mile Little Mis Tor was reached. Also known as Wain Tor, this is a compact granite stack with superb views. The stony track used by military vehicles ends here but although not marked on OS Maps, a grassy path continues to the expanse of Great Mis Tor ahead.

A white van was parked at the end of the track and a red flag flying on the tor. The latter indicated live firing in the Merrivale Range, which meant I couldn't go much beyond Great Mis Tor and the former, I rightly assumed had some connection with the military's activities.

The tor is easier to climb from the north so I took a path skirting it to the right, a magnificent view into the central northern basin opening up before me. With clear sky, clean air, the sun shining and the moor in winter shades of brown, this was Dartmoor at her best.

To the left was the beautiful Walkham Valley. Beyond this were Lints Tor and Standon Hill, then over the Tavy, Ger Tor, Tavy Cleave Tors and Hare Tor. The mass of Amicombe Hill was due north and in the distance behind it, almost eight miles way, High Willhays, the highest point in Southern England. Fur Tor, Dartmoor's remotest tor, was easily located four miles away, with Cut Hill adjacent. To my right, across the Cowsic River, Devils Tor could just be picked out, with Beardown Tors to the east. Distances were deceptive and it is only when measured on the map or walked, that one realises quite how far away these places are. What I did know was that even if the moor wasn't closed for firing, with few paths, rough ground and bogs, it would be a hard walk to reach any of them. There was virtually no

View from Great Mis Tor

sign of human activity. Writing in *Dartmoor Captured* Michael Hedges talks of this view towards High Willhays, Fur Tor and Cut Hill, describing the intervening landscape as, '*some of the wildest and most barren in the whole of England*'. Surely I was looking into a wilderness?

I approached the two military huts which stand beyond the tor, not far before a line of red and white poles indicating the range boundary. As I stood taking in the awe-inspiring view a man emerged from the hut. His job was to tell people not to enter the range. I was the first person he'd seen all day. We chatted for some time while his dog Jack, an eleven-year-old collie, sat patiently by us.

The man (I wished I'd asked his name) was employed by Landmarc, who provide services to the military, including guarding the boundaries of Dartmoor's ranges. It was his van at the top of the track. His job was to sit in the little hut, challenging anyone who walked by and using binoculars check for persons who may put themselves in danger by entering the range elsewhere. He didn't have the power to stop anyone but said that whilst some people get '*arsey*', when the risks are explained they generally agree to turn back. If necessary he contacts the military who have to cease firing and send soldiers to escort the 'trespasser' from the range. I recently read an account by someone who had just popped over the boundary on Cut Hill for five minutes to find a letterbox, assumed he was out of sight, but soon after passing out of the range was rapidly approached by two running soldiers who gave him a severe lecture.

Today firing was in a limited area around Baggator (we could hear the bangs) but if it's more extensive the range has to be cleared of sheep and cattle. This is mostly done with the help of dogs but it can be a real problem to stop the cows wandering back into danger. Jack was once his range dog but is now retired. Horses were regularly used to assist but are now only occasionally employed. The metal building close to the hut is a stable.

The chap told me that he was a farmer on the northern moor but could no longer make a living from farming alone and would have had to sell up if it wasn't for the range work. The various impacts of Brexit (although he didn't mention the word itself) means it may no longer be viable at all soon.

He was able to answer one question which I've always wondered. What is to stop livestock from straying all across the moor, far from their home farms. He explained that sheep and cattle tend to stay where they are put, although he once had a sheep appear that had wandered seven miles. The farmer traced the owner by the smit mark and it was collected but within a few days was back again.

After talking for half an hour I said farewell to this most interesting man. The chap and his dog returned to their little hut where they'd stay until it was almost dark, as the observation posts are only manned in daylight hours, although they're allowed to leave time to get back to their vehicle before nightfall. For the observer on Rough Tor he said this is an hour as it's quite a walk.

I headed back to the tor, ascending the main stack with suitable care. After the Butter Brook incident I'd decided that I wouldn't climb tors anymore but this was fairly easy, there was no wind and something I wanted to see at the top.

Mistor Pan is one of Dartmoor's finest rock basins; a depression in the rock forming a pool that fills with water – or today, with ice. Granite has a layered structure and if water penetrates cracks then freezes, its expansion widens the crack. Where the rock is flat the freeze-thaw process can undercut the crack, eventually forming and widening a depression, which becomes a small pool. Whilst the process still continues slowly most of the erosion took place in the Ice Ages, so Great Mis Tor's rock basin has sat atop the rocks for many thousands of years. It is about 3 feet across by 6 inches deep and of course being on Dartmoor has its associated legends.

Like many of the moor's stories, the Devil is involved and is said to have used the small pool for his evil rites. The basin is also known as the Devil's Frying Pan, as after riding across the moors with his hounds, he would stop at Great Mis Tor to fry breakfast. This story may have arisen as a small portion of the rock basin's wall is missing, giving the appearance of a handle for the frying pan – or maybe it was indeed used for frying satanic sausages. A more macabre story is that the rock basin was cut by ancient Druids before Roman

Mistor Pan

times, who used it as a receptacle for blood from their human sacrifices. The missing portion of wall would have acted as an overflow. Another suggestion is that more recent Druids collected pure rainwater from the basin for use in their ceremonies.

The red flag fluttering in gentle breeze indicated that the 'wilderness' ahead was out of bounds, so I returned down the path, the temperature dropping markedly as the December sun went down. The three mile walk however felt inadequate, so after eating the cake that I'd brought with me from the Police Station Café, I decided there was enough light for a quick exploration of the Merrivale antiquities. Possibly the finest collection of Bronze Age remains on Dartmoor, they are close to the road but many drive by oblivious to the history nearby.

Exiting the rear of the old school grounds through a pinch stile, a V-shaped gap in the wall designed to allow people but not sheep to pass through, I stepped across the Longash Leat on a small clapper bridge. The leat was built to provide water to cottages at the bottom of Longash Hill. It was cut in the 1880s, with granite slabs along the sides added later to prevent leakage and still acts as a water supply.

I followed the leat downstream, passing another clapper which was modified in 2021 to allow access for mobility scooters and soon reached the complex of Bronze Age remains. Most striking are two double stone rows which run either side of the leat. The northern row is about 200 yards long and the southern one 300 yards. Like all Dartmoor's stone rows, their purpose is a mystery. Both run roughly east to west but are not entirely parallel and neither align with a significant sunrise or sunset.

I stopped to talk to a gentleman who was pacing the distance between stones. He comes here often and was keen to tell me that this arrangement of parallel stone rows is unique not only on Dartmoor but throughout the UK. Following the row on the left I soon reached a kistvaen which lies beside it. One of Dartmoor's largest cists, the granite chest was excavated in 1895, when a flint knife, scraper and whetstone (sharpening implement) were found. Unfortunately, in an act of 19th century vandalism, the large capstone was split and the central piece used to make two gateposts.

Merrivale Kistvaen

A path curves diagonally left from the cist towards a standing stone, just before which is Merrivale Stone Circle. Consisting of eleven fairly small stones, this well-preserved stone circle was excavated in the late 19th century. Nothing of interest was found within the circle but a series of pits nearby suggested that there may once have been larger stones outside. A single stone nine metres to the south-east of the circle may have been an outlier that was used in astronomical sightings. The purpose of the three-metre-high menhir (standing stone) is also unknown.

Turning right at the menhir, I returned to the stone rows, pausing to inspect a kistvaen inside a retaining circle midway along the southern row, a most unusual feature within a stone row. As the light failed and with no one else around, a calm but slightly mysterious atmosphere fell over the Merrivale antiquities. I wondered what tales the stones could tell.

Chapter Thirteen

LEIGHON TORS

This was a day of changing plans. I set out with the intention of a short morning walk from Trendlebere Down but on checking my phone at Bovey Tracey found that Torquay's match at Plainmoor had been postponed, so there was no need to get back for the 3pm kick off. Now having all day, I decided on longer walk, so diverted along the road to Moretonhampstead, intending to head to Postbridge.

Near East Wray the car in front came to a halt. The road was flooded. I got out to investigate. It was hard to see how deep the water was but the flood extended round a bend and a small car appeared to be abandoned in the water. The occasional cars coming towards us were splashing through but most arriving from Bovey Tracey turned round on seeing the water. One driver said she'd been there a while and thought that each time a vehicle splashed through it lowered the level a little. I waited a while, contemplating whether to risk the water or turn back.

A lorry pulled up behind us, the driver a little irate to be held up when he could easily get through. We pointed out the broken down car blocking his way. He muttered about having a job to do. With good timing, four people, two in wellies and two with bare feet and rolled up trousers, promptly splashed their way through the water to push. With the car removed the lorry went on its way and a succession of four by fours came through the flood. Several stopped to give advice. It conflicted but most considered that it would be unwise to take a small car through. Mine was only tiny – and it was hired. The friendly people at Simple Car Hire might not be so amenable if I had to admit that their car was stuck in a Dartmoor flood. I turned back, a decision that proved to have been wise when later that day I read a warning from Moretonhampstead Fire Station that the water was over a foot deep. Enough to float a car.

My plan had been to buy lunch at the excellent deli in Moretonhampstead, so not wanting to set out on the moors without food, I returned to Bovey Tracey. Here an intended purchase of a sandwich seemed to turn, without much resistance, into an excellent late breakfast at Brookside Restaurant.

Having now seen reports of flooded roads all over Devon and with a biting cold wind and threatening clouds, I decided to revert to my original plan and headed for Trendlebere Down. My objective was Leighon Tor, one of the lesser-known tors in Max Piper's book.

East Dartmoor is a part of the National Park which receives little attention in literature. It is not the 'wilderness' that is often associated with Dartmoor but contains woodland, rivers and fields, as well as patches of higher moorland. It is a beautiful part of Devon but one that is often ignored by Dartmoor walkers. In its valleys, on its hills and particularly hidden in its woodlands, East Dartmoor is however rich in tors, although many are little known, some only recently discovered and most not named on maps.

Max Piper, a remarkable young man, has taken it upon himself to seek out

Lower Leighon Tor looking to Hound Tor

and document these rocks, many of which are hard to find or are on private land and has gathered together snippets of information including long-forgotten names. His book may become a Dartmoor classic and perhaps invites a challenge for others to visit as many tors as they can.

I chose not to delve into East Dartmoor's wooded valleys but to visit two of Max's lesser-known tors on open moor. Leighon Tor and Lower Leighon Tor are rocks that I'd been close to but never actually visited and seemed a good objective for a short walk on a wild day.

Leaving the car in a car park on Trendlebere Down, I headed uphill on a path that got gradually narrower and wetter. The source of shrieks from further up the hill became apparent when I passed a young couple descending, the girl volunteering that the path was extremely slippery and she'd fallen several times.

I recalled walking near Trendlebere Down some years ago when it was a mass of black, burned by a huge wildfire. Other than fire breaks, put in to limit the size of future blazes, one would not know that major fires in 1997 and 2015 left the land black and seemingly dead. With careful management heather and gorse returned, followed by birds and insects and one bonus of the fire was that previously unknown prehistoric remains were uncovered. The 2015 fire was a result of a controlled burn which spread until extinguished by the Fire Service.

The use of controlled burning to remove overgrown gorse, heather and dead vegetation, allowing new growth and improving the land for grazing, is known as swaling. It is a controversial practice, causing carbon emissions, destroying wildlife, stopping shrubs and trees from growing and precipitating wildfires but without it, especially with current reduced grazing levels, Dartmoor would look very different.

Tom Greeves' 2006 paper, *Swaling on Dartmoor – An Historical Survey* tells us that people have been using fire to modify the vegetation on Dartmoor for thousands of years. Analysis of pollen and charcoal from several sites revealed enhanced deposition of microscopic charcoal between 7700 and 6100BC and Greeves concludes:

Lone tree below Leighon Tor

'The potential for further detailed work on Dartmoor's prehistoric vegetation and the influence of humans is very considerable, but the evidence accumulated so far indicates that some form of 'Swaling' has been practised for approximately 8000 years. The earliest historic record of burning on Dartmoor dates to the end of the fourteenth century and is complemented by two other mid-fifteenth century records.'

After crossing the lane from Haytor Vale I picked up a track towards Leighon Lodge, centre of the 783 acre Leighon estate. In 1902 this was purchased for £9,500 by Washington Singer, of the sewing machine family who once owned the building which contains our Torquay flat. In 2021, now half the size, Leighon was for sale at a guide price of £4.5 million.

After a short distance I took a path on the left which runs along the side of Black Hill, a view to Hound Tor soon opening up, and reached my first objective after ¼ mile. This was Lower Leighon Tor, an extensive tor spread along the north-west slopes of the hill but which isn't shown on OS maps. The upper part of the tor is formed from huge rocks in which signs of splitting by the tare and feather method can be seen.

This method was first used on Dartmoor around 1800 and involves a line of metal wedges with tapered shims (feathers) either side hammered into holes drilled in the granite. Eventually a crack line appears and the stone splits. A short distance below the upper outcrop is a striking pyramidal shaped rock and below these but partly concealed by trees are more huge flat-topped rocks.

It is only recently that commentators have documented the tor, William Crossing being the sole early writer who appears to have mentioned it, referring to the rocks as the place where Rev. Prebendary Wolfe, then a resident of Leighon, saw thirteen buzzards settling. The first record of the tor's name seems to be as recent as 2000, in an article by Tim Jenkinson which appeared in *Dartmoor Magazine*.

I could have spent longer exploring the rocks but was getting quite cold in the biting wind, so resumed my walk towards Leighon Tor. This was a further quarter mile along the side of Black Hill, although no path seems to lead to it from any direction. It is only about 250 yards below Black Tor but is clearly a separate tor, however was not marked on the OS map until Max Piper managed to get it included in 2022. It was however shown on Lt. Col. William Mudge's map of 1809, where it is recorded as Leighn Tor. This is yet another tor on this part of Dartmoor to command superb views, particularly of the Becka Brook valley and the majestic Hound Tor beyond.

The elevated position also gave forewarning of dark clouds scuttling across the sky, so donning full waterproofs I set off back to the car, which I was glad to reach before becoming too wet or cold. Whilst I've walked on the moor in all weathers I no longer find battling the elements to be an enjoyable challenge so temper walks accordingly.

Max Piper's lesser-known tors provide some excellent objectives for short walks and promises intriguing hunts for hidden rocks.

Chapter Fourteen

VIXEN TOR

On 21st February 1972 my father and I walked from Walkhampton, through Samford Spiney, to Vixen Tor, then on to the Merrivale antiquities, returning along the Princetown railway track. Dad's notebook records that we approached Vixen Tor via Heckwood Tor, that it was *'surrounded by farm'* and that we saw a kistvaen north of the tor. Sadly and very controversially, no longer can walkers, climbers and those seeking to visit the Bronze Age burial chamber, access the tor. The owner doesn't want them.

For many years the public enjoyed unrestricted access, then in 2003 the land was purchased by Mary Alford of Moortown Farm near Tavistock. Soon stiles were removed, barbed wire erected and *'Private Property – Keep Out'* spray painted on rocks. Mrs Alford's 'justification' was apparently that the land is part of a working farm and she could be sued by anyone who injured themselves on the tor. Surely this was an excuse? It's a concern that other Dartmoor landowners don't seem to share, perhaps because to successfully sue one has to prove negligence which would be most unlikely on a natural rock formation.

As one of the most striking outcrops on Dartmoor and the tallest free-standing granite pile, which from some angles resembles a sphynx, Vixen Tor was a popular destination for both walkers and climbers. Neither group was prepared to give up access without a fight and the battle was taken up by the Ramblers Association, British Mountaineering Council, the DPA and others.

In 2004 Mrs Alford was prosecuted by Defra under the Environmental Impact Assessment (Uncultivated land and Semi-natural areas) (England) Regulations 2001, for carrying out agricultural improvements without the necessary permission. It was alleged that she had failed to undertake the

Vixen Tor

environmental assessment which is required by law to safeguard plants, wildlife and archaeology.

After a two-day trial, in which the judge concluded that the land was uncultivated, she was convicted at Plymouth Magistrates Court and fined £1,000 with £5,000 costs awarded against her. Mrs Alford had spread some of the land with manure and calcified seaweed, changing it from moorland to semi-improved pasture, an action which potentially negates its wilderness characteristic. Defra regards uncultivated land as a very precious resource and referring to the Vixen Tor case was quoted in the *Western Daily Press*:

> *'If anybody wants to agriculturally intensify land, to basically change its use, they need to complete an environmental impact assessment. That would highlight any of the adverse effects. If (the change) is deemed unsustainable for whatever reason ... it is possible that it would not be allowed to go ahead. When someone cultivates the land without completing an assessment they could be prosecuted. We are talking about the heritage of the countryside.'*

The matter of access went to a Planning Inspectorate Inquiry where Mrs Alford appealed against inclusion of Vixen Tor as Access Land under The

Countryside and Rights of Way Act (CRoW). In September 2004 *The Tavistock Times* reported that:

'She is concerned that public access to the tor, which would be enforced next August under the act, would leave her open to expensive lawsuits from people injured on her land.'

The inspector ruled that the area was not, *'wholly or predominantly unimproved'* moorland and, although the decision was finely balanced, he found in the Alford's favour.

Walkers and climbers were dismayed and DPA Chief Executive John Bainbridge was quoted in *The Guardian*:

'I don't think anybody who knows anything about Dartmoor would think Vixen Tor is not moorland. Anybody who thought they were getting a right to roam on moorland and went to look at Vixen Tor and was told it did not apply would be absolutely astonished.'

The DPA reported with dismay and anger on the Inquiry's decision in its spring 2005 newsletter, *Dartmoor Matters*, describing the decision as *'absurd'*:

'The decision by inspector David Pinner and his assistant Janet Forbes, a qualified botanist and ecologist, followed a week-long inquiry in January into the appeal by Mary and her son Daniel Alford against the inclusion of Vixen Tor on the provisional map of access land. At the inquiry the Countryside Agency, represented by Jeremy Cahill QC, defended its inclusion of the land on the map. The other objectors to the appeal were the Ramblers' Association represented by lawyer Michael Horwood of Foot Anstey Sargent, ecologist Michael Hughes and the energetic and meticulous Devon Area access officer John Skinner. The DPA, British Mountaineering Council and Open Spaces Society also objected.

The inspector was required to decide whether the land qualified as predominantly mountain, moor, heath or down. Janet Forbes studied the area carefully and considered the 'ecological survey undertaken on behalf of the Ramblers' Association .....' 'to be the most reliable ecological evidence presented at the inquiry'. This survey estimated that 55.2 percent of the area was qualifying habitat. Ms Forbes was less sure of the actual amount, although she thought it was likely 'that more of the land consists of relevant qualifying vegetation than not'. The inspector was equally cautious and gave the benefit of the doubt to the Alfords. So although both inspectors admit that the land is likely to qualify, it does not go on the map. This cannot be what the government intended, or the public expected, would be the result of CROW.'

With reference to the illegal spreading of seaweed and manure the article added:

'One cannot help wondering whether that treatment of the land swung the access decision in her favour.'

The British Mountaineering Council were more forthright:

'But the Planning Inspectorate's decision to ignore Vixen Tor's illegal improvement in hearing Ms Alford's appeal now opens the door for other landowners to use similar tactics – flouting the law to help get their land removed from open access designation.'

Several mass trespasses were organised. On 1st January 2004 an informal group, 'The Friends of Vixen Tor', gathered at the tor in a peaceful protest which caused no damage. One of the 'Friends' spoke for many who love Dartmoor; *'No one can own a beautiful tor like this. He/she can only be custodian'.*

On 24th September 2005 a representative of the British Mountaineering Council led around forty climbers and ramblers who ignored the signs and clambered over the barbed wire. Mrs Alford was seen to be observing the trespassers from Windy Post. Some climbed the tor and unfurled a banner saying, *'Vixen Tor for all to Enjoy'*, while others picnicked at its base. The police and DNPA Rangers were on hand in case any trouble occurred but the event went peacefully.

One mass trespass however was said to have resulted in violence, with a climber allegedly assaulted and a rope cut. Police were called and arrests made. *Tavistock Today* reported on 8th December 2005 that Mary Alford was accused of attacking climbers, her son charged with assault on a climber causing actual bodily harm and Francis Yeo, also of Moortown, of criminal damage for allegedly cutting a climber's ropes. All charges were dropped by the CPS at Plymouth Magistrates Court.

New Year's Day protests continued and in 2006 twenty-five people visited the tor but left when approached by Mrs Alford.

The matter eventually went to a public inquiry, held at Princetown in 2011. Campaigners tried to get the land dedicated as Access Land under CRoW, which like most of the open moor, would allow anyone to walk on it. Crucial was whether two footpaths across the land, identified by Devon County Council in 2009, had been used continuously for a period of at least twenty years. Fifty nine witnesses gave evidence that they had used the paths in the 1970s but aerial photography didn't show clear paths and Planning Inspector Mark Yates concluded:

> *'Overall I accept that people have walked to Vixen Tor and used routes through the enclosure.' 'However, I am not satisfied that, on balance, the evidence of public use of the order route, either in whole or part, presented to the inquiry is sufficient to demonstrate the dedication of this route at common law.'*

Ramblers Chief Executive, Tom Franklin, summed up the disappointment of those who wished to walk to the tor or climb on the rocks:

> *'We are obviously disappointed with the inspector's decision and saddened that there is no further access of any sort to this scenic setting. Vixen Tor has a long history of visits by the public and an almost mystical status as a local landmark. It is a great shame that access to this iconic tor has been restricted.'*

Mrs Alford had got her way and despite much ill feeling access to Vixen Tor, one of the gems of Southern Dartmoor, remains barred to the general public, unless of course they choose to trespass, which some did (and indeed still do).

Shortly before my visit someone posted a photo of Vixen Tor on a Dartmoor Facebook page. These were the comments:

> 'Great picture. So near and yet so far.'

> 'Lovely spot. Twas only last week I was sat on top with a nice coffee and an iced bun.'

> 'I thought it was a private tor?'

> 'Pfft. I saw a tor and decided that's where I wanted a coffee and bun break.'

I decided I should take a bun on my walk.

For many years, contrary to common belief, trespass was not a criminal offence. *'Trespassers will be Prosecuted'* signs may have acted as a deterrent but as trespass was a civil wrong and not a criminal offence, trespassers could not be prosecuted. Hence, unless if the individual committed a separate criminal offence such as abusive and threatening behavior, or damage to property, it was not a matter for the police.

The 2022 Police Powers and Protections Act however made certain types of trespass a criminal offence, punishable by up to four months in prison. The Act though is aimed at encampments and an offence will only be permitted if a person over the age of 18:

> *Resides or intends to reside on land in or with a vehicle (including a caravan) without consent; and*
> *Fails to leave and/or remove their property (or re-enters the land) as soon as reasonably practicable when asked to do so; and*
> *Has caused, or is likely to cause significant;*
> *Damage to land/property/the environment*
> *Disruption to the use of land/supply of utilities; and/or*

Distress via 'offensive conduct', such as the use of threatening words or behavior.

Sitting atop a Dartmoor tor eating an iced bun doesn't appear to be included.

I decided that as a responsible walker I should write to Mrs Alford and ask for permission to visit Vixen Tor and the nearby kistvaen. She didn't reply.

A few weeks later I set off from Merrivale, followed the footpath along the Grimstone and Sortridge Leat, then beside the barbed wire-topped drystone wall that divides the farm's enclosures from open moor. The first gate to the enclosure in which stand the massive rocks of Vixen Tor was padlocked. Vixen Tor Cist, a three-thousand-year-old burial chamber which was declared a Scheduled Ancient Monument after it was damaged in 2003, lies close to the gate but with access prohibited.

After a short distance I reached some large rocks, outliers of Vixen Tor and the only ones that may be legitimately visited. These are the rocks which have been defiled with red spray paint; *'No Public Access'* on one and *'No Access'* on another. The paint was reapplied in 2020, repeating an act of vandalism and defacing the moor. This would be an easy point for a trespasser to climb over the wall were it not for a horizontal barbed wire fence protruding from the wall.

Close to the rocks is a boundary stone, inscribed 'SB' and 'WB', which marks the extent of Sampford and Whitchurch Bounds. Just beyond here a wooden pallet rested against the wall, a potential breach in the defences allowing trespassers to clamber over.

The gate at the bottom of the enclosure wasn't locked. An overgrown footpath runs to Vixen Tor Farm, now a holiday cottage in a fine location, although access to the tor is not permitted even for those staying here. Just a fence and thick bracken stood between me and the tor standing proudly in its enclosure.

At this point I feel it is best for the reader to draw their own conclusions as to what I did next:

- Did I obediently view the tor from outside the gate?
- Did I make a token incursion onto the private land, just to make a point?
- Did I enjoy an iced bun sitting on the tor?

Legally Mrs Alford has the right to ban the public from her land. Morally however many disagree. Standing looking at the immense rock pile I considered what I'd do should I ever be in the fortunate position of owning an iconic Dartmoor tor that wasn't on Access Land.

The easiest option would be to ban visitors and keep it to myself, friends, family and maybe a few sheep (not cows, I'm a bit scared of them). There would be none of the potential problems of inconsiderate visitors, litter, campers, barbecues and damage to the rocks. Or perhaps I could open it occasionally, allowing people to visit the rocks once in a while. Or maybe charge for admission like the owners of Becky Falls. If the rocks were in my back garden perhaps I'd allow limited visits by arrangement but Vixen Tor isn't in anyone's garden. It stands on the moor, albeit within a large walled enclosure where sheep sometimes graze. It is in a National Park and as the landowner I would consider I had a moral obligation to allow free and unfettered access.

There were a number of comments after I posted photos of my walk to Vixen Tor on a Dartmoor Facebook page. Most considered that the tor should be open to the public but a few supported the landowner. One poster said that it had been made private after someone injured themselves on the rocks and tried to sue the owner but they declined to elaborate and I could find no report of this anywhere else. I have since been advised by a well-informed source who was present at the inquiries that neither a claim nor threat of claim was mentioned. One poster said they knew the owner and why she'd banned access but chose not to tell us. My letter to Mrs Alford gave her the opportunity to explain why access to the public is not permitted. Having received no reply I cannot comment on anything other than press reports which stated her justification as being concerns regarding liability should a person be injured on the tor.

The owner of course is perfectly within their rights not to allow the public to enter their land and has no obligation to give a reason for doing so. Many

Vixen Tor

people however consider that there is a moral duty to allow reasonable access in a National Park, so to try to facilitate this for Vixen Tor I wrote to Mrs Alford, this time by recorded delivery, offering to pay for public liability insurance for a trial period of one year. Once again there was no reply.

A few weeks later I sent a third letter, explaining that I was looking for an appropriate Dartmoor legacy in memory of my father and asking if Mrs Alford would consider selling the enclosure which contains Vixen Tor. For the third time there was no reply.

The controversy looks set to go on for many years and could fill a book on its own. I shall however end this chapter by relating one of the legends of Vixen Tor.

Many years ago there lived in a cave at the foot of the tor a wicked old witch named Vixana. She was tall and thin, had a large hooked nose, two fangs for teeth and naturally was quite evil. Each morning she would emerge from her cave, climb to the summit of the tor and scan the moor looking for unwary travellers. Vixen Tor stood on the important path from Tavistock to Ashburton which pre-dated the road. When a traveller reached the bog at the foot of the tor she would wave her stick, summoning a mist that enveloped them so that they lost their way and fell into the mire. Once she heard their awful cries as the bog sucked them into a terrible death, Vixana would lift the mist and enjoy watching their struggles. The last sound the doomed traveller would hear was the cackles of the evil witch.

Fortunately every such story also requires a hero and this was a moorman, who of course was handsome and who in return for helping the pixies had been given special powers. Hearing of the misfortunate of those who had strayed too close to Vixana's tor, he set out to deal with the evil witch. She spied him walking across the moor and waited until he reached the bog, at which point the witch sent down her usual impenetrable mist. Vixana was however unaware of the young man's special powers, one of which, quite conveniently, was the ability to see through thick mist. Hence he remained safe, not straying from the path. On seeing him emerge unharmed the witch let out a scream of frustration and started to weave another of her evil spells. At this point the man hurriedly made use of the second power which had been bestowed upon him by the pixies, slipping a ring onto his finger and immediately becoming invisible. Confused, the witch leaned over the tor as she looked for the man but unbeknown to her, he had crept round the back. Catching Vixana unaware he climbed the rocks and pushed the evil witch to her death.

To complete the story an even happier ending is required. The people of the moor were so grateful to be rid of Vixana that they gave the young man enough money to buy a farm of his own. Before long and with an element of predictability, he met a beautiful young lady from a neighbouring village. With him being so handsome and her so pretty, they fell in love and soon married. Travellers were always welcome at their farm and whenever anyone was lost on the moor he was always the first to volunteer to search.

Is there a handsome young man who without recourse to pushing anyone off the top, can help reach a mutually agreeable solution that would allow the public access to the iconic Vixen Tor?

PART 6

THREE DARTMOOR WOODS

After the last Ice Age most of Dartmoor was covered with trees. These were gradually removed by early settlers, after which blanket peat bog formed on much of the higher moor. Most of the high moor remains largely free of trees, an environment influenced by altitude, climatic changes and from human intervention, with grazing of farm animals restricting new growth. The open views are a huge part of the attraction of the wild moorland. Around ten percent of the National Park is now tree-covered, largely fitting into three types and on the whole adding to the moor's diversity and with arguably some exceptions, its beauty.

Dartmoor's three high-altitude oak woods, Black-a-tor-Copse, Piles Copse and Wistman's Wood, are internationally important for their plant and animal life. With diminutive, wind-twisted trees, carpets of moss, lichens and liverworts, they are enchanting places and form the highest concentration of this type of wood in the UK. These are remnants from the woodland which covered most of Dartmoor until removed by people, mainly in the Bronze Age, to develop grazing pasture. Most of the remainder were cut down in the 12th century for charcoal used in extracting and smelting tin.

Broadleaf woods cover the steep-sided valleys of Dartmoor's rivers as they flow from the higher moor to the surrounding villages. Most class as ancient, dating back to at least the 17th century and support many nesting birds including wood warbler and pied flycatcher.

More recent and more controversial are the large forestry plantations, notably Bellever, Burrator and Fernworthy. Some were planted around reservoirs and all are commercially harvested for timber. Mainly coniferous, with few native trees, these plantations are generally less attractive to both people and wildlife. In the 1960s more of Dartmoor could have been lost to coniferous forests through the tax avoidance schemes that caused so much harm to the Flow Country in Scotland and we are fortunate that areas such as High House Waste were saved.

I selected walks visiting one of each type of Dartmoor's main woodlands; Piles Copse, Bellever Forest and Fatherford Wood.

Chapter Fifteen

PILES COPSE

Located in the beautiful valley of the River Erme, Piles Copse is often bypassed by those walking on the Redlake tramway higher up the hill, but is well worth a visit, although access is not as easy as it was.

Like much of Dartmoor, Harford Moor is privately owned, but is a 'Common of Pasture' meaning that local farmers have the right to graze livestock and designated as 'Access Land' where anyone can walk freely. Since 1931 it has been owned by the Howell family of Lukesland, an estate on the road from Ivybridge to Harford. Their enchanting woodland garden is open to the public in spring and autumn and I can thoroughly recommend a visit.

For many years walkers were able to park in an old gravel pit at the top of a narrow lane from Harford. It was known as Harford Moor Car Park but in February 2021 closed signs suddenly appeared. The car park had been shut arbitrarily by the landowner, who it seemed considered there were too many people walking on this part of the moor. There was no consultation with those who had used it for years. Initially this appeared to be temporary but before long more permanent signs were erected and walkers advised to park in Ivybridge, adding 2½ miles in each direction to their walks. The owners cited congestion in the lane, erosion of paths and antisocial behaviour by campers at Piles Copse.

Signs on the moor asked people to spread out, rather than using eroding paths, potentially impacting on ground-nesting birds and the opposite of advice given in busy areas like the Lake District. There however the paths are maintained by organisations such as the National Trust and few people want Dartmoor's grassy paths to be paved or gravelled. The alternative was said to be paths eroding down to the rock beneath, with peat and soil washed into rivers.

Many of those who had used the car park as an easy access point to the southern moor were outraged. Not everyone is able to add five miles to a walk and for many it would mean this part of moor was effectively inaccessible. It was pointed out that cattle cause more erosion than walkers, especially around gateways and if people use common sense damage can be minimised. The car park's capacity of around a dozen cars didn't allow hordes to access the moor.

I avoided any problems by taking the train to Ivybridge, a taxi to Harford and walking up the lane to the moor gate. Here I met a DNPA ranger who was adding to the proliferation of notices, so took the opportunity to discuss the controversial closure of the car park. DNPA were well aware of the problem he told me but there were no funds for a solution. They had no power to force the landowner to allow parking and no money to purchase a suitable piece of land should one be available. My suggestion of a minibus from Ivybridge had been considered and they'd spoken with the community transport people who run a 'dial a ride' type service towards the coast but nothing could be arranged – certainly not without funding. The one success they had achieved was to get agreement for walkers to have free use of Ivybridge station car park but there appeared to be no prospect of a better solution to access on this part of the moor.

And so to my walk. Picking up a path that runs north from the 'car park' and continues beyond the wall, I headed along the valley of the River Erme, one of the most picturesque on Dartmoor. After half a mile the path passes a well-preserved kistvaen then goes through a gate into an enclosure known as Lower Piles. Originally Bronze Age enclosures, the substantial walls of Lower Piles, and Higher Piles a little further up the valley, were erected when they were farms in the Middle Ages. Both were abandoned in the 19th century, leaving a complex of stone walls amongst which are Bronze Age boundaries and hut circles.

Approaching the tiny Piles Brook I glimpsed a flash of movement – a roe deer. Until a few years ago I'd never seen a deer on the open moor but this was the second time I'd spotted one in this area and they are becoming more common. Deer and I stood dead still for several minutes, perhaps both thinking that if we didn't move the other wouldn't notice us, until it blinked first and lolloped off down the valley.

The path took me into Piles Copse and what a wonderful place this is. The trees are larger and less wind-twisted than the more exposed Wistman's Wood, but grassy glades and fewer rocks allow easier access. The clitter (granite boulders that over millennia have tumbled down the hillside) prevents sheep, cattle and ponies from nibbling young shoots, allowing the wood to self-sustain. A path runs close to the river, the clear flowing water adding to the wood's incredible beauty. I walked slowly, stopping frequently to enjoy the vistas and serene atmosphere. The river divides around a small island and hopping over the almost dry channel I investigated the little cascades, pools, rocks, trees, grasses and flowers that combine to make Piles Copse such a magical place. My notes questioned whether this was the best spot in the wood.

Just before the end of the copse however I found an equally beautiful place for lunch; a grassy bank by a deep, brown pool, with a low waterfall feeding it and the steep-sided valley beyond. Fish plopped out of the water, dragonflies darted about and birds sang. Sheep on the hillside stayed respectfully quiet as if they understood this was a place just for wildlife. I sat quietly, conscious

Piles Copse

Piles Copse

that I was the only human in the wood and honoured to be amongst nature in such an idyllic spot.

I wrote in my notebook, *'Is this the most beautiful place on Dartmoor?'* but on emerging from the wood looked at the view across the hills of Southern Dartmoor and wondered if perhaps the tors and hills trump the rivers. After due reflection I concluded that Dartmoor's beauty could be divided into the near view – flowers, mosses, lichens and grasses, the middle views of streams, waterfalls, trees, and the far view, the tors, valleys and expanses of wild moor, but that one cannot truly compare the various aspects of the moor's beauty.

Sadly not everyone treats the moor with the respect it deserves. Piles Copse had become a popular site for campers but some left rubbish, cut firewood from trees and caused damage with fires. The copse could not sustain the level of use and abuse, which made it impossible for the landowner to fulfil their obligations as custodians of a Site of Special Scientific Interest, so in January 2020 a temporary ban on camping was announced. Not everyone heeded the signs and Dartmoor Marshals were brought in to patrol the wood. On one occasion a large family group was asked to move on after being caught pitching camp despite having read the signs. Others removed stones from a wall to make a fireplace and illegal campers damaged trees for firewood, a criminal offence in an SSSI.

Conservation work was carried out to restore the damage, with fire sites reseeded and walls repaired. Fences were erected to keep out grazing animals. Thanks to this work and the limited number of visitors, I had found Piles Copse to be in excellent shape. In time it must be hoped that a compromise can be found that enables easier access but if a minority persist in selfish activities that damage the wood one can understand the landowner continuing to impose some restrictions. Perhaps more effort should be made to educate, deter and catch the miscreants, rather than punishing the majority. Closing the car park was however an act that few have sympathy with.

It's hard to get a taxi back from Harford in the afternoon as they tend to be busy with school jobs, but I was happy to walk the extra couple of miles across the moor to Ivybridge. Mostly downhill, it's a pleasant walk and one which I took slowly on what had become a very hot afternoon. I paused by the trees that surround the now disused Ivybridge reservoir (this was on open moor when I first remember it) to view a fine collection of hut circles, the sheltered valley by a stream evidently a good place for Bronze Age dwellers four thousand years ago.

This was my first visit to the Butter Brook since I'd ended up prone

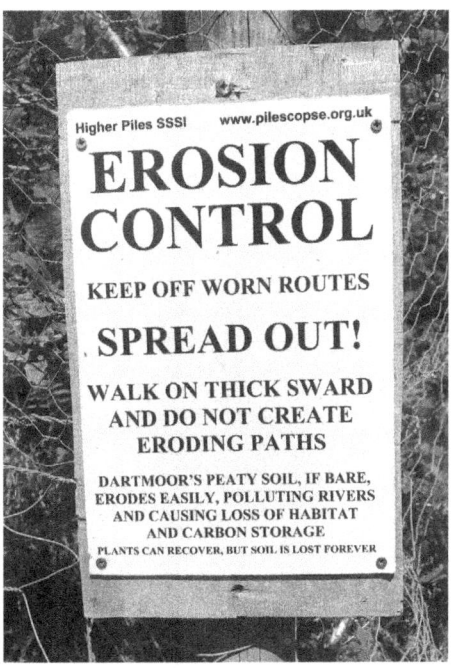

Erosion sign, Piles Copse

across the stream with my legs in the water and my face on a rock. Taking great care, this time I used the stepping stones and made the crossing without breaking even one bone. With plenty of time until the train I joined two herds of cows and a flock of sheep who had stretched out along a narrow strip of shade by wall beneath Western Beacon. Over the wall was Lukesland, home of the owners of Harford Moor and the wonderful Piles Copse. They have a difficult job in managing the land to balance the needs of farmers, nature and sustainability, with the increasing numbers of people who wish to visit the moor. Their conservation work and restrictions had added to my enjoyment of the day but for others it means that a visit to one of Dartmoor's gems may not be possible.

Surely some way can be found to facilitate the reasonable access to a National Park that people expect but with no legal obligation to allow parking the landowners hold all the power – too much power many would say.

Chapter Sixteen

BELLEVER FOREST

Bordering the main road from Tavistock to Moretonhampstead, Bellever Forest lies close to Postbridge and almost in the centre of the National Park. Unlike Dartmoor's ancient woods, the forest is neither old nor natural. It was one of many planted across Britain after the First World War to replenish the country's depleted timber stocks and continues to be harvested. The first trees were planted in 1924 and the forest much expanded after Bellever Farm was purchased by the Forestry Commission in 1931.

Planting of the forest in this area rich in antiquities was opposed by the DPA and it was eventually agreed that a strip of land from Kraps Ring to Bellever Tor would be left unplanted. It remains controversial as an unnatural incursion into wild moorland which has left other prehistoric relics hidden in the trees. Tim Sandles on his excellent website *legendarydartmoor. co.uk* speaks for many when he says, *'One of the biggest travesties as far as Dartmoor archaeology is concerned must be the forestation of the area around Bellever'*.

On a warm summer's day Deb accompanied me for a circular walk to explore the forest and some of its Bronze Age remains. Leaving the car at Postbridge, we crossed the road and followed a gently rising track between the trees.

Whilst lacking the beauty of natural deciduous woods, the forest was not as dark and dead as some coniferous plantations appear. Enough light was getting through to allow limited growth beneath the trees but it wasn't an environment that invited one to explore away from paths.

At a crossroads half a mile from the forest car park we turned right onto a narrower path that soon emerged onto the open moor of Lakehead Hill. The hill would have been covered in conifers were it not for the objections of

Bellever Forest

conservationists. This was far better – real Dartmoor, with fine views across the moor and Bronze Age remains to explore.

A small copse provided shade for lunch in an attractive natural environment, after which we continued a short distance to a cairn circle, a burial site with a ring of stones around it. The next stop was a short stone row almost on the summit of the hill, then another cairn circle, this one containing a cist. Descending the strip of moorland we passed more Bronze Age remains in the form of hut circles, settlements and enclosures. All would have been hidden amongst trees had the foresters got their way.

A short ascent on a well-worn path took us to Bellever Tor from where we enjoyed remarkable 360-degree views across the moor. One of Dartmoor's finest tors, with several huge rock stacks, it can be picked out standing above the trees from many points on the moor, hence the views from it are outstanding.

Bellever Forest

Our return route turned right below the tor onto a path through the forest, bypassed the hamlet of Bellever by crossing fields, then picked up a path on the far side of the lane, coming out at Postbridge clapper. The last section was quite rough, down steep and eroded steps.

After duly viewing the clapper bridge and perusing the visitor centre, we agreed that an early dinner at the Warren House Inn, the highest in Southern England, would make a fitting end to our Dartmoor day out. It did indeed.

Returning to the controversy of Bellever Forest, two articles in *The Ecologist* provide contrasting views.

The environmental journalist Tesni Clare questions whether Bellever is even a forest, a word which in her mind summons the, *'feel and smell of diverse old-growth, towering moss-clad beeches and twisted oaks, dense undergrowth overwhelmed with insects and fungi'*. If this is her definition then Bellever doesn't meet it, but a *'large area covered with trees'* would be a more common description.

Clare goes on to lament how some forests no longer match her childhood memories of, *'rich, tangled, ancient woodlands'* - '*It seems now that a 'forest' can be orderly rows of skinny, non-native conifers, planted too close together for any sunlight to penetrate the forest floor'*.

I have much sympathy for her view, however the parts of Bellever through which we walked were not the dark, austere landscape, with nothing appearing to live at ground level, that I have so disliked when walking through parts of Fernworthy, Burrator and Beardown plantations.

Mike Seddon, Chief Executive of Forestry England, responded a month later, initially with sadness that Tesni Clare had not enjoyed her walk through Bellever Forest in the way that many thousands do each year. He agreed that the forest is mostly conifer, saying it produces excellent, sustainable construction-grade timber but adds:

'Bellever Forest has Bronze Age archaeology sites; populations of rare and protected birds; and open access so people are free to roam and

Bellever Tor (Debbie Caton)

explore. Alongside the conifers, it also has gnarly moss-covered broadleaf trees and open meadows. The forest hums with insects and is bursting with wildflowers, fungi, lichens and ferns.'

Seddon accepts that mistakes were made in the effort to create a strategic timber reserve after the First World War, with conifers planted in huge numbers, many in places that we now see as inappropriate, but says that much has changed in the last hundred years:

'We understand the value of forests beyond the price tag of timber. We recognise that our forests are crucial for wildlife to survive. We value forests for the spaces they provide for people to be active, connect with nature and rejuvenate.'

After reading such contrasting views I went back to Bellever Forest on a cold afternoon in January, walking along paths to Kraps Ring, a settlement of Bronze Age huts within a ring wall. This impressive prehistoric remain would have been indiscernible had the original plan to forest the whole of the hill been allowed to proceed and is the only Bellever settlement that has been relatively undisturbed by the forestation. A plan of 1891 shows fifteen huts enclosed by the ring wall, of which eleven can still be seen.

It had been a pleasant walk on paths through gaps in the woodland but on my return I left the paths and walked beneath a few broadleaf trees that

Bellever Tor (Debbie Caton)

border the open hillside and into the forest amongst closely packed pine trees. In some places sufficient light penetrated to allow a carpet of mosses to grow on the ground but in others there was just a thick covering of dead pine needles and little sign of life. Devoid of greenery until a great height, this seemed an alien environment of tree trunks and little else. It could even be called a man-made wilderness, although would not be what we have in mind when describing the moorland of Dartmoor.

Mike Seddon is right that Bellever is a diverse forest but so too is Tesni Clare when she writes of, *'eerily empty spaces holding singular species efficiently grown for human need'*. It is good that there is now more understanding that we should move on from the dismal monoculture conifer forests which are largely inhospitable to both wildlife and people, and that management now aims for forests to be biodiverse and attractive places to visit. I still maintain however that Dartmoor isn't the place for them.

Bellever is one of the most popular places on Dartmoor and there is no doubt that it has beauty and atmosphere. I would however suggest that accessibility is a factor in the forest's popularity and it is mainly the streams, tor, open areas of moorland and edges of the forest that most people enjoy, not the areas of dense conifers.

The final word I shall give to Harry Trude, the man who planted the first conifers at Bellever and Fernworthy, who Judy Chard quotes in *Along the Dart*:

> 'They've altered the look of the land though. They take away from Nature, the natural look of the moor.'

Chapter Seventeen

FATHERFORD WOOD

My original plan was to visit Yarner Wood in East Dartmoor, England's first National Nature Reserve. It is a beautiful place, as are many of the woods on that part of the moor but I changed my mind and decided to explore one of the wooded valleys where rivers run off the higher moor. These are very typical of Dartmoor and the sort of landscape that would be extended if those who wish to see the moor rewilded get their way. I chose Fatherford in the East Okement Valley as it's a walk easily accessed by train.

It was a good decision not to head to the open moor from Okehampton as the Ten Tors event was setting up and it would have been far from quiet. The lady in the visitor centre on the station told me that the bus from Bude this morning had been delayed in the traffic and missed its connecting train to Exeter but the passengers didn't really mind. No doubt they, like me, headed for the Bulleid Buffet.

A late breakfast duly consumed, I picked up the bridleway which starts immediately on the right of the road into town and runs high above the East Okement. It soon passes through a gate and enters Tramlines Wood. Owned by the Woodland Trust, this 14 acre linear wood covers the steep slope between the river and railway but sitting just north of the A30 it is just outside the National Park.

The ancient wood is thought to have had its origins in the 12th century Okehampton Deer Park and is a good example of western upland oak woodland. The woodland has received little management in recent decades which has allowed holly and hazel, along with the ubiquitous brambles to grow beneath the high forest structure. Historically cattle had access to the wood which would have helped to control species like holly. There are a number of significant older trees that could be deemed to be of veteran interest. Looking down the steep slope into the trees I could see bird's nests, gnarled and twisted branches and green vegetation on the floor. This varied habitat is home to an abundance of wildlife and plants, including pied flycatchers, dormice and lichens.

At the start of my walk through the woods the sounds of boys shouting as they played a rugby match on the school field below filtered through the trees. Once these were out of earshot the unwelcome muffled roars of traffic from the A30 above intruded into the peace of the wood. After passing through a gate which marks the boundary of the Woodland Trust's ownership, the path descended to a delightful meadow speckled yellow with dandelions. This beautiful area beside the river is owned by Okehampton United Charities, *'for the benefit of people in the town and surrounding hamlets'*.

From here the track curved right, passing a large chicken coop and reaching Fatherford Viaduct, where the railway crosses the East Okement. The track on which I'd walked was once a tramway, built to bring materials for construction of the viaduct and giving its name to the wood.

In this pretty spot are not one but three bridges over the river, as well as a ford. The largest and most impressive is Fatherford Viaduct, a stone structure dating from the 1870s which carries the railway high above. Just behind this is the far less attractive (ugly would be a better description) concrete bridge over which cars and lorries thunder by, bringing their unwelcome noise and pollution to Dartmoor.

The third bridge has a sad story. It was opened in 2011 in memory of twelve-year-old Charlotte Saunders, who was swept away and drowned when her pony Jake stumbled as she crossed the ford in 2001. Normally a few inches deep, heavy rain had swollen the river to a depth of around three feet and it was running very fast, washing poor Charlotte downstream where she became entangled in rocks and branches. Unlike the narrower footbridge which it replaced, this can be used by horse riders. Named Charlotte's Bridge, her name engraved is on the fence.

From the bridges the path ascends towards open moor, passing through a gate by a signpost indicating East Okement Valley and Klondyke Corner.

East Okement, Fatherford Wood

The fast-flowing river runs through the steep-sided, tree-filled West Cleave Gorge – a beautiful place. Fatherford Rocks, a largely hidden tor, could be spotted amongst vegetation at the top of the right bank. Trees on the valley floor were mostly small but some on the side were enormous and looked ready to slide down when no one was looking. Rivulets ran down rocks on the valley side and the Okement splashed over a series of cascades as it tumbled off the moor. Pebbles had been deposited as the flow slowed on a bend forming a stony beach. With the river, rocks, greenery and ancient trees, this was a natural and very beautiful place. My notes recorded, '*so much better than Bellever*'.

After half a mile of thoroughly enjoyable walking from the viaduct I reached a clam bridge which crosses the Moor Brook, a small stream that rises on the slopes of Rowtor and passes Okehampton Camp. Here I sat down to think. It had been a lovely walk but one that I reluctantly realised I should curtail due to an injured foot. Each step was painful and a Google search (not necessarily a good idea for medical matters) had suggested tendonitis and that excessive walking could cause long-term damage. Not wishing to add another chapter to my mishaps section, I had been walking slowly and trying to choose a point to turn back based on the balance of my desire to enjoy the valley but not cause (too much) further injury.

I could have continued beside the Moor Brook and made a circular walk via East Hill but with the pain in my foot increasing decided that the most sensible option would be to turn back following my outward route and make a longer walk another day. As I walked slowly back to the viaduct I considered how Fatherford and Tramlines Woods compared to Piles Copse and Bellever Forest.

East Okement Footbridge

Without intending to do so, I had chosen to visit 'woods' from three different categories; a copse, a forest and a wood. The definition of a forest was considered in the Bellever chapter. According to Oxford Languages, a copse is a *'small collection of trees'* and a wood *'an area of land, smaller than a forest, that is covered with growing trees'*. Piles Copse is the smallest of the three, although it could be argued that it merits 'wood' status, and Bellever Forest by some way the largest. Size is however not the most significant difference.

Bellever is a largely coniferous commercial forest. It has areas of beauty but others that are dark and of limited value for nature. Fatherford and Tramlines are what one might consider to be traditional British woods, with tall, native, deciduous trees. These are typical of the woods that surround Dartmoor's rivers as they run off the moor, often through a gorge, or cleave as they are sometimes called in Devon. Fatherford is a beautiful place but not unique to Dartmoor. The smaller oaks of the high-altitude Piles Copse, along with Wistman's Wood and Black-a-tor-Copse, are however rare environments and in my opinion the most attractive, meriting the description of being magical places. It is interesting to consider rewilding and how the woods would fare without human interference.

The conifers of Bellever are not a natural environment but if they were to be felled and unmanaged (other than removal of newly seeded conifers), the land would eventually revert to moor, scrub and broadleaf trees. To an extent the mix would depend on whether grazing animals were controlled. It would form a more biodiverse environment than the present forest but if livestock were excluded the area's prehistoric remains may soon become hidden.

All three of Dartmoor's ancient high-altitude woods require a degree of human management to maintain them as they are, although much of this is necessitated by our own activities, either directly or through our livestock. Wistman's has actually increased in size but management is required to prevent footfall damaging the delicate mosses and lichens. The owners of Piles Copse have made access more difficult and put right the harm caused by inconsiderate people. Areas of Black-a-tor-Copse have been fenced off to prevent the more adventurous sheep from getting amongst the clitter and

Dartmoor resident

nibbling oak seedlings that allow the wood to regenerate. Without human intervention the woods would spread, regaining some of their prehistoric territory but only if we remove our grazing animals and limit our own access. The growth of ground-based vegetation in Tramlines Wood shows how lack of human management will allow a more diverse but impenetrable environment to form. If grazing animals were removed Fatherford Wood would eventually extend onto open moorland further up the river valley, increasing biodiversity but changing the moor's character.

It was only four weeks later when I was able to go back to this lovely gorge and with my foot now recovered, to continue onto the open moor. The difference in the wood was quite striking and with the trees now in full leaf it was an even more beautiful walk. Far more than the conifers of Bellever, the natural cycle of deciduous trees means that every month the views and atmosphere in the wood change, with each season bringing its own beauty. Sunshine on the vivid green leaves of early summer gave the wood a magical feeling and as at Piles Copse, I stopped by the river to enjoy lunch.

This time I crossed the bridge over the Moor Brook, soon following a steep path that ascended beside waterfalls as the East Okement crashes down off the moor. I thought of the man working in Haytor Visitor Centre who told me there aren't any waterfalls on Dartmoor.

Another wooden bridge took me over the river to a path that doubles back on the open moor, passing Scarey Tor and descending to the Okement where it meets the Black-a-ven Brook. From here I walked a short distance downstream to a small pool, known as Cullever Steps, a popular wild swimming spot. Set in a natural amphitheatre, surrounded by rocks one side and a grassy bank on the other, it is a beautiful spot to sit for a while even if you don't fancy a dip. The natural pool was enlarged by a dam which was built to deepen it for swimming and this afternoon two lads and an older lady were enjoying a swim.

Making a circular walk I followed the track up the hill, overtaking the swimming lady as she climbed very slowly, returning to her car which was parked by a military track. I thought once more about public use of these roads. If not permitted the lady might not be able to enjoy a swim at Cullever Steps but the two lads who soon drove past me could probably have walked from off the moor. Cars parked on the moor allowed people access but impacted on its wildness, the roads and cars effectively meaning that any wilderness area couldn't start until further into the moor. It is a difficult balance and I wondered how I'll feel in say twenty years time when I won't be able to walk so far. Would I be content to know I could never get into wilder Dartmoor or would I prefer to know that by keeping my car off the moor I wouldn't be affecting its wildness for others?

Nun's Cross Farm

PART 7

THREE REMOTE HOUSES

As one walks, rides or drives along Dartmoor's roads an isolated house or farm may be spotted a little way into the moor. There is no doubt that these homes are remote but as recently as the mid-20th century there were houses lived in on the moor where the only access was a rough track. Dotted across the moor are the remains of historic Dartmoor dwellings which were possibly the most isolated homes in England.

Some like Nun's Cross and Teignhead were farms, where the occupiers eked out a living from sheep and cattle, growing vegetables for their own consumption. Others were associated with Dartmoor's industries and the largest number were warrens, where rabbits were farmed for their meat and fur. Several of these are mentioned in other chapters as I've walked past them but for this section I chose to visit two remote former farmhouses and the home to the manager of a peat works.

Brown's House, possibly the shortest lived and most remote of Dartmoor's farms, made for a superb walk either side of the West Dart Valley. Nun's Cross Farm was combined with a walk along the Devonport Leat, and the isolated remains of the aptly named Bleak House beside the Rattlebrook stream reached from the Dartmoor Inn near Lydford.

Chapter Eighteen

NUN'S CROSS FARM

Deb dropped me on the road to Whiteworks and I followed the half-mile track across the moor to Nun's Cross Farm. It is hard to imagine why John Hooper chose to build his farmhouse at this remote spot. He wasn't a Dartmoor man but saw potential to make a living here, leased a smallholding from the Duchy of Cornwall at £2.10s per annum, built enclosures and a house overlooking Fox Tor Mire, moving in with his wife Sarah in 1871. After buying a cow his limited funds had virtually disappeared but over time he made a success of the venture, bringing up a family here and eventually selling a hundred pounds' worth of cattle each year.

After Sarah died in 1889 he moved to Princetown, living with his daughter Anna Marie and her husband Edward Worth, of the well-known Dartmoor family from nearby Peat Cot. It is likely that John continued to work at Nun's Cross Farm and when he died in 1895 Edward took it over, extending the cottage and converting it into a cattle shed. In 1901 he built the substantial two-storey, three-bedroom house which still stands today and moved his family here from Princetown.

Several residents followed the Worths, the last being Mr and Mrs Phillips and their son Jack but after World War Two the farmhouse was abandoned and soon fell into disrepair. In the 1970s and 80s it was used by the Royal Navy as a camping base for training and it is now owned by Mount Kelly Independent School and available for hire as a bunk house. With basic facilities it accommodates up to thirty-six people, although there is no electricity and visitors are directed to the leat for water.

A 1968 photograph in Elisabeth Stanbrook's very informative *Dartmoor Forest Farms*, shows the original cottage largely intact, so probably was in a similar state when I first visited with my father in 1971, having walked from

Nun's Cross Farm

Dousland via Eylesbarrow Mine, but now just rubble remains. Standing starkly on the remote and wild moor, the newer farmhouse is one of the most isolated buildings remaining on Dartmoor.

Close to the farm is Nun's Cross, at seven feet high arguably the most impressive of all Dartmoor's crosses. Dating from either Saxon or early medieval times, it is one of the oldest crosses on the moor. It was originally known as Siward's Cross and 'SIWARD' is engraved on the eastern face. Dartmoor has many crosses and whilst none are alike, Nun's Cross is remarkable not only for its age but also for its unusual appearance. Both arms are short for its great height, and one deeper than the other, giving a slightly lopsided appearance. The shaft has been broken and repaired, the damage occurring in 1846 when two lads pushed it over. There is no known connection to nuns, either in history or legend.

A grassy path from the cross took me over the brow of the low hill, through tin workings, crossing from the watershed of the Dart to the Plym. Behind me was wildest Dartmoor and ahead the slightly tamer moorland of Walkhampton Common and a glimpse of the sea.

I paused to look at a ruined building beneath a beech tree which is known as 'Old Farm', a name it was referred to by former residents of Nun's Cross farm. The origin of the building varies according to sources. Although in an area of extensive mining, it is larger than tinners' huts and considered by some to have been a small farm. The ruin is however generally thought more likely to have been a blacksmiths used by workers constructing the Devonport Leat.

Constructed in 1790 to take fresh water to Plymouth Docks, which became Devonport Dockyard in 1824, the leat meanders across Dartmoor, descending slowly around hillsides, the water flowing gently off the moor. It originally ran for 27 miles, supplying more than two million gallons of fresh water a day and whilst the lower section is long-disused, the moorland end still serves an operational purpose. Water is picked up at three headweirs, starting on the West Dart near Wistman's Wood, then collecting from the Cowsic and Blackabrook streams, eventually feeding into Burrator Reservoir.

A few yards beyond the ruin is a narrow gorge into which the leat emerges from a tunnel through a stone arch. For most of its length the leat makes a series of loops as it gently descends from the high moor but the 18th century engineers had to find a way to take it from the Dart watershed at head of the Swincombe Valley into the upper Meavy Valley. Their solution was a tunnel. The original linked several existing adits (horizontal passages) from Nun's Cross Mine. This was replaced around 1850 by the current stone-lined tunnel that runs for 640 yards under the hill and was constructed with the help of tinners.

On rounding a bend a cross appeared on the skyline. Standing beside the leat, this is Hutchinson's Cross. Much more modern than most of Dartmoor's crosses, it is cut from a single piece of granite and stands in a large boulder, occupying the socket of an ancient cross that once stood here. The current cross was erected in 1968 by Lt. Commander B. Hutchinson R.N. as a memorial to his mother Mrs S.L. Hutchinson. The shaft bears the inscription 'S.L.H' on the western face and '1887 – 1966' on the eastern.

The slow-moving leat picks up water draining off wet ground as it bends round the hillside, reaching Older Bridge where thousands of pond skaters stood (or skated?) on the water's still surface. The track crossing the bridge

Hutchinson's Cross

is known as the Monks' Path and is marked by crosses at intervals across the moor. It is said to have once linked Buckfast and Tavistock Abbeys but this section would also have been used by miners and farmers and was known as the Peat Cott Track, being the only track to this remote hamlet prior to construction of the road from Princetown.

At an ancient cart bridge I diverted left to view Crazywell Pool, which dates back to tin mining times and is probably a flooded mine excavation. There are many legends associated with this steep-sided, mysterious body of water, the best known being that it is bottomless. When villagers from Walkhampton decided to investigate and tied all the church bell ropes together then fed them weighted into the pool, it was estimated that their full extent of 540 feet had failed to reach the bottom. However, in the particularly dry summer of 1844 the pool was almost emptied to supplement the Devonport Leat and the bottom found. Its depth was estimated at a mere 15 feet. It may have a bottom but is another legend true – that the level rises and falls with the tides in Plymouth Sound? Unsurprisingly, it is not. The level is fairly constant, the pool being fed by an underground spring. Perhaps it is true that sometimes at night an articulate voice is heard calling out the name of the next person in the village to die. Or that anybody who looks into the water on Midsummer's Eve will see an image of the next parishioner to die. Maybe it is haunted by a witch who does nothing more sinister than offer bad advice.

I paused here for cake, looking down on the pool where a group of ponies enjoyed a drink. Exchanging pleasantries with a couple of walkers, we agreed that the pool was the lowest we'd ever seen it – but still bottomless of course.

Returning to the leat, I soon reached Raddick Falls where the water drops spectacularly 50 metres towards the River Meavy. It crosses the Meavy on a metal aqueduct known as Iron Bridge, which is still supported by the granite piers of the original wooden aqueduct that was built in 1792. I first saw the aqueduct on a wet day in 1971 and recall seeing a succession of crosses looming out of the mist, being impressed with the leat falls but somewhat disappointed with the aqueduct. I'd imagined it would be a huge stone viaduct.

Leaving the open moor the leat enters Stanlake Plantation, one of the areas of forest planted around Burrator to aid drainage. It's a very pleasant walk with a wide path beside the faster flowing leat. Here I experienced a little incident that could easily have made my Dartmoor mishaps section.

I'd been carrying my map and opened it up to check the route. It's laminated and a combination of slippery surface, cold hands and wind (possibly with a little help from my own carelessness) resulted in the map falling from my hands and dropping into the leat. This is one of the faster flowing sections of leat and the map hurried off downstream, pursued by its owner. A handy rock allowed me to lean over and grab it. Unfortunately, just as I regained ownership of the map a bottle of water fell from my pocket and bobbed its way downstream. Once again I set off in pursuit, keeping keep pace with the bottle until finding a spot where it was close enough to the bank to reach. Just as I was leaning over the water to retrieve it a couple walking behind caught me up, and presumably having viewed the entire debacle, asked if I was OK. Having established that I was merely a little stupid or unfortunate, depending on how one wishes to view matters, they continued on their way. Both items were returned to the safety of my rucksack and the trousers that somehow got wet in the rescue operation soon dried. All ended well and on this occasion there was no need to attend A&E.

Glad to be reasonably dry and still in one piece I continued through the plantation, approaching close to Burrator Lake, with views to the iconic Sheepstor. A lane took me down to the lake and past another waterfall, this one also fed by the leat as it ends its journey across the moor in the reservoir. My journey ended by the dam where Deb soon arrived to pick me up.

Chapter Nineteen

BROWN'S HOUSE

It was one of those early autumn days which could turn out hot or cold, dry or wet, calm or windy, or anything in between. After much deliberation and two changes of mind, I set out from Two Bridges in sunshine wearing two layers, with three more in the bag, plus the foil survival blanket I always carry. Knowing how quickly Dartmoor weather can change, my increased caution with advancing age tends to tip the balance from minimising weight in the bag towards ensuring I'll be warm and dry whatever elements may arrive.

Leaving behind tempting odours of lunch drifting from the Two Bridges Hotel and two anglers carrying their rods to the Dart, I followed the track towards Crockern Farm, then branched left onto a path gradually rising towards Littaford Tors. An American couple returning from their walk stopped to chat. This was their first visit to Dartmoor and they loved it. I was soon carrying my light jacket, a T-shirt being all that was needed as the sun shone brightly.

Littaford Tors stand at the start of a striking two mile ridge punctuated by rocks that are easily identified from many places on the moor. The plural 'Tors' is generally used as there are several granite stacks, the first of which is also known as Little Bee Tor. Next on the ridge is the massive Longaford Tor. Formed of grass-covered earth as well as rock this is slightly unusual in being cone-shaped. It's easily climbed and well worth it for the superb views from the summit. My father's notebook records that I first climbed the rocks in August 1970, when all the family walked to Wistman's Wood and Dad and I made a quick extension to the tor.

Bearing right, I ascended the gentle slope to Higher White Tor. There is a stone row on the right but the stones are small and the grass tufty, so it's not easy to spot. The first time I located it was when the stones protruded through a light covering of snow. The view from Higher White Tor was a wonderful 360-degree panorama, including both the West and East Dart valleys, Cut Hill and Whitehorse Hill in the centre of Northern Dartmoor, Ryder's Hill and the low hills flanking the Swincombe basin to the south and the distinctive ridge of Hameldown to the east. The walk from Two Bridges and the views from Higher White Tor are amongst my favourites on the moor.

After crossing a stile over a newtake wall I gently descended to Lower White Tor from where I sent a photo to my cousin who had passed by here the previous week on his big walk from Okehampton to Ivybridge. I stopped for lunch, first greeting the leader of a group of youngsters who were completing a circular walk from Princes Hall. By the time I'd finished my sandwich sun had given way to wind and dark clouds. A considerable drop in temperature prompted me to put on not only the jacket but also a small waterproof. The shared opinion with the group leader twenty minutes ago that it was an ideal day for walking looked as if it may have been wrong.

The ruin of Brown's (or Browne's) House was now visible ahead on the side of Wildbanks Hill, reached by a path that bears left from Lower White Tor. Parts of this can be quite boggy, especially in the dip before a tinners' hut on the left. The hut is quite well preserved, but unlike many areas of Dartmoor where tin extraction took place, there isn't a great deal of evidence of mining here. Alluvial cassiterite (tin ore) deposits would have been collected from on or close to the surface, rather than the excavations or deep mines that disturbed the ground. The ore was washed down when Dartmoor was mountainous, settling in valley bottoms and people have exploited these alluvial deposits since Bronze Age (bronze being an alloy of copper and tin). Medieval tinners ventured into the remotest areas of the moor to stream the deposits and gain the valuable ore for smelting in blowing houses. Their huts around the moor would have been used for storing tools, shelter and sometimes overnight accommodation.

I waved to a couple who were leaving nearby Brown's House, heading towards Hollowcombe Bottom and maybe Postbridge, then left the tinners' hut to explore the more recent remains of the house. It's a desolate spot and

Brown's House

not where one might choose to build a dwelling - possibly the most isolated to be built on Dartmoor, or indeed anywhere in Southern England, since prehistoric times. The two-roomed single-storey stone house was constructed by a Dr Benjamin Brown and probably stood for no more than two decades.

According to legend Mr Brown had his own good reason for choosing to live in this isolated place. He apparently was not the best looking of men but was fortunate to meet a beautiful young lady who agreed to be his bride. Obsessed with jealousy and perhaps realising his good fortune, Brown would not allow another man to even cast eyes upon his beautiful wife. To keep her safe from potential admirers he built the farmhouse on remote Dartmoor. Local people were apparently amazed that he should choose to live in such a place and what Mrs Brown thought of living in a 'wilderness' one can only guess.

What became of his pretty wife is unknown but records do show that a Dr Benjamin Hayword Brown of Withecombe near Chagford did indeed build the house, after applying to the Duchy of Cornwall for a lease in 1810. It is thought that his venture was an attempt to 'improve' the moor by building enclosures to be farmed, as was being successfully achieved in less exposed areas of Dartmoor.

Unfortunately he started work on the farm before the lease was granted and the Duchy showed their displeasure by setting the rent at an uneconomic 1s 6d per acre, rather than the more usual shilling. Eventually they reduced it to 1s 3d on the condition that Brown built a 2½ mile access road at his own expense.

Cattle was probably the farm's main concern and according to local tradition milk and butter were sold to French prisoners interned at Princetown during the Napoleonic Wars. The enterprise was however never likely to be profitable and the cost of building an access road would have made the undertaking even less viable.

The road was never built and in 1812 Brown sold the lease for the not inconsiderable sum of £700 (equivalent to £65,000 in 2024). Over the next seventeen years the farm changed hands several times but disappeared from records after 1829, presumably abandoned to the moor as a venture that could never be profitable.

Just piles of stones and low walls of the building remain but the outline of the house and surrounding enclosures can be made out. A slotted gate post,

Tinners' hut near Brown's House

leaning at an angle, stands at the entrance to an enclosure but little remains of the house where Dr Brown brought his pretty young wife and a succession of tenants tried to make money from the moor.

The Anglican priest and novelist Reverend Baring-Gould wrote of Brown's House in his *A Book of Dartmoor*, first published in 1900:

'There are those still alive who remember when the chimney fell; and had heard of both the building, the occupying and the destruction of Browne's House. Few indeed have seen the ruin, for it is in so remote a spot that only the shepherd, the rush-cutter, and the occasional fisherman approach it.'

Rush-cutters are few and far between these days and it would be rare to find a fisherman this high up the Dart. A farmer might pass by, as do a few walkers, but it felt right that I was alone, with no sight of another person, as I sat by the isolated ruin.

Choosing to make the walk circular, the Dart was easily crossed and I commenced the steep ascent of Rough Tor. Fortunately the ever-changing view necessitated frequent stops. Haytor, Saddle Tor and Rippon Tor could now be seen and the cone shape of Longford Tor was particularly striking from this angle. After a while Brown's House came into view once more, its location looking even more remote from across the valley. A distant low noise also prompted me to stop and soon an army helicopter appeared low over the hills to the north, sending sheep scattering in all directions as it flew down the Dart Valley.

Rough Tor is also known as Row Tor and generally pronounced this way. Its rocks are neither large nor high but it commands fine views and is distinctive from afar as two military huts and a flagpole give it the appearance of a submarine. I turned left here, following a rough path along the line of military posts marking the boundary of Merrivale Range, then veered left to Crow Tor. Dutifully sitting atop the highest rock was a lone crow.

My first visit to the tor was on a wet day in 1975. My father's notebook records that it was 15th August and that we walked to Two Bridges from Princetown,

Edge of Wistman's Wood looking to Crow Tor

which we'd reached by Mr Striplin's independent bus from Tavistock. We passed Beardown Farm and clapper, then followed the Devonport Leat and on to Crow Tor where we ate lunch, sheltered from the rain. Dad's notebook says, *'wet weather – rain all the time after entering moor at Beardown'* and my only recollection of the walk is being at a very damp Crow Tor.

Some say that the tor's name comes from its resemblance to the bird. Dartmoor authority Eric Hemery however disagrees, saying that the common local pronunciation is not as the bird but accentuates the 'ow' and that it is also known as Croughtor. The tor's distinctive shape is largely due its unusual geology, with some of the rocks containing aplite, a fine-grained granite, that has fractured leaving an overhang that can provide useful shelter to walkers.

Crow Tor was home to one of the first Dartmoor letterboxes, which was placed here in 1962. My father and I signed it in 1975 and should we care to delve into the archives in Plymouth library, could probably find our names listed. I spent a while looking in nooks and crannies for the book (I seem to recall it was under the overhang but that was almost fifty years ago), however was unable to find the current letterbox. Apparently it has been removed.

From Crow Tor I descended towards the Dart, using what appeared to be a new ladder stile. Despite recent rain, crossing the River Dart on rocks was quite easy and within the bounds of my new-found caution following the Butter Brook incident. I could therefore take a direct route to Wistman's Wood, then the well-used path above the wood and on to Two Bridges.

I wondered what the effect on the wilderness characteristics of the Upper West Dart Valley would have been had Dr Benjamin Brown built the road to his house as the Duchy requested. It could potentially have opened up the moor, although it seems unlikely that even with easier access a house in such a remote location would have remained inhabited for long. Of all Dartmoor's remotest dwellings only Nun's Cross Farm and Ditsworthy Warren still stand and it is very probable that Brown's House would still have been a long-abandoned ruin. Arguably, whilst inhabited the house detracted from wilderness but as a tumbledown ruin no longer has a significant impact. It is a question I asked myself many times – does human activity many years ago impact on its current wilderness status?

Chapter Twenty

BLEAK HOUSE

Bleak House sounds the sort of place that might be in a wilderness – although of course some may say that the presence of a house may preclude an area from such status.

The house was built in or just after 1879 for the site manager of The West of England Peat Company's works in the upper Rattlebrook Valley. Until the works closed in 1930 they would have been a busy, noisy and ugly blot on Dartmoor's landscape and Bleak House not the lonely ruin in a quiet valley that it is now. Could somewhere that was once decimated by human activity revert to wilderness almost a century later? I walked to the ruin with this question in mind.

My walking guide includes a route to Bleak House from Sourton but this time I chose a walk from my father's book, starting at the Dartmoor Inn near Lydford. I first visited this part of the moor in 1968, as his notebook records:

April 17th with Peter

Train to Bridestowe. Walk to Nodden Gate. Crossed Lyd on stepping stones. Ascended Arms Tor. Descended & crossed Lyd by bridge above Dartmoor Inn. Saw Lydford Castle & walked to Lydford Station. Train back.

This was one of my earliest walks on Dartmoor but although I was just seven I still have several strong memories. The first was my surprise at the Lyd being so small. I'd seen the Thames in London and thought that's what all rivers were like! The second was the wind. It was very strong and blowing in our faces as we climbed Arms Tor. I didn't like it and eventually we turned back. The third was passing Lydford Castle and the fourth was asking Dad if frying was allowed on Lydford station. We'd brought bacon to cook on our little spirit stove but it had been too windy on the moor and I didn't really understand why it wasn't OK to fry our lunch at the end of the platform.

I left my little hire car in the car park on High Down behind the Dartmoor Inn and walked across the Down to the River Lyd. Three boys were messing around in the river by the stepping stones. Their mum and I agreed that it was a good place to play. Then I crossed the wooden bridge and set off along the path that bisects Arms and Brat Tors.

As I stopped to apply sun cream a chap went by on a mountain bike - illegally – this is not a bridleway. Contrary to the beliefs of many cyclists, unless permission is given by the landowner, bikes are only permitted to be used on public bridleways or other designated routes. It is illegal to cycle on open moor or common land and the many cyclists who ignore this cause significant erosion. It is a contentious matter. Soon he passed me on his descent, which we agreed was much easier.

The path was not as clear as I recalled and I lost it completely after having to divert to avoid a cow who was clearly protective of her very young calf. I strayed close to Brat Tor, with the unusual Widgery Cross on its summit.

River Lyd footbridge, High Down

The highest cross on Dartmoor, this was erected to commemorate Queen Victoria's Golden Jubilee in 1887 and is constructed from blocks rather than a single piece of granite.

Picking up a path on the ridge I proceeded to John's Cairn, a modern cairn at a crossroads of paths. Here I turned right, heading into wilder Dartmoor, with a fine view to Amicombe Hill, Great Links Tor and Sharp Tor. Passing through extensive remains of tinning works I wondered if this historic human activity detracted from wilderness, or whether the deep gulleys that made it harder to traverse made the land more wild.

After passing a boundary stone, incised 'L' for Lydford on its north side and 'BS' for Bridestowe and Sourton on its south, the path descended into the Rattlebrook Valley, running just below Lower Dunna Goat Tor. Approaching the tor I stopped to take in a view of part of the moor's central northern 'wilderness'.

Fur Tor, Dartmoor's most remote tor stood out to the south-west. It looked a short hop to reach it but appearances can be deceptive on Dartmoor. To reach the tor would require traversing almost three miles of rough and often miry ground, with no paths. Cut Hill to its left, considered the centre of Northern Dartmoor, looks benign from afar but is an inhospitable place, with few features and a mass of peat hags. Other than the loss of trees, my view into the central moor gave very little indication of human activity. All I could list, unless I looked slightly to the right where a military range pole stood rudely on the hillside, was North Hessary Tor television mast high above Princetown, the remains of tinning activities from centuries ago, a few paths and some cows. If Dartmoor is a wilderness then this wild area is part of it.

I dropped down to the Rattlebrook where by a clapper bridge I met the first people I'd seen since the cyclist on the slopes of Brat Tor. A man with his two daughters were finishing their lunch. They were enjoying a few days on the moors and had walked up from the Fox & Hounds. I told him how my father had introduced me to Dartmoor and how good it was to see his girls enjoying the moor. They were keen on wild swimming and I suggested Black Rock on the Lyd.

Bleak House

Bleak House

After crossing the stream I approached Bleak House, a hundred yards or so upstream. Constructed of granite cut from the tor above and originally known as Dunnagoat House, Bleak House was thought to be a more appropriate name for this remote Dartmoor dwelling. The house is now an atmospheric ruin with its chimney stack lying across the floor. Grass-covered depressions on the slope above the house show areas where peat was removed.

In 1998 DNPA carried out work to remove dangerous masonry and stabilise the building, work which some people had been requesting for twenty years, but the house remains very much a ruin which without attention will eventually crumble. Like many remains of Dartmoor's industrial past opinions vary as to whether it should be maintained or the stones allowed to return to the moor.

I sat by the Rattlebrook to eat my lunch. Deep in the valley with the stream splashing over rocks, sheep-cropped grass and granite boulders randomly scattered on the bank, this seemed too pretty to be wilderness. Whether the ruined house behind me meant that the valley didn't qualify anyway I shall consider later.

On previous visits I'd found the track from Bleak House to the peat works, a public right of way, was so boggy that it was almost impassable, however work was carried out in 2018 to improve it. Sections of boardwalk were laid

Above: Bleak House 1935 (Jeffrey W. Mallim *The Romance of Dartmoor*)

Below: Bleak House & Green Tor

between the peat works buildings and the remote Kitty Tor on Amicombe Hill, assistance for walkers but more human interference in the 'wilderness'.

Making a circular walk, I recrossed the Rattlebrook and headed upstream to the remains of the peat works. Peat cut from the surrounding moor was brought here to be dried in kilns before shipping off the moor. At its peak around a hundred men worked here. The peat works were demolished by

the army in 1961 at the request of farmers who feared for the safety of their animals and now just some low stone walls and rusting equipment remain.

My return route followed the well-preserved track of the Rattlebrook Railway which was constructed to carry the peat to the main line at Bridestowe. Built to standard gauge, for most of its life trucks were hauled by horses, but in latter days a petrol locomotive converted from a lorry worked the line. Its final job was to remove the rails when the railway closed in the 1930s. The cost of the line, which rose 1,000 feet over its 5 mile length, was a major factor in the peat works failing soon after they opened, although further attempts to run the enterprise took place over the next fifty years.

In order to avoid the steep gradient of Corn Ridge the line was built with a reversing point where the trains doubled back. A grassy path cuts off this corner but somehow I missed it, as had a chap who I met walking up the track. It was a very pleasant descent, passing below the distinctive domed Great Nodden hill, then fording the Lyd and following it back to High Down Bridge. It had been a wonderful walk, passing through picturesque spots on the edge of the moor and into wild areas on the edge of its 'wilderness'. Whilst it seemed that when I'd stopped near Lower Dunna Goat Tor to take in the view towards Fur Tor I was looking into a wilderness, the question remains, was and is Bleak House itself in wilderness?

Writing in 1907 Eden Phillpotts considered it so:

'The men followed this stream, and so approached a solitary grey cottage that stood nakedly in the very heart of the wilderness. Stark space

surrounded it. At first sight it looked no more than a boulder, larger than common, that had been hurled hither from the neighbouring hill at some seismic convulsion of olden days. But, unlike the stones around it, this lump of lifted granite was hollow, had windows pierced in its lowly chambers, and a hearth upon its floor.'

Eric Hemery in *High Dartmoor* wrote of the romantic beauty:

'When the works first gave promise of financial success and the railway from Bridestowe was built in 1879, the manager was provided with a house eight hundred yards downstream; in this short distance the dreary surroundings of Rattle Brook Head were exchanged for a site of romantic attractions, the valley narrowing, the sides steepening and the now leaping brook excavating a defile through which came a fine prospect of middle Tavy country. 'Dunnagoat Cottage', they called it, known ever since in its dereliction as 'Bleak House'.

Of course the beauty of which Hemery writes and that I had just experienced does not preclude it from being wilderness but it was still in my mind that wilderness equated with starkness, and a wild, barren landscape met my perception more than a pretty river valley, even if the latter equally complies with dictionary definitions.

It depends how one interprets the various definitions as to whether the area around Bleak House qualifies as wilderness, regardless of the more subjective (and possibly irrelevant) aesthetic factors. If one considers that human activity which altered the land a hundred years ago precludes it from being wilderness then this valley does not qualify but I am inclined to the view that a wilderness can include ancient works taken back by nature.

Later in the week I came back to the River Lyd, this time with Deb and my brother and his family. As we picnicked close to the river a chap with two girls walked by saying hello. After a few seconds we both realised that we'd met two days earlier at Bleak House. What a coincidence. They had taken up my suggestion of a swim at Black Rock and his youngest daughter told us this was the best place she'd been to in her whole life.

PART 8

FOUR BATTLES TO SAVE THE MOOR

If this book was written four thousand years ago it might have discussed saving the moor from felling of its trees, an action by prehistoric people that totally changed its character. Five hundred years ago I might have written about the miners who churned up the moor seeking tin. In the 19th century and early 20th century it could have been quarrying for granite, deep mines, peat cutting, china clay extraction and the tramways that cut across the moor to service them. All of these activities damaged the moor but now provide interest as we explore it, although potentially impact on its wilderness characteristics.

I have instead written about four areas where conservationists sought to save parts of the moor in the second half of the twentieth century, with chapters about threats to the moor from two reservoirs, china clay extraction and planting with coniferous trees.

The recent campaign to 'Save Dartmoor' was prompted by a ban on wild (backpack) camping and concerns about access but perhaps stretched the definition of 'save'. By 'saving' Dartmoor do we really mean keeping it exactly as it is now? We certainly don't want reservoirs or developments that may change the moor permanently and resist anything that might cause more temporary damage. We don't think that these things should be allowed in a National Park but we still need it to be managed to ensure that it remains a wild and natural area for wildlife, for us and for future generations. And of course we want access – ideally unfettered access. It is a difficult balance.

West Okement Valley looking to Meldon Viaduct

Chapter Twenty-One

SWINCOMBE

As I walked round the final bend in the little lane from Princetown to Whiteworks on a cold winter afternoon, one of Dartmoor's great vistas opened up ahead. This is not however a view of majestic tors, pretty valleys or heather-covered slopes. It is wildest Dartmoor, an awe-inspiring landscape, the basin of Fox Tor Mire surrounded by low hills. Today's swirling low clouds added to the atmosphere of this magical place, where the rocks of Fox Tor stand guard over the mire through which flows the infant River Swincombe. It is hard to believe that little more than fifty years ago this could all have been lost, flooded by erecting a huge dam, that along with associated engineering, would have ruined much of Dartmoor.

This was the greatest ever threat to wild Dartmoor and conservationists, led by the DPA and its dedicated but controversial chair Lady Sylvia Sayer, took up the fight. There was a need to enhance South Devon's water supply, particularly in summer when tourists boost the population and many local people considered that a reservoir in a desolate part of Dartmoor was preferable to losing farmland elsewhere. Lady Sayer was deeply unpopular amongst farmers and many ordinary Devon folk.

As I walked beside the Devonport Leat, looking across a mire that could be described as desolate but equally as wild, majestic, a place of ever-changing raw beauty and indeed a wilderness, it was hard to imagine that all this could have been under water.

This is such an important story that I shall leave the telling of it to two longstanding campaigners for Dartmoor.

The first piece was written by the environmental campaigner Kate Ashbrook, a former Secretary of the DPA, Chair of Ramblers and Campaign for National

Devonport Leat & Fox Tor Mire

Parks and longstanding General Secretary of the Open Spaces Society. I recall meeting Kate in the mid-1970s at a meeting of the London Group of the DPA. She was then a student I was impressed by her enthusiasm and her idea to push a wheelbarrow of china clay waste from Dartmoor to London. The following is based on an article Kate wrote for the DPA in 2004 and is reproduced with her kind permission.

At about 3pm on Thursday 3 December 1970, a small joyous figure appeared at the Ramblers' Association's office in Crawford Mews, London. 'I'm walking on air,' said Sylvia Sayer to the Ramblers' chief and fellow-campaigner Chris Hall. She had just come from the House of Commons where the bill to destroy the Swincombe valley had—against all the odds—been rejected.

The proposal, from Plymouth Corporation and the South West Devon Water Board, was to create a 754-acre reservoir in the Swincombe basin. The vast dam would cross the valley about 250 yards downstream from Stream Hill Ford. The reservoir itself would form a huge triangle with each side stretching for nearly two miles but, as it would be shallow, the draw-down would leave an ugly margin around the waterline. Water was to be stolen from the West Dart, Cowsic and Walkham rivers, via the concreted and widened Devonport and Prison Leats. Much more was proposed by way of tunnels and pumps. This would, of course, devastate the moor—and all to provide Plymouth with water, much of which was being lost through leaky pipes.

A collection of officials visited the proposed reservoir site in the late 1960s. Syl was there and she wrote about them in Wild Country: national asset or barren waste (1971):

"There they all stood, on the rim of a great natural amphitheatre, looking out across the wilderness; a group of good worthy citizens in Homburg hats and raincoats and pointed town shoes. 'Just a barren wilderness', said one stout alderman to another 'and a perfect site for a reservoir', and I think he voiced the opinion of the majority of that particular party. But a minority of those present felt—and said—that he could only have produced that remark out of a totally barren mind."

In those days such works had to be approved by Parliament, and the DPA led the fight against the bill. It jointly petitioned with other national and local bodies; and Devon County Council and the landowner, the Duchy of Cornwall, also objected. All were represented by counsel. The bill was considered by a parliamentary committee of four MPs for 17 days. DPA members from Devon and from its newly-formed London Group were present throughout.

As Syl wrote in the DPA newsletter of May 1971, at the conclusion of Plymouth's 17-day-long case the committee chairman, John Hunt (Conservative, Bromley), 'courteously asked to have the committee room cleared ... so everyone except the four MPs of the committee went out of the room, down the flight of stone steps into Westminster Hall, to wait for a torturing ten minutes while Dartmoor's future hung in the balance.'

They returned to hear Mr Hunt say 'We have come to the conclusion that the promoters have not made out the case for the bill, and in the light of this we feel it would be contrary to the public interest to allow the proceedings on the case to be continued.' Syl rejoices: 'With

> *that stunningly straightforward statement, those Four Just Men saved Dartmoor from the worst threat it has ever had to face.'*
>
> *Syl thus never had the opportunity to present her case, but her evidence remains in the archives and is wonderful reading, together with its meticulously drawn and coloured maps. 'Foxtor Plain is a great natural amphitheatre ... a place of immense spaciousness and wildness: it has nothing to do with "prettiness"; its character is one of austere beauty, challenge and inspiration—Dartmoor itself'. She describes the archaeology and public paths in loving detail. She emphasises the national importance of this precious place. And she condemns the Country Landowners' Association and National Farmers' Union for falsely claiming the alternative sites were high-quality agricultural land and for using their influence on the Water Resources Board to insist that the reservoir should go on Dartmoor.*
>
> *Indeed, even after Swincombe was saved, the NFU and CLA continued to press for it, and it was not until the Roadford reservoir was given the go-ahead in 1983 that Swincombe was finally reprieved.*
>
> *Back in December 1970, Syl didn't know that. The day after the victory, she and her husband Guy walked to the dam site, wandered among the antiquities, found again the tinner's hut inscribed 'HC 1753' near Swincombe gorge, and drank in the quiet landscape, saved from the ravages of the water board.*
>
> *I hope such destruction is now inconceivable, but whenever we walk around that 'great natural amphitheatre' we must remember the great battle, and the DPA's part in it.*

Secondly some extracts from an article written in tribute to Lady Sayer by my father, Michal Caton, who at the time was chair of the London Group of the DPA.

> *Dartmoor has faced many threats but none greater than the proposal by the SW Water Board in the late 1960s to construct a 750 acre reservoir in the Upper Swincombe valley south of Princetown.*

Because of its size and central location, the scheme would have destroyed much of Dartmoor's great asset as the only extensive area of wild country in the Southern half of England and as such a place of refuge for those who seek peace and quiet in an increasingly urban society and for people of all ages wishing to experience a sense of adventure and explore with map and compass. It would also have inundated many prehistoric and historic remains, including the famous Childe's Tomb and the ruins of Foxtor Farm, setting of Eden Phillpott's novel, The American Prisoner.

The Water Board's case was put forward through a Parliamentary Private Member's Bill, the Second reading of which took place in the House of Commons on 14th April 1970. To quote the DPA Newsletter of August 1970 'The Second reading debate was a disaster. The excellent speakers against the Bill, led by Mr Carol Johnson, were in a marked minority. Plymouth's spokesman Dame Joan Vickers, persuaded many MPs that Swincombe was merely an expendable bog, and at 10pm the big battalions of the farming and landowning lobbies came trooping in and all voted for the Bill to proceed, though most of them had not heard a word of the debate.

My father also described the dramatic minutes when after seventeen days of the Bill's Committee stage, the Chairman asked for the room to be cleared, then after a short time invited everyone back to hear that Swincombe had been saved. Dad's article continues:

I was privileged to be present at this moment of triumph and to witness Sylvia's expression of joy at hearing the wonderful news. Swincombe had been saved but this was a victory with much wider consequences. It had shown in no uncertain terms that wild and beautiful countryside can be saved, through effective application of the democratic process, by those who care about it against the desire of powerful vested interests. It was a victory for all National Parks. For this we are indebted to Sylvia Sayer.

I'd only planned a short walk today, just to take in the atmosphere of the Swincombe basin once more and chose Goldsmith's Cross as an objective. Leaving the leat at Sunny Corner, I turned left beside a long wall on a path that dips as it crosses several streams feeding into the mire. After the second

Fox Tor Mire from close to Goldsmith's Cross, looking to Whiteworks

of these I headed left towards the cross which is about ¼ mile away. The going was far from easy – huge clumps of grass, too unstable to stand on, with very wet ground between them. This was just the edge of Fox Tor Mire. I struggled on until about 100 yards from the cross, then thought, what's the point? I'd been there before and to continue would just make my feet even wetter. Furthermore, I could see the cross, as marking the monastic route from Buckfast to Tavistock, it was designed to be visible. I turned back. The cross, which stands in a boulder, was re-erected by Lt M. Lennon Goldsmith in 1903 after he found part of it lying here. It would have been submerged had the reservoir been built. What a disaster for Dartmoor that would have been.

I returned via Nun's Cross Farm and Cross where the ground was somewhat drier, reflecting as I always do when I walk on this part of Dartmoor on how close we were to losing it and the debt we owe to those who fought to save it. It is not '*just a barren wilderness*' but a wilderness to be celebrated.

Chapter Twenty-Two

MELDON

'Surrounded by steep sided banks and approximately 900 feet above sea level, Meldon Reservoir offers some of the most breathtaking scenery that Dartmoor has to offer'. So the South West Lakes Trust tells us. To some this may be true but to others it is an intrusion into the wild moorland that has flooded part of one of Dartmoor's most beautiful valleys.

Standing on the 201-metre-wide, 51-metre-high concrete dam, an impressive piece of engineering in its own right, one can make the comparison. On one side is the reservoir, an attractive lake surrounded by moorland hills. On the other is a deep, steep-sided valley with the West Okement River splashing its way off the moor - part of Dartmoor's natural beauty. I know which I prefer.

In 1962, just eleven years after Dartmoor gained the National Park status that most people believed would protect it from such developments, North Devon Water Board announced that its favoured location for a new reservoir was the West Okement Valley at Meldon.

Initially permission was sought to sink boreholes to test the rock formation but this was denied by the Dartmoor National Park Committee. The Water Board were urged to consider a site outside the National Park but they wanted Meldon and appealed to the government. An inquiry was held at very short notice, giving the ten organisations who objected little time to prepare. It was held at Okehampton in January 1963 and many witnesses couldn't get through deep snow to attend. Those that did were frustrated that the inquiry's terms of reference did not include the reason for the boreholes – creation of a reservoir. The Minister duly gave approval but it seemed to objectors that the inquiry had simply been a mechanism to go through the 'democratic process' to reach a pre-determined conclusion.

Reservoir from Meldon Dam

In June 1964 the government published the Draft Meldon Water Order proposing construction of the dam. Immediate objections were raised and a public inquiry held the following year. The DPA's booklet *The Meldon Story* summarises the main reasons why the reservoir was opposed:

'The objectors to the Meldon Water Order based their case on the inestimable value to the nation of this wonderful wild valley, which the proposed developments would destroy; on the principle, pronounced by successive Ministers, that a national park should not be invaded unless it can be proved beyond all doubt that there is no other alternative; and on the fact that the Board had not fully investigated other potential water sources.'

The possibility of siting the reservoir at Gorhuish, north-west of Okehampton and outside the National Park was discussed at some length, however a detailed comparison with Meldon wasn't possible as the Board hadn't released their limited technical data on Gorhuish. The inquiry was presided over by the Ministry's water engineering inspector Mr Wood, with their senior planning inspector Mr Johnson sitting beside him. The two men came to different conclusions but Richard Crossman the Labour Minister of Housing and Local Government, was responsible for the decision. He ignored the advice of his planning inspector, accepting instead the recommendation of the engineering inspector to approve the Water Order.

All however was not lost. It came to light that a rarely used parliamentary procedure would allow the original objectors to lodge a petition against the Draft Water Order when it came before Parliament, allowing for a Select Committee hearing and a debate in either House.

Representatives of objectors to Meldon convinced the Select Committee to delay the Order for eight months while a thorough investigation into the technical viability of the Gorhuish site and its cost relative to Meldon would be carried out. In the Committee's view Meldon should only be chosen if Gorhuish turned out to be impractical or significantly more expensive.

Unfortunately for Dartmoor the investigation was far from independent. Anthony Greenwood, Crossman's replacement as Minister, had told Lady Sayer that it would be run by the Ministry but it was actually conducted by the Board itself in conjunction with the Devon River Authority. The DPA's engineering consultant was permitted to attend some of the sessions but not the site tests, nor to contribute to the report. Mr Wood, the Ministry's chief engineer at the public inquiry, the man who had signed the Ministry's letter approving Meldon, chaired the discussions and presented the final report to the Ministry. This stated that to build the reservoir at Gorhuish would cost as much as £1 million more than Meldon, sufficient grounds for rejecting the former. It has been strongly suggested that some estimates from which this figure was derived were skewed against Meldon.

Before the Minister had received Mr Wood's Gorhuish report campaigners against Meldon were given another hope when high levels of arsenic and lead were found in the spoil heaps from long-abandoned 19th century mine workings within the reservoir's catchment. The somewhat controversial response of Mr Peter Mills, Conservative MP for Torrington and supporter of the reservoir, was that, *'it is grossly unfair to my constituents that these fears should be raised'* and that, *'we cannot all live on fresh air and a view'*. The Water Board considered that its purification process would reduce the concentration of toxins below recommended levels but warning of the potential health hazards, the Council of the Royal College of Surgeons expressed concern that long-term exposure to relatively small doses could have a cumulative effect. Devon River Authority's Pollution Officer said that it would be best to err on the side of caution and locate the reservoir elsewhere but eventually the Water Board agreed to remove the spoil heaps from the area to be flooded and seal off the old mine workings.

In November 1968 the Minister's decision letter backing the Meldon reservoir was published. A last ditch attempt to appeal through the Parliament Ombudsman that an injustice had been done failed. Whether the case for Meldon had been fairly considered is a matter of dispute but in March 1970 the bulldozers moved in.

Writing in *Dartmoor News* the author and former DPA Chief Executive John Bainbridge sums up the views of many who lament the loss of this beautiful valley:

'Now I know this artificial lake has its fans, but they tend to be people who don't remember the magnificent valley that was lost when the dam was built. As a result of a short-term solution to Devon's water-shortage, and promoted by local jobsworths who seemed to have a real hatred of the National Park, Dartmoor's most beautiful valley was lost for ever.'

My walk commenced at the car park close to the dam, a good starting point for Dartmoor walks. Following a path on the east bank, I crossed a footbridge over the Fishcombe Water, a small stream running off Homerton Hill, then passed an artificial island, a nature reserve formed from spoil when Meldon was constructed. The original course of the West Okement was to the south of the island. In the very dry summer of 2018 the water was so low that people had walked onto the island and written their names with stones on the dried mud, a practice that is generally frowned upon.

The head of the reservoir is reached after just over a mile, then the valley floor becomes a wide grassy plateau. An arched stone bridge crosses the river but the gate the other side is locked and topped with barbed wire. Until 2011 it was possible to make a circular walk along both banks of the reservoir. It was a popular route, enjoyed by around 15,000 people the previous year but the moor here is not Access Land. The farmer who owned South Down received about £700 a month as part of an access agreement with DNPA but when this ended he stopped allowing walkers to use the path. DNPA couldn't afford the higher sum demanded by the farmer to renew it and the government had ceased to offer payments for access as part of Higher Level Stewarding funding. No resolution has been found so access alongside the reservoir remains prohibited. There is still an excellent circular walk along the other side of South Down but this is longer and more demanding, so fewer people can manage it.

After a further ¼ mile I reached a weir with a narrow bridge that can be crossed on foot. Above this the river tumbles over huge boulders as it descends through a steep-sided wooded valley. About 200 yards from the weir the stream divides, running either side of a 90-metre-long rocky island – The Island of Rocks. Early 20th century writings and postcards refer to the Island of Rocks and Rocky Valley, although neither name seem to be in regular use now and Valley of the Rocks a more common name for this magical glen. It is one of Dartmoor's lesser-known beauty spots, although in Victorian times was a popular picnic place on an advertised tourist trail. William Crossing's words in *Gems in a Granite Setting* provide a poetic description of this spectacular Dartmoor valley:

'At every step the scene becomes more impressive, and the beautiful and the romantic unite in a manner that cannot fail to cause the most supreme delight. It is a mingling of oak tree and fern; of mountain-ash and bushes of the wild raspberry; of sturdy thorns and withies that bend to the breeze; of briar, and ivy, and heather, and whortleberry, half-shrouding grey masses of granite; of rushing river and gleaming foam, and deep pools; of rugged tor and hills that shut out the world.'

The island is best seen in winter when the bracken has died down and leaves fallen from the trees, hence my choice of February for this walk. Summer foliage and sunshine may add to the beauty but access is harder and views obscured. The first time I came here was in August 1969, when I was eight, before either Meldon Reservoir or the Okehampton Bypass were constructed. My father's notebook records:

Island of Rocks with Peter
Weather, sunny periods, some rain

Train to Okehampton. Walked onto slope of East Hill above station & to road past military camp. Along slopes of Rowtor, West Mill Tor & Yes Tor (tall heather & boggy in places) to just short of Black Tor. Descended to West Okement just below Black Tor Copse & along river to Island of Rocks. (Lunch). Back – ascended river to weir. Ascended & crossed moor along Homerton Hill & Longstone Hill. Picked up track along Red-a-Ven Brook across Black Down. (Went near pools on Black Down). On to military camp & back to Okehampton Station.
(7 hours - long stop for lunch as Peter not well).
(I vaguely recall having a headache and a sleep on the moors.)

There are a number of stories attached to the island, some of course involving pixies, but a particularly sad event occurred in January 1866. Richard Allen, a resident of Sourton, decided to take a shortcut across the moor while walking to Sticklepath but the weather was bad and he failed to arrive. The next day a farmer was gathering sheep when his dog alerted him to something by the Island of Rocks. It was Allen's body, sat under a rock with an umbrella at his feet. It is assumed that he took shelter here and died from the cold.

Meldon Reservoir & island

I returned downstream and picked up a track that runs along the steep hillside, giving fine views to the wooded gorge below, with glimpses of white water cascading over rocks. Whilst winter gives the best views of the water, it is a spectacular walk at all times of the year.

The track ends just above a waterfall where the river runs through a walled area around a water intake that predates the reservoir. I remember seeing this in 1969. Just inside is a weir, behind which is a small pond but the enclosure is overgrown with trees, bracken and brambles so one cannot see far into it. The gate is padlocked and the walls keep out both people and grazing animals. This is what much of the lower moor would become were it not grazed – rewilded and unmanaged. An environment that supports more diverse wildlife, particularly birds, although not those such as snipe and skylarks which nest on the ground. Potentially a fully rewilded Dartmoor could be more of a wilderness than the open moorland that formed after its trees were felled by Bronze Age dwellers, a concept that is considered later.

I sat on a rock to eat my cake, looking up to Black Tor which drifted in and out of mist. For a brief moment a patch of dim sunlight appeared over the rocks but before I could consider re-taking photos in the better light the mist was back. *Walks Discovering Lesser Known Dartmoor* includes several options for circular routes returning via Black-a-tor-Copse and over Longstone Hill, but today I opted to go back the way I'd come, considering again what was lost when the Okement Valley was flooded.

As I walked back by the lake I realised there is one blessing - unlike some of Dartmoor's earlier reservoirs, Meldon was not surrounded by conifers. The moorland hills run down to its shore, giving the lake a natural appearance. There is no doubt that it is a place of beauty but the Meldon gorge that was flooded was even more so and was true Dartmoor.

Chapter Twenty-Three

HIGH HOUSE WASTE

In July 1964 the DPA distributed the following leaflet.

An Appeal to All Dartmoor Lovers
HIGH HOUSE MOOR *is an area of about 142 acres of open moorland, bordered by beautiful valley oakwoods, on Southern Dartmoor, about 1½ miles north of Cornwood village. For three years past a battle has been fought to save it from commercial afforestation.*

It recently became apparent that afforestation could be averted only if someone was prepared to buy the land. This was the only way in which this wonderful stretch of open moorland could be preserved in its present state. There was moreover no time for an Appeal to be made to the public for financial help.

It was in these circumstances that a member of the Dartmoor Preservation Association, who prefers to remain anonymous, signed a contract to buy the land in order that it may be saved for the Nation. Under this contract the purchase price is to be paid by instalments over a period of two years; the signatory of the contract has paid the first of three equal instalments. It is proposed that in due time the land should be offered to the National Trust or some similar body or be vested in trustees so as to be preserved as on open space for the public generally.

Meanwhile the Dartmoor Preservation Association has resolved to make an appeal to the public for contributions towards the cost of purchase. The Association does not think it right that the price which has to be paid to preserve High House Moor should fall upon a single individual, however public-spirited. They believe that there will be many Dartmoor-lovers who will rejoice that High House Moor has been spared and will welcome the opportunity of sharing in its preservation.

The amount we want to raise is £2,000 – to cover the purchase price (£1,500) a half share in a fence to be erected on the Eastern Boundary (approximately £200) and certain other general and legal expenses. Any monies raised in excess of the sum actually required for these three purposes would be put aside as a fund for the management of High House Moor for the public benefit.

We believe that there will be many organisations and individuals throughout the land who will share the view that preservation of High House Moor represents a signal victory for the principle of sensible land use, and a notable event in the unceasing battle for the defence of our country's heritage of natural beauty. This piece of moor has outstanding qualification as "access" land, it is exhilarating country for walking and riding, with magnificent views of Dartmoor and South Devon. A charming rocky stream, Broadall Lake, borders its eastern boundary. It is entirely wild and unspoilt and most of it is above the natural tree line. Artificial planting here, up to and above the 1100 foot contour, would have been a conspicuously unnatural intrusion. The Moor contains, too, some very notable pre-historic and historic sites – a large Bronze Age settlement and a twelfth century ruined farmstead (the original High House which gave the Moor its name) with associated enclosures and a "hollow way" leading up to the open land above. These national assets have now been saved from obliteration. Part of High House Moor has been listed by the Nature Conservancy as a Site of Special Scientific Interest. Our Atlantic moorlands are vegetational units not to be found anywhere else in the world.

High House Moor must be saved – for all time and for the enjoyment of this and succeeding generations. Will you play your part in this achievement by sending a contribution to:

THE HIGH HOUSE MOOR FUND
LLOYDS BANK
PLYMOUTH
DEVON

W.G. Hoskins
President of the Dartmoor Preservation Association

The appeal was successful. The DPA purchased High House Moor, preventing it becoming a commercial conifer plantation and saving it as moorland for all to enjoy.

The land was part of the Blanchford Estate, owned by Wing Commander Cyril Wolrick Passy, a decorated World War Two Hurricane fighter pilot. He had sold High House Waste to Economic Forestry Ltd for tax-avoidance coniferisation, a scheme by which wealthy people could invest 'tax efficiently' but which caused great damage around the country, notably in Scotland's Flow Country. Their plan to fence and plant 360 acres of High House Moor caused an outcry. The Dartmoor National Park Committee resolved to purchase the land but their decision was overruled by Devon County Council, its parent body. It was the DPA and the many people who contributed to the appeal that saved this corner of Dartmoor. To quote Kate Ashbrook, '*And so this magical place was saved from becoming a dreary blanket of impenetrable conifers, unlike the neighbouring Dendles*'.

I'd never been to High House Waste (waste is a South Dartmoor word for enclosure) and on a sunny May morning was quite excited to be exploring this special corner of the moor. It didn't start well.

After parking at Heathfield Down near Cornwood I started to sort out my rucksack and footwear but quickly realised something was missing – my drinks were still in the fridge back in Torquay. So were my walking socks! Yes I know it may sound strange but to keep my can of drink cool I slip it inside a sock. Remembering a conversation with a gentleman I'd met on Harford Moor the previous summer, on a warm day I was reluctant to set out without anything to drink. He had once forgotten his drink, become disorientated through dehydration and was fortunate to be just about able to call his wife who came to rescue him. Safety first, I got back in the car, set out to find a shop and was most relieved to find a small village shop in Cornwood. (Sadly, soon after my walk this closed, hopefully only temporarily.) Now equipped with bottles of water and cartons of juice, I set off up the quiet lane towards the moor.

After the tiny settlements of West Rook and Middle Rook the lane narrowed and whilst still tarmacked was impassable to cars – a pleasant approach to the moor. At East Rook Gate I entered the open moor and skirted the lower slopes of Penn Beacon to the Ford Brook which borders the east side of High House Waste. The path took me to Oliver Sayer Gate one of four gateways to the enclosed land, all named after people who have contributed to Dartmoor.

Oliver Sayer was son of Sir Guy and Lady Sayer, who like his parents devoted a huge amount of time to campaigning for Dartmoor, including as treasurer for the DPA. He died of cancer aged 63.

Frank Beech was elected secretary of the DPA in 1973 and was heavily involved in the unsuccessful campaign to prevent the Okehampton Bypass being built in the National Park. He died suddenly in 1980. On taking over as secretary he wrote these very relevant words in the DPA newsletter:

'Finally, as a life-long rambler who still derives his greatest pleasure from tramping in the "last wilderness" around Cut Hill, Fur Tor and Cranmere as well as in the gentler parts of the moor, I am not in the least troubled by accusations of being a "preservationist". Today all national parks, not the least our beloved Dartmoor, are in greater danger than ever before and we cannot afford to allow any threat, however small it might appear, to pass unchallenged.'

Neil Main sadly died in his early forties. He was a good friend of my father and amongst Dad's papers I have found the notes he prepared when he and Mum walked to High House Waste with Neil's parents for dedication of the gate. Dad wrote that Neil was a loyal member of the DPA London Group, that he had a great knowledge of Dartmoor and it was a delight to be with him on the moor. He recalls that Neil used to lead walks and how he put his love of the moor into practice sending 150 handwritten letters to MPs when Swincombe was threatened.

Matt Collins was a major in the Irish Guards. He was tragically killed in action in Afghanistan on the 23rd of March 2011. He was thirty-nine at the time and left a wife and two young children.

The Oliver Sayer Gate is at a lovely spot beside the Ford Brook and I stopped here for lunch before setting out to explore High House Waste and its remains of archaeological interest, notably a number of Bronze Age reaves (field boundaries) and two scheduled ancient monuments – the ruin of High House farmstead and a Bronze Age settlement.

First I headed east towards the farmstead, making my way between tall gorse bushes to a grassy area criss-crossed with low walls. Amongst these are the ruins of High House, which is thought to have been built on the site of a longhouse and to date from no earlier than 16th century. Three rooms can be discerned in the ruin, as well as various outbuildings and field systems. The excellent website *dartmoorexplorations.co.uk* provides detailed analysis of the site.

Most striking was the superb view across the steep valley of Broadall Lake, to Hawns and Dendles Waste and beyond these, Stalldown, on which the stone row could be picked out. With the sun shining and a carpet of bluebells, this was a good time to enjoy one of Dartmoor's wonderful views. Twenty-five years earlier the view would have been somewhat different.

Whilst the DPA purchase saved High House Waste, in the early 1960s Dendles Waste and Hawns were ploughed up and planted with conifers, creating an environment of little use to wildlife or walkers. The lovely Broadall Lake Valley which I was looking down to lost its biodiversity as a piece of Dartmoor became a dull coniferous plantation.

Fortunately Dendles Waste and Hawns were later acquired by Nature Conservancy (now Natural England), then taken over by DNPA and the conifers were harvested in 1997. Their plan for the land was to plant broadleaf trees at the lower end, leaving the upper parts of the two areas to revert to moorland. Trees were planted, with deer fences protecting them, and whilst a few conifer stumps remain the land has returned to open moor. Lack of funding has however limited DNPA's management, resulting in a degree of rewilding and diverse habitats.

Thanks to Lady Sayer (it was she who initially purchased the land) and the DPA, High House Waste remained free from conifers and much of it is unaltered moorland. It had been intended that the land would be passed

High House Waste looking to Stalldown

on to the National Trust or a similar body but the DPA later decided to retain ownership and manages the land for, *'nature, archaeology and public enjoyment'*. Regular volunteer working parties clear gorse, bash bracken and carry out swaling to prevent the gorse from becoming dominant, so allowing growth of heather, bilberry (commonly known as whortleberries on Dartmoor), moorland grasses and other flowering plants.

My exploration of High House Waste continued as I walked north, along the side of the valley to the Bronze Age settlement at the top of the enclosure. This consists of five irregular enclosures with eight hut circles within them and has been dated at circa 1500 BC. The wiggles in the 18th century newtake wall show that its builders made use of the walls of the Bronze Age settlement. This being before it was considered important to preserve such ancient structures, it's thought likely that several hut circles were lost when their stone was taken for the newtake wall.

Oliver Sayer Gate

I returned through the gorse to the Oliver Sayer Gate, which with the stream hurrying by provided a suitable spot to enjoy my afternoon cake whilst reflecting on the beauty and history of High House Waste.

Rather than a direct route back to East Rook Gate, I stayed higher up the hill with the intention to visit Rook Tor, one of Dartmoor's tors that I'd never been to. It's marked on the OS map, although with no specific location but one would assume that a stack of granite would not be hard to spot. Not the case – I couldn't find it! I've spent many hours combing Dartmoor for kistvaens and other small or hidden remains but had never failed to find a tor. It was only when I got home and looked it up on *torsofdartmoor.co.uk* that I found out why. There is no tor as such. All that remains are scattered rocks. The rest has been stolen by quarrying.

Looking west from the slopes of Penn Beacon I could see (and hear) the ugly consequences of china clay extraction on Lee Moor. A lorry on the skyline of a huge white tip epitomised the destruction of this corner of the moor and we must be grateful to the DPA and others who successfully campaigned to prevent the china clay extraction from spreading well into the southern moor.

As Carter and Skilton wrote in *Dartmoor The Threatened Wilderness*, '*Ultimately, perhaps the conservation of British wilderness will depend on those who love and understand it and can argue on its behalf from the strength of a hard won affinity*'.

Chapter Twenty-Four

AREA Y

To most readers this must be a strange chapter name but to seasoned Dartmoor campaigners it signifies a celebrated victory for conservationists. If it were not for their efforts a beautiful hillside, part of Shaugh Moor, would have been lost to Dartmoor.

China clay, formed by the breakdown of feldspar in granite, has been extracted from Dartmoor for 150 years. Works at Red Lake in the centre of the southern moor were a major operation, with a hostel for workers, locomotive shed for the railway that served it, office and dining room, as well as all the buildings associated with the extraction of china clay. Whilst this closed almost a hundred years ago, the spoil heap remains visible from many miles around and footings of buildings can still be seen – interesting industrial archaeology but marks of human interference to the moor.

The operations at Lee Moor are however on a different scale and a huge scar on the south-west corner of Dartmoor. Clay is extracted by high pressure water jets from material dug out of immense quarries. The operation is noisy, dusty and creates an alien white environment. For each tonne of china clay extracted seven tonnes of waste is produced and this piles up in huge white heaps.

Leaving the car near Beatland Corner, I climbed to Hawks' Tor, a fine viewpoint looking down to Plymouth Sound. A large slab of granite forms a shelter, which this morning was occupied by a single horse, while another and two foals stood outside. Steve Grigg (*Dartmoor Explorations*) tells us that rock shelter was said by Richard Hansford Worth in the 1940s to be a natural group of rocks but that Rowe (in 1848) regards it as a cromlech (megalithic tomb). Eric Hemery suggests that the 'artificially' placed slab might have been a shelter for a shepherd. Like so many places on Dartmoor

Hawks' Tor

there are several explanations. It would be a very unusual cromlech so this seems unlikely and an artificial shelter, as other sources suggest, is most probable.

Continuing to the top of the hill I reached an alien world of whiteness. This was once moorland like the hillside behind me. Now it's ruined. Such destruction of Dartmoor almost brought tears to my eyes. Behind me was moorland with heather, gorse, grasses, ponies and prehistoric remains. In front were piles of white china clay waste, a huge hole in the ground, no sign of wildlife and virtually no vegetation – perhaps the greatest contrast of environments on the moor. In time, as has happened in Cornwall, the artificial white hills will grass over and some sort of 'natural' environment will return. But this will never be Dartmoor as it was and the long-buried history is gone forever.

This is what so nearly happened to Shaugh Moor. Back in the 1800s few people worried about the effect of industrial activity on Dartmoor. By the 20th century there was opposition to schemes that damaged the moor, but perhaps not to the extent that we would see now. Unfortunately this came too late to save Lee Moor but there was an outcry when plans were later announced to tip china clay waste on Shaugh Moor.

Back in 1951 Devon County Council had given permission for two china clay companies, Watts, Blake & Bearne (WBB) and English China Clays (ECC), to win and work clay on about 5,000 acres of south-west Dartmoor, including 150 acres of Shaugh Moor. When in 1971 the companies announced detailed plans to tip waste on Shaugh Moor, the DPA, led by Syliva Sayer, spearheaded a campaign to save what had become known as Area Y, highlighting the unspoilt nature of the land, its many antiquities, the fine views it provided and its use by walkers and horse riders. Quotations were gathered from eminent people and everyone with an interest in saving Shaugh Moor urged to write to the press and ministers. In November 1975 a letter from archaeologists Sir Mortimer Wheeler and Jacquetta Hawkes was published in *The Times*:

> *'We are of the united opinion that the loss of these antiquities would constitute little less than a national disaster and in the circumstances would most urgently urge the Minister to revoke the planning permission, or at the very least to call a public inquiry.'*

Three years later the companies agreed to share alternative tipping space, Area Y was saved – but only for thirty years. Whilst ECC were willing to make their part of the agreement legally binding, WBB were only prepared to give the County Council a written undertaking not to tip waste here for 30 to 40 years. Shaugh Moor was only safe until 2008.

As the deadline approached campaigners ramped up their efforts to save Shaugh Moor from disappearing under mountains of waste and part of the Blackabrook Valley to be lost to a 'super-quarry'. Protests were organised by the DPA and Ramblers Association, supported by many other organisations and on 19th September 1999 over five hundred demonstrators gathered at Cadover Bridge.

Circumstances had changed since the original permissions were granted. When the National Park was founded in 1951 Shaugh Moor was outside the boundary, influence of the clay companies considered by many to be a factor in where the line was drawn. It was when the boundaries were reviewed in 1994 that Shaugh Moor became part of the National Park, strengthening the case of those who fought to save it from tipping. The Environment Act 1995 required that old permissions were reviewed and crucially that environmental impact assessments had to be completed.

On 20th June 2001 WBB and Imery (formerly ECC) both announced that they had given up their rights to work the Blackabrook Valley and Shaugh Moor. Their decisions were made after analysis of Environmental Impact Assessments showed that it would not be possible for them to quarry the area in an environmentally friendly way. A great victory for Dartmoor and those who fought so hard and without whom this corner of the moor would have been lost.

I left the land of white clay, walking back down the hill and finding a nice grassy spot to eat lunch. Looking down to the village of Shaugh Prior with its 15th century parish church the desolation behind me seemed unreal. How could this have been allowed to happen?

Looking into Southern Dartmoor from Saddlesborough

Shaugh Moor is criss-crossed with ancient field boundaries and I followed one to Saddlesborough Summit, on which stands a trig point and prehistoric cairn, from where on a beautifully clear day there was a superb vista into the moor:

Trowlsworthy Warren and tors, Sheepstor, Gutter Tor, Ditsworthy Warren, Hen Tor and up the Plym Valley towards central Southern Dartmoor - Plym Head and Crane Hill. A view into Dartmoor's wilderness? From this distance, other than North Hessary Tor mast, I could see no sign of human activity beyond Ditsworthy Warren. Shell Top and Penn Beacon were to the east but below them the china clay works defiled the moor. Locally these are known as the White Hills. It is not considered a term of endearment!

A few yards north of the summit is a small tor, sometimes known as Luxton Tor but more often simply as Saddlesborough. It is more notable for its views than rocks. After taking another set of photos from this slightly different angle I followed a reave down the hill. Another reave soon branches to the left. Both were bracken-covered but well preserved. Several hut circles lay either side - evidence that the hillside was once lived on. I followed a stone row which runs NNE from the reave. It is indicated by a silver star on a post and apparently there was once a plan to mark prehistoric remains in this way right up the Plym Valley. That's just not done on Dartmoor! The stones are small but the row well defined – another significant historic site on Shaugh Moor.

The stone row, hut circles, settlements, cairns, reaves, a medieval homestead and Saddlesborough would have been covered by mountains of waste had campaigners not fought to stop the dumping. As I walked back to the car I thought, as I had at Fox Tor Mire and High House Waste, of the debt we owe to all those who worked so hard to save the moor.

The battle against Meldon was lost, High House Waste was saved from afforestation but much of Bellever covered with conifers and the A30 built inside the National Park. The damage from china clay extraction has been limited but most important of all, Dartmoor was saved from the Swincombe reservoir which would have decimated so much of the southern moor and seriously impacted its wilderness. More recent battles have been to ensure access and the right to backpack camping on the moor and whilst not impossible, it is hard to imagine such a damaging proposal as Swincombe being put forward again. It is however vital that we remain vigilant to protect the National Park from threats both small and large and we must be forever grateful to those campaigners past, present and future whose efforts preserve the moor we so love.

Grimspound with visitors

PART 9

TWO DARTMOOR VILLAGES

Dartmoor has been occupied since early Bronze Age times and by the Middle Bronze Age (1700 – 1200 BC) was fairly well populated, people living in huts, with land divided by reaves. The huts (known as hut circles or round houses) tended to be grouped together and often inside an outer wall forming a pound. The best known and best preserved (restored) of these Bronze Age villages is Grimspound.

Whilst there was limited Neolithic, Iron Age, Roman and Saxon activity around Dartmoor, they tended not to live on the moorland. In medieval

times longhouses were built on Dartmoor and villages grew up around the moor, forming the basis of most current settlements. New houses continue to be built, although not without controversy, there being a difficult balance between the desire to keep Dartmoor's villages unspoilt and the need for housing. Demand pushes up prices, meaning local people often can't afford to stay in the villages where they were brought up but developers prefer to build more profitable larger properties.

There are of course many Dartmoor villages of interest for their history, some of which are very picturesque with beautiful old buildings in a moorland setting. Much has been written about these and I chose to visit the remains of two long-abandoned settlements on the open moor - Grimspound as the best example of a Bronze Age settlement and the remains of Hound Tor medieval village which was abandoned more than 500 years ago.

ABOVE: Frozen bog above Strane River looking to Whiteworks
BELOW: Stalldown Stone Row

Great Mis Tor observation hut looking into Central Northern Dartmoor
ABOVE: Winter   BELOW: Summer

ABOVE: Great Mis Tor
BELOW: Leighon Tor

LEFT: Bellever Forest looking to the East Dart Valley (Debbie Caton)

CENTRE: Arms Tor & Brat Tor above the River Lyd

BOTTOM: River Erme, Piles Copse

Nun's Cross Farm

Oke Tor looking to Taw Marsh

Fox Tor Mire, Fox Tor & Ter Hill

ABOVE: High House Waste looking to Dendles Waste & Stalldown

BELOW: An alien world. Lee Moor china clay works above Hawks' Tor

Powdermills (*Debbie Caton*)

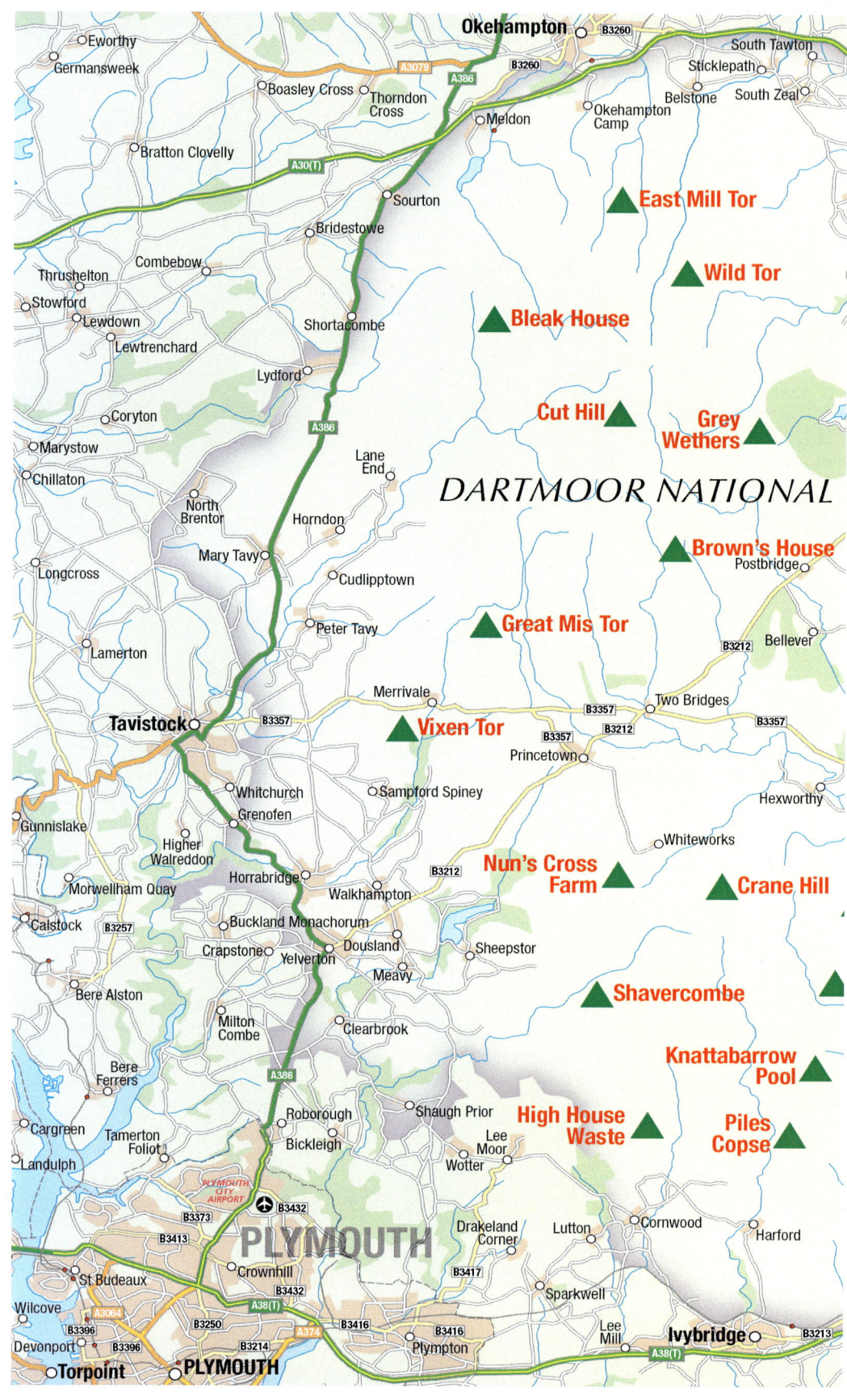

ABOVE: Sourton Tors Ice Works looking to Meldon Reservoir

BELOW: Shavercombe Waterfall

Devil's Cauldron, Lydford Gorge

BELOW: Becky Falls (September – after rain)

ABOVE: Cater's Beam, Black Lane (2015)

BELOW: Nun's Cross & Ivybridge Lane

Bog at foot of Cut Hill

Cut Hill summit

Fur Tor from Cut Hill

ABOVE: Ugborough Beacon looking to Three Barrows & Central Southern Dartmoor

BELOW: East Mill Tor looking to Okement Hill with military track

ABOVE: Nun's Cross Farm

ABOVE: Looking to Great Mis Tor from slopes of North Hessary Tor

BELOW: East Mill Tor looking to Oke Tor & Steeperton Tor

Chapter Twenty-Five

GRIMSPOUND

Grimspound lies in the dip between Hameldown and Hookney Tor and is only a short walk from the Challacombe Road but I chose a more interesting route with added Bronze Age interest.

Leaving the car at the popular Shapley Common car park I climbed towards Shapley Tor, soon passing three hut circles which were occupied by Bronze Age farming people around 3,500 years ago. These are almost as well preserved as those within Grimspound but receive a fraction of the visitors.

After stopping for lunch on Shapley Tor, with a panoramic view across Northern Dartmoor, I continued to Hookney Tor where a large Bronze Age burial cairn stands close to the summit. It is one of the few of Dartmoor's cairns to have incorporated a natural rocky outcrop and includes a rubble bank on its south face. As I crested the tor the circular settlement of Grimspound came into view.

The best-known prehistoric settlement on Dartmoor, this dates from the Late Bronze Age, most likely around 1300BC. The remains of twenty-four round houses can be seen inside a 150 metre diameter wall. Averaging 3 metres thick and 1.5 metres high, the pound's stone walls are by far the strongest on the moor but its situation in a valley suggests that this was not for defensive purposes. Excavation by the newly formed Dartmoor Exploration Committee in the late 19th century showed that they were actually two separate walls with a gap between them and it seems that the purpose was to keep domesticated animals in and wild creatures out.

The Committee excavated sixteen of the houses, finding numerous structures and artefacts, including paved floors, hearths, cooking holes, raised benches, charcoal, flint and pottery. The distinctive style of pottery helped date the site to the Bronze Age, however there have been no recent excavations to recover organic material for more accurate radiocarbon dating. Signs of human occupation were found in thirteen of the huts and the remainder were likely to have been for keeping animals.

The site was partially reconstructed after excavation but using contemporary assumptions as to how it originally looked, so there are thought to be some inaccuracies from how the settlement was in Bronze Age times. Archaeological practice has changed since the 19th century and remains would now tend to be left as they are, not rebuilt. The walls were probably not much higher than they are now but the huts would have had conical roofs made from thatch or turf. The Grim Lake, a tiny stream, runs through the north of the settlement and would have provided water.

Grimspound is owned by English Heritage. Its name is relatively recent and attributed to the Cornish clergyman and poet Rev. Richard Polwhele, who in 1797 was the first to record it. The name probably derives from Grim, the Anglo Saxon God of War.

Grimspound looking to Hookney Tor

I descended from Hookney Tor and walked around the enclosure to the main entrance on the south side. Here can be found Grimspound Cross. This small cross, just six inches high, is inscribed into a large rock on the right-hand side of the entrance. Little appears to be known about it and it isn't mentioned in the main Dartmoor reference books. After various fruitless attempts to discover its origin I obtained some information from Dartmoor guide and editor of *Dartmoor News*, Paul Rendell. Paul told me that the cross is believed to have been carved by the Dartmoor Exploration Committee (DEC), part of the Devonshire Association, when Richard Hansford Worth and others carried out the archaeological dig in 1893. *Dartmoor News* suggests that it may have been a baseline to which the survey was done or possibly the logo of the DEC.

The cross raises an interesting question. If it had been recently carved it would be considered an illegal act of vandalism to an ancient monument. If it too was very old it might be seen a historic addition. At around 130 years old maybe it falls between the two. Is it history or desecration? Its age and the people who carved it gives the cross historical interest but also illustrates how attitudes of archaeologists have changed over the years.

Whilst not as busy as the likes of Haytor and Postbridge, it is rare to visit Grimspound and find no one else there and today, as is the norm, groups of people were sitting inside hut circles chatting or eating. It seemed appropriate to find my own hut and enjoy a cake.

Grimspound from Hookney Tor

We don't know exactly when Grimspound ceased to be inhabited but it is thought to have been around 1000BC and even that along ago, as a result of human influence on the land. The forest that once covered Dartmoor had been gradually removed by Bronze Age people who used the open land for grazing their animals and growing crops but in doing so they exposed the fragile moorland soil. Dartmoor's heavy rainfall slowly washed away the soil's nutrients, limiting its use for agriculture and hence the density of population that the moor could support.

A small incident as I left Grimspound could easily have been my third mishap. For some years this corner of the moor has been home to Highland cattle who are well suited to Dartmoor's harsh conditions. With shaggy coats, big horns and a placid temperament, they are particularly photogenic and popular with visitors. Although they look fierce, they tend to allow people to approach quite close and hence I wasn't concerned to find some on the path. Had they been Dartmoor's 'normal' cows I'd have taken a detour but didn't think the placid Highlands would mind a walker passing by. One did! As I approached slowly it charged, no doubt considering whether merely to toss or impale on its horns this impudent walker. Let's say I was a little perturbed. Fortunately it opted to stop just in time a few feet short of the rather worried walker, then stand and stare. I didn't stand still for long!

Chapter Twenty-Six

HOUND TOR MEDIEVAL VILLAGE

On a warm and sunny September day it was a pleasant surprise to find plenty of space in the car park at Haytor Visitor Centre. Two pounds to park all day seemed a bargain (it's gone up since) and whilst many disagree and some boycott charged car parks, I don't mind paying knowing that the money will be spent on looking after the moor. Ideally I'd like to see it funding better public transport to reduce the need to take cars to Dartmoor.

Whilst most visitors head to Haytor Rocks, I took the grassy path directly opposite the car park entrance, towards rocky mounds half a mile ahead. The path merges onto a stony track which reaches a gate by a large heap of rocks. Through the gate is Haytor Quarry, a place of great history and now of great beauty. It is a different world to the tors and moorland that epitomise Dartmoor. In what once was a hive of industrial activity, sheltered by the huge rock faces is an oasis of serenity, beauty and wildlife. I followed the narrow path to the flooded quarry where water lilies add to the pool's beauty. Deb has swum here but is less keen to return now she's learned that leeches live in the water. There used to be goldfish, presumably released by some well-meaning person, but as an invasive species that ate insect larvae and tadpoles, these were removed.

Haytor Quarry was worked from the late 18th century but was busiest in the mid-19th century. Granite from here was used on a number of iconic London buildings, including the British Museum and the old London Bridge. The last stone to be extracted was used for the Devon County War Memorial, which was unveiled in 1921. Various relics of the quarrying operation have survived for over a century, notably a metal winch which still turns, albeit somewhat noisily. A large piece of timber with metal fittings on one end lying at the edge of the pool was once part of a crane used for lifting rock.

I was able to advise two ladies standing by the pool that they could exit the top of the quarry to make a circular walk. Of course we agreed that this was a lovely spot. They both worked at Paignton Zoo, one looking after the birds and the other the gardens. We had an interesting chat, agreeing that it was a shame the little train that ran round the zoo's lake had gone.

Sitting on the grass to eat my pasty, for a while I had the whole quarry to myself, the peace quite a contrast to what must once have been a noisy and dusty working environment. Then a lady arrived with a lad of about eight. She was of that age where she could have been either mother or grandmother. The boy, as all children do, turned the winch handle, the grinding noise echoing around the enclosed quarry. Soon after they had departed an elderly couple arrived, the gentleman walking very slowly with a stick. We too agreed that it was both a lovely day and a lovely spot.

A gate at the top of the quarry leads onto the open moor. This had replaced a stile a few years previously, assisting those who are less mobile. A *'Miles Without Stiles'* sign on the gate into the quarry indicated that this is one of the stile-free routes suitable for those with limited mobility. It's easy to forget what a barrier these can be.

A grassy path, one of many on this popular part of the moor, took me to the granite tramway that served Haytor and Holwell Quarries, then on to Smallacombe Rocks, from where there are magnificent views across the moor. To the right of the tor is a prehistoric settlement consisting of four Bronze Age round houses (hut circles) and a reave. Pottery and flint tools were found when the site was partly excavated in the 1890s. By the rocks I met the two zoo ladies again and we resumed our chat. I mentioned that no child can resist turning the quarry winch, to which the bird keeper lady admitted that she'd done the same.

From Smallacombe Rocks I followed a steeply descending path through heather, turning left towards Greator Rocks at a grassy clearing. A signpost at the next clearing pointed along two paths indicating *'Public Bridleway'*. It might have been of greater assistance had it said to where they led but for many people part of the appeal of Dartmoor is that walkers have to navigate their own way. Signposts make the moor less 'wild'. (When I walked this way again a year later it had gone.) Bearing left I descended through trees to the Becka Brook, a very pretty stream that runs through Becky Falls before joining the River Bovey. It was once known as the Little River Becky.

A squat, two-span clapper bridge crosses the stream, after which I commenced a fairly steep ascent through trees. On emerging through a gate the massive Hound Tor stood ahead, Greator Rocks to the left and below them the Medieval Village, which was reached along a narrow path through bracken that stood considerably taller than me.

The small village was established in the 13th century when a combination of favourable weather and population growth seems to have encouraged people to move higher up on to the moor. The land had previously been farmed in the Bronze Age and in Roman times may have been used for summer grazing.

The settlement contained four traditional granite longhouses, in which people lived at one end and their animals at the other. A passage ran between the two living quarters and a drainage channel down the middle of the animal

Hound Tor Medieval Village looking to the tor

section. The human areas were divided into two rooms, one much larger than the other. Roofs would have been thatched with straw or rushes and smoke from the open central hearth dispersed through the eaves. The rooms, passages and doorways can easily be distinguished. Several smaller buildings may have been dwellings and closest to Hound Tor are the remains of a barn, with a corn drying oven and kiln. Fields close to the buildings were used for growing crops, including corn, something that wouldn't be possible in today's climate.

The village was only discovered in the 1950s, by surveyors working for the Ordnance Survey and was excavated in the 1960s. The life of the permanent settlement may have been short and pollen evidence suggests that cereal farming had ceased by 1350. Some sources say that it was abandoned as a result of the Black Death which killed at least a third of England's population. It might not have affected this settlement directly but the people may have moved lower down to take over vacant houses. A more common theory is the worsening climate which meant it was no longer possible to successfully grow crops on Dartmoor, or it could have been a combination of factors that led to the village's abandonment. A recent re-examination of the pottery however suggests occupation to the end of the 14th or early 15th century.

After its discovery the village received significant damage from both humans and animals. Thoughtless visitors climbing on the ancient walls dislodged stones and on one occasion some people decided to build their own longhouse with stones they removed from the old walls. In 1997 DNPA not only repaired the site but glued the stones together to minimise further damage, adding soil and grass seed making it look as if the buildings had never been touched.

Like the quarry, there was just me at the village as I sat eating a cake and enjoying the views. It is an historic and atmospheric place that's well worth a visit and another corner of Dartmoor where peace has replaced the activity of many years ago. A thousand feet above sea level, this would have been a wild location when the wind blew in from the north-east and the villagers huddled in their stone houses, but today in the shelter of Hound Tor and Greator Rocks, it seemed an idyllic place to live.

Looking to Greator Rocks & Hound Tor

Descending back to the clapper I spoke to a young couple from Belgium who had stopped for a rest as they climbed towards the village. This was their first visit to Devon and although in Belgium there are the hills of the Ardennes, these are mostly tree-covered and they'd enjoyed discovering Dartmoor's open moorland.

Resting on the bridge I met a group of five walkers from London who had arrived at Newton Abbot on a coach at 5am, were camping out for two nights and ending up at Okehampton. They were seasoned walkers, familiar with Dartmoor, Exmoor, the Lake District and Scotland, so I asked them the big question. Is Dartmoor a wilderness? They were unanimous and without doubt – '*Yes – it's vast and unaltered*'.

PART 10

TWO DARTMOOR CHURCHES

Symbols of religious activity on Dartmoor may go back as far as the Bronze Age, the stone circles and stone rows quite possibly being of spiritual importance, although we don't know whether any worship was of the sun, stars and nature, or of a supreme deity.

Saxons built Christian churches around the moor, although none remain intact. Harford church, which I often wander into on my way to the moor, was built on the site of a Saxon church, as was St Petrock's at Lydford. An earlier building here was destroyed by Vikings but the current church retains a late Saxon font. Likewise Viking raiders may have burned down the Saxon church that stood on the site of Bovey Tracey's large medieval church.

The Normans built churches around Dartmoor: St Peter's in Meavy and St Michael de Rupe at Brent Tor, which stands prominently atop an extinct volcano, still retaining considerable Norman structure.

As medieval villages grew up on the edges of the moor, each had a church built, nearly all of which still stand today, although usually with more modern additions. Most still hold regular services and remain central to village life.

In the 18th century John Wesley was foremost in the founding of Methodism and his frequent visits to the West Country led to the opening of chapels, many of which are still active today. Small chapels such as those at Peat Cot and Poundsgate were built on Dartmoor and Methodist churches are still a part of the community in its surrounding towns.

My walks took me past several Dartmoor churches and I have written about some in other chapters but for this section I chose two very different places of worship; St Leonard's at Sheepstor, a traditional small village Dartmoor church, and a tiny open air chapel that was built on the open moor in the early 20th century.

Chapter Twenty-Seven

ST LEONARD'S CHURCH SHEEPSTOR

I've passed through the tiny village of Sheepstor many times on my way to the moor but today it was my destination for a short walk. I parked at Burrator and walked over the dam but there was no time to stop and enjoy views across the reservoir, as rather than looking inside an empty church, today I was actually attending the service. I arrived at five to eleven and received a friendly welcome. My attendance had boosted the morning congregation to thirteen, not bad for a village of just fifty people, although I was told that only one actually lives in Sheepstor, the remainder coming from homes dotted about in its surrounds. I wondered how the church manages to keep going.

On a very cold day I chose my seat well - nicely in line with an infra-red heater that kept me warm throughout. The service was formal, in that it was mostly read from a book but with an informal atmosphere and some laughter when the wrong reading was started. As a Methodist I'm used to less structure in worship but the archaic language did not seem out of place in a 15th century building.

The earliest record of a church at Sheepstor is of a chapel in 1280 but no signs of this remain. The present Grade 1 Listed Perpendicular Gothic-style building is thought to date from around 1450, a time when there was wealth in the area from wool and tin. It has a prominent granite tower which houses bells that are still rung. Internally the church is dominated by pillars supporting arches and a magnificent wooden rood screen. This is not the original which was removed when the church was 'restored' in the 1860s, but a replacement commissioned by Rev. Hugh Breton, who in 1914 raised £440 to have a copy made by Hubert Reed of Exeter. Rev. Breton was vicar of Sheepstor from 1907 and with a village population of only 95, found ample time for walking and writing about Dartmoor. The proceeds of his five books written whilst vicar here were used for restorations in the church.

Leaving the other twelve members of the congregation to enjoy coffee and biscuits, I stepped outside to explore the churchyard. A cross outside the church porch is a war memorial commemorating the three men from Sheepstor who died in the two World Wars. Three tombs lying within railings are of particular interest. These are of the Rajahs of Sarawak, the grandest grave, which is made from red polished Aberdeen granite, being that of James Brooke. It is an interesting story that connects Sarawak, now a state of Malaysia, with Sheepstor, a tiny village on the edge of Dartmoor.

Of course being Dartmoor, there are two versions of the story. According to a plaque inside the church James Brooke was born in Bengal in 1803. After being badly wounded in the Burma War he bought a schooner and travelled in the Far East, sailing to Singapore in 1839. Here the Governor asked him to take gifts to Rajah Muda Hassim of Sarawak, then part of Borneo, as thanks for the Rajah's kindness in assisting shipwrecked British sailors. Sarawak was ravaged by tribal wars and Brooke's advice and experience were most helpful to the local administrator, who eventually asked him to stay on and become Rajah. He served for 22 years, in which time he helped prevent piracy and slavery and brought a degree of peace between warring tribes.

Other accounts however cast Brooke in a rather less favourable light. His involvement with Sarawak came in 1839 when higher taxes demanded by the Sultan of Brunei had led to widespread rebellion. Brooke was requested to assist the Sultan's uncle, Pangeran Muda Hashim, to restore order and a treaty was signed surrendering Sarawak to Brooke as Governor. At this point he seemed to have somewhat exceeded his authority, attacking Kampong Ayer, the capital of Brunei, which resulted in the Sultan having to apologise to Queen Victoria.

Both accounts agree that Brooke retired to Sheepstor in 1863 where he was buried in 1868 and that upon his death his nephew Captain John Brook Johnson became Rajah. John however died within a few months and his younger brother Charles Anthony Johnson took over as Rajah of Sarawak, a role which he undertook with success for almost fifty years.

St Leonard's Church, Sheepstor

Just outside the churchyard is the village cross, erected by Rev. Hugh Breton and the men of Sheepstor to commemorate the coronation of George V. It is consecrated so can be used for outdoor services. Before leaving I walked along the lane to find one more item of interest which I recalled from childhood walks; the Holy Well of St Leonard which stands on the outside of the west wall of the churchyard. Fed by a spring and dating from medieval times, it is thought to have been moved from inside the churchyard for the convenience of villagers and now sits within part of the church's old east window which was removed during the Victorian restorations.

My visit to the hamlet of Sheepstor complete I returned along the lane to Burrator, passing an organised group of walkers, then three girls running, all of whom headed down the road which circles the reservoir, a popular circuit for a Sunday morning. The lake was full, with water rushing through the dam outlet, quite a contrast to my last visit a few months earlier when the reservoir had been at only half its capacity. Some people thought that a lost village, drowned when the valley was flooded in 1898, would appear but this is just another Dartmoor legend. Farms and houses, including the 15th century Longstone Manor were inundated but there was no church and those who claim to hear bells ringing on stormy nights are clearly mistaken.

Turning right at the end of the dam, I followed the road on the west side of the reservoir, soon passing the running girls who had almost completed their circuit. Just beyond the Discovery Centre I took a small lane on the left, gaining excellent views across the reservoir to Sheepstor, then completed my short morning walk following the Devonport Leat and returning along the Princetown Railway track.

On returning to my car there was not a parking place to be had anywhere near the dam. This is a popular spot and many people drive out here from Plymouth. They seem to like Burrator as it is, although South West Water, through their front organisation South West Lakes, have repeatedly sought permission for commercialisation with car parks, a visitor centre, interpretation boards and signed trails. After objections from several hundred individuals, a number of parish councils and conservation organisations,

Grave of James Brooke, Rajah of Sarawak

plans by South West Water to construct a visitor centre, café and car park were rejected by DNPA in 2000. DPA News commented:

> 'We hope that this arrogant company will remember in future that Dartmoor is a National Park and not a theme park.'

Some visitors walk up onto the moors, while others stay around the reservoir but few explore the little village of Sheepstor, which is all the better for its quiet isolation. Of course if there was a car park, café and a bit of marketing, people would come, especially if they knew it was featured in Steven Spielberg's film *War Horse*. They'd look at the Rajahs' graves, wander into the church and probably put some coins in a collecting box. I love it as it is but wonder if the small band of loyal people who keep St Leonard's alive ever wish that their church was somewhere more visitors might come and help boost its finances.

On another Sunday morning a few weeks later I walked through the even smaller hamlet of Harford and stopped to look in the church. I'd missed the service but two men were doing some work. One told me that they'd had nine in the congregation, although as there is only a handful of houses in the 'village' and most of the parish is moorland, this is not surprising. The men were working on a toilet that was being installed in the church and told me that it had taken years of fundraising but as this was the only public building in the parish, it was needed.

This is perhaps the key to how churches survive in such small villages. They are not just places of worship but part of the community. Most villagers care enough about the church as part of village life to want it to continue, hence it is not just the few attending services who support it.

Sheepstor church is supported by The Friends of St Leonard's which was set up in 2010, with Lord Tanlaw, grandson of the third Rajah, as its patron. A secular group, their aim is to, '*support the Parochial Church Council in maintaining the fabric and furnishings of St Leonard's Church and its environs*'.

They recognise that, '*Many people, in addition to the regular, small congregation, have an attachment to St Leonard's Church. Some can only attend services occasionally, others are visitors and local residents who have an affection for the building which has stood here since the middle of the 15th Century and its continuing associations with Sarawak and its former Rajahs'.*

Such support enables village churches to survive, when often the shop, post office and pub have gone. These all need to make some profit, whereas churches can benefit from the generosity of sympathetic donors to keep them as living places of worship and not simply empty shells or museums of the past. Like railway branch lines and local post offices, not everyone uses them but few want to see them disappear. They still however rely on a congregation and willing volunteers and the big question is how this will continue without younger people joining them? As one who feels an affection for Sheepstor I joined its Friends.

Chapter Twenty-Eight

HUNTINGDON CHAPEL

I started my walk from what I and many Dartmoor walkers refer to as Cross Furzes, at the junction of the lane to Buckfast on the Wallaford Road. From here the most famous of Dartmoor's ancient tracks, the Abbot's Way which linked Buckfast and Tavistock Abbeys, descends through trees to Dean Burn. Cross Furzes is however marked on OS maps and a signpost as where the lanes to Coombe and Hayford diverge 250 yards beyond this point. Another of Dartmoor's many anomalies.

I walked up the lane past Hayford Hall, then along the track and onto the moor through Ludgate, without seeing a soul. This isn't the busiest part of Dartmoor but is easily accessible from Buckfastleigh and one normally passes a few people on a walk. Today I was to see sheep, cows, ponies, a tiny foal, a heron and a baby frog, but not one person.

Following the track towards Huntingdon Warren, I paused at Little Man, a small standing stone. Also known as Kit's Stone or the Lone Piper, it is a guide or boundary stone, however Dartmoor legend gives us another story. Many years ago when merriment on the Sabbath was strictly forbidden, a group of youngsters climbed the hill dancing to a piper. Angry at such blatant sinfulness, God sent a blinding flash and instantly turned them all to stone. The rocks on top of Pupers Hill are the dancers and Little Man the piper.

The easy-walking track continues over the rise between Pupers Hill and Hickaton Hill, from where the enclosures of Huntingdon Warren came into view in the valley of the Western Wella Brook. The warren house is long gone and a large sycamore tree stands in its place.

The first Huntingdon Warren house was a two-storey thatched building constructed in the early 19th century by Thomas Mitchelmore. Rabbits were successfully farmed here, miners working on the moor providing a ready market, but the original house was largely destroyed by fire in 1890. Its replacement was constructed at a cost of £34 and remained in use as a warren until after the Second World War but was later abandoned and accidentally burned down by naval cadets in 1956.

For much of the first part of the 20th century the warren was run by John (Jan) Waye and his wife Caroline (Carrie), who raised their family here. As the price for rabbits fell Jan supplemented their income with employment at Red Lake and Left Lake china clay works, where he looked after the horses. After they left the warren in 1939 the Wayes moved to Moorside Cottage near Lud Gate, where my father once met Mrs Waye, who told him about life at Huntingdon Warren. On another occasion we both met her daughter Stella (then Mrs Coles) who was brought up at the warren and used to ride her pony to school in Coombe.

The final resident of the warren, Frederick Symes, son of a Methodist minister, was an interesting character. He moved into the empty building in 1942 to live a spartan life as a hermit. Apparently he used to correspond with the Abbot of Buckfast in Latin but also wrote to himself. Mr Symes, or Mooroaman (or MoorRoaMan) as he liked to be called, would go down to Buckfastleigh Post Office, where he'd post a self-addressed letter so that the postman had to walk across the moor to deliver it next morning. It's said that after attending market and spending the day drinking Symes would often fall asleep on the way back, but his faithful horse knew the way so well that he'd bring him home safely. Adrienne Yelland, writing in *Dartmoor News*, describes him as, *'dressed in a stained old raincoat tied around the middle with rope, a sprightly figure with white hair and sparkling eyes'*, and says when he made the twelve mile round trip to collect provisions he carried them in a pack on his back. The remains of the cart used by Mr Symes (and maybe his predecessors at the warren) can be seen behind a gate by the site of the warren house.

When I first visited Huntingdon Warren one could wander freely around the enclosures. However, after the walls were rebuilt to make them stockproof under a management agreement between the tenant and Duchy the public were no longer allowed in the fields, which were not classified as CRoW

Access Land when this was designated in 1994. The DPA, DNPA and English Nature become involved as the tenant wished to build a hay barn on the site and there were fears that this could lead to a better track and maybe a house being built. There seemed no need for a barn and one wonders if there was another agenda. No building was erected but the tenant was granted his wish to improve the land by adding fertiliser but only for the purposes of stock grazing. A consequence is, as Paul Rendell wrote in *Dartmoor News*, '*The area stands out from a distance and takes away from the wild place*'.

I wouldn't be visiting the warren today but branching off to find a tiny chapel further down the valley.

Descending towards the river the extensive mine workings of Huntingdon Mine are passed. Known as Avon Consols when it opened in 1854, then as Devon Wheal Vor, after a period of closure it was revived as New Huntingdon Mine in 1864. Tin was mined at several levels and the engine shaft sunk to a depth of 64 metres. It closed for good in 1868 but extensive workings remain.

Huntingdon Chapel

I left the track by a deep pit and large mound (about 100 yards short of the stream), turning onto a narrow path above the mine workings. There are several indistinct paths and approaching Huntingdon Chapel the ground can be wet. The chapel is easily missed, especially if one is looking for something more grand than the tiny open air building. It lies in a dip inside a small raised area about fifty yards above the Western Wella Brook and a hundred yards beyond a dry leat that runs roughly in line with the most southerly wall of the warren (across the river).

The very simple chapel comprises drystone walls, a stone seat at one end and an incised cross at the other. It was built early in the 20th century by a group of young clergymen who used to camp near Huntingdon Warren each summer. They would dam the stream, making a pool to bathe and catch the plentiful trout. Like the warren, from where they got supplies of bread, eggs, milk, plus the odd rabbit, the young men received a daily postal delivery.

The clergymen named the spot Matins Corner and held services here every morning. The chapel was named after one of the clergymen, William Keble Martin, who is best known for *The Concise British Flora* which he published aged 88 after 60 years fieldwork.

Huntingdon Chapel Cross

After more than a hundred years vegetation has covered the granite floor and had volunteers not periodically cut back the bracken and reeds the chapel might not be recognisable. It could perhaps be mistaken for a mine building, but the stone cross, cut into the granite with a cold chisel and hammer, confirms the religious significance of this little building that is unique on Dartmoor.

In recent years a wooden plaque was placed in the chapel and read:

Keble Martin open air Chapel 1903
Divine worship last held here 11th July 1982
Thou God Seest Me Gen. 16 v13

I found today that it had disappeared, I hope for good reason and not stolen as a Dartmoor memento.

In May 1990 the blessing of a marriage was held in the chapel. Caroline Atchley and Derek Newman had first met by the Ten Commandments Stones on Buckland Beacon. Their marriage ceremony took place at Newton Abbot Registry Office and the blessing in Keble Martin's chapel. Derek camped out overnight and was joined the next day by Caroline, their guests and Reverend Eric Carless, who walked across the moor to perform the blessing.

I've visited the chapel many times and find it a tranquil place to say a prayer or give thanks for the beauty of the moor. Cards and flowers are sometimes left as tributes but since my father brought me in 1976 I have never seen another person here. This may be the most rudimentary of Dartmoor's many chapels and churches, and definitely the most remote, but it was and for some is still, a true place of worship.

I always feel a reluctance to leave the little chapel but after a suitably reverent period of time set off to look at a larger stone building a little further down the valley. This narrow rectangular structure was the wheelhouse of Huntingdon Mine and housed a wheel which operated pumps that prevented the shafts from flooding. It tends to be surrounded by mires and hence not easy to reach. Today I chose to keep my feet dry and carried on, following little paths close to the river. It's often boggy here but was the driest I'd known it for some time and my toes remained dry.

There are two points of interest by the confluence of the Western Wella Brook and River Avon.

The first, Dartmoor's newest clapper bridge, spans the Wella Brook just before it enters the Avon, allowing walkers to negotiate what could be a difficult crossing. A small plaque on the bridge states that it was erected in 2018 by Dartmoor National Park Authority, funded by legacies made to

Huntingdon Warren

Totnes Ramblers & S. Devon Ramblers. It is certainly helpful to walkers, as on occasions it's been hard to find anywhere to cross safely below the clapper at Huntingdon Warren.

The bridge provides easy access to the second item of interest, Huntingdon Cross, which stands beside a stone wall a few yards away. It's a relatively small cross and is thought to have been placed here around 1550 as one of four boundary markers erected by Sir William Petre to mark the extent of the Manor of Brent. The Manor was originally owned by Buckfast Abbey and came into Petre's possession soon after the dissolution in 1539. The cross also acts as a waymarker for the Abbot's Way path.

The wall was erected in 2000 and caused some controversy, as it obscures the view of the cross when approaching down the Avon Valley – the route of the Abbot's Way. The tenant farmer was concerned about damage caused by another farmer's cattle who tended to stand around the confluence of rivers and contacted DNPA. They suggested a fence but the stone wall was put up instead and as this is common land they had no legal power to intervene.

Making a circular walk, I returned along the Abbot's Way, passing above Avon Reservoir. This unwelcome intrusion into the wild moor was formed when the river was dammed in 1957. It is an attractive lake but a matter of opinion whether the reservoir enhances or spoils the moor, however served by a private road, there is little doubt that it impacts on the area's wilderness characteristics. Submerged beneath the water are a number of Bronze Age hut circles, a fine blowing house and the remains of a summer retreat used by monks from Buckfast.

The Abbot's Way took me across Brockhill Ford, over Gripper's Hill and past Water Oak Corner, a small plantation which was merely a handful of scraggy trees when we used to come this way in the 1970s. After a pleasant walk over the grassy Lambs Down, I descended into the wooded Dean Burn valley and crossed the 18th century clapper bridge. An ancient lane climbs through the trees and soon reached Cross Furzes, completing my walk and still not having met even one person on the moor.

PART 11

TWO WALKS EXPLORING INDUSTRIAL ARCHEOLOGY

It is only relatively recently in its history that Dartmoor has been considered as a place which should be preserved for nature, recreation and its prehistoric remains. The moor has been grazed by livestock since Bronze Age times. Attempts have been made to cultivate it, with limited success in times of favourable climate or sheltered spots around dwellings, but arguably it has never really been tamed.

Dartmoor has however been extensively harvested for its minerals, although fortunately most of this was before the days where more modern methods would have caused even greater damage. It could be said that the mining, quarrying and extraction that took place on the moor has scarred it but it has also left us with much industrial archaeology of great interest. In most cases it has taken a century or more, but eventually nature has reclaimed Dartmoor, leaving relics of industry and perhaps increasing the diversity and beauty of parts of the moor.

Tin extraction dates back to Bronze Age times when alluvial deposits were taken from streams. It was a huge industry in medieval times, dominating many parts of the moor but the last mines closed before World War Two. Copper, iron and other metals such as arsenic were also extracted, and many of my walks passed relics of Dartmoor's mining history. The moor's granite has been quarried and used in the construction of many notable buildings, but this too has now ceased. China clay extraction however continues, scarring the south-west corner of the moor and it is fortunate that campaigners prevented this from spreading up the Plym Valley. China clay extraction at Red Lake close to the centre of Southern Dartmoor ceased in the 1930s, leaving spoil and ponds that have eventually become places of beauty, although arguably detracting from the moor's wilderness. Peat has been extracted for fuel and to be distilled into naphtha oil, with tramways built to take it off the moor but whilst this could still be a valuable resource, we now understand the importance of leaving the carbon deposited in the ground.

I have mentioned all of these in my walks but it is two of Dartmoor's less likely industries that I have focussed on for this section; ice and gunpowder.

Chapter Twenty-Nine

SOURTON TORS ICE WORKS

On a wintry January day I secured the last pasty at Hog & Hedge Services on the A30, which with hail lashing down I chose to eat in the warmth of their café rather than on the exposed moors. Wearing plenty of layers and with more in my bag, I set off from Sourton to visit the remains of one of Dartmoor's more unusual industrial enterprises – an ice factory.

Taking a track to the right of the church, which crosses over the old Southern Railway line (now the Granite Way cycle route), I passed through a gate onto the moor and continued uphill between the two walls of a strole. The path is part of the West Devon Way, a 37 mile route from Okehampton to Plymouth. Ahead were the spectacular jagged outcrops of Sourton Tors, formed of metamorphic rock, not the granite of most tors on the central moor. Unlike most of Dartmoor there isn't a gradual change from fields to moorland here, but a sharp transition from green pasture to the wilder slopes of Sourton Tors. This close to the village and road it isn't wilderness but over the hills it may well be.

Beyond the wall the track runs through a low cutting then around the left side of the tors. It is hard to imagine horses hauling carts loaded with blocks of ice down the hill but grassy mounds at the crest of the rise are remains of Sourton Tors Ice Works.

As Britain's population grew in the 19th century there was a growing demand for ice to preserve food and cool drinks. Mechanical refrigeration was not yet commercially developed but most large houses had their own ice house for storage. Natural ice was imported, mostly from Norway, which at its peak exported over a million tons a year, however shipping was expensive and of course the cargo diminished as it travelled.

Sourton Ice Works

In 1875 Scotsman James Henderson, a former lieutenant colonel in the Royal Engineers, constructed a 'factory' on the edge of Dartmoor to produce ice. It was whilst working as a mining engineer and surveyor in Cornwall that he had the idea for harvesting natural ice and he chose the exposed north facing slopes of Sourton Tors for his works. It is one of very few to have been built in Britain and as a very rare survival of 19th century industrial ice production is listed as a Scheduled Monument. After his initial application had been refused Henderson was granted a 21 year lease by the Duchy of Cornwall, commencing in February 1875. The rent was £10 per annum with royalties of two pence per ton if yearly sales exceeded the annual rent.

The works consisted of terraces cut into the hillside, in which 32 small rectangular ponds were dug. These were fed with water brought by leats from a nearby spring. In winter ice from the ponds was collected, cut into blocks and kept in trenches, then transferred to a well-insulated stone storage building before being taken off the moor, mostly to be shipped by train to Plymouth for sale to fish traders.

Henderson's enterprise was however slow to show any return on his investment. Collection problems resulted in only a small amount of ice being harvested in the first three years, then two mild winters meant that little was produced. A cold winter in 1878/79 however enabled ice sheets of up to eight inches to be produced and 171 tons was sold to fish buyers in Plymouth, plus 20 tons elsewhere. In the following year 300 tons were sold but competition from mechanical refrigeration companies had forced the price down from a peak of £3 to only £1 per ton.

A combination of mild winters, losses during transit and the falling price from 'artificial' ice meant that the business was never really profitable and in 1886 Henderson put it up for sale. After only three people attended the auction and none made bids, he had little choice but to shut it down.

Before moving on I spent a while poking around the remains of the works buildings in hollows beneath the mounds, walking up and down some of the ponds and enjoying views to the summits of West Mill Tor, Yes Tor, High Willhays, Fordsland Ledge, Black Tor and Shelstone Tor in West Okement Valley. The workers had fine views but out on the exposed moor in a location specifically selected for its coldness, it cannot have been the most enjoyable employment.

Just beyond the ice works is the King Way, an ancient track used by the King's Messengers to travel between Okehampton and Tavistock, a much

Branscombe's Loaf

easier route to ride than muddy lanes in the valley. Following the track south, after a quarter of a mile I reached a gulley close to which are three points of interest.

A small pool, which being of roughly circular shape, located on a saddle between hills and close to Bronze Age remains, may well be a sacred pool formed by prehistoric people. It is included on Tom Greeves' list and its location on a plateau of land close to Bronze Age remains fits his criteria.

Just to the left of the gulley is half of an apple cider press. Carved from granite to crush apples for cider, this is one of a number of presses abandoned on and around the moor. The presses were operated by a horse pulling a stone wheel to crush apples as it rotated around the trough, which sloped inwards allowing the juice to be collected in the centre.

By the path to Corn Ridge, about 40 yards south-east of the apple crusher, is Sourton Tors Stone Circle. This is a large stone circle of 32 metres diameter. Most of the stones lie flat on the ground and the circle isn't obvious but it would be an impressive monument were they to be raised.

I continued past the stone circle, commencing the climb up Corn Ridge with frequent stops to enjoy the view. Rainclouds were approaching and I donned waterproofs ready for a soaking but this time it was not hail but merely light rain. It had almost passed by the time I reached burial cairns on the summit from where the massive Great Links Tor came into view. Looking back it was striking how small Sourton Tors seemed from height of Corn Ridge, yet they tower above the church and road.

Continuing for a short distance I reached Branscombe's Loaf, an isolated tor on the ridge with fine views into the northern moor. Other than the tors, the moor ahead in its winter shades of brown, was largely featureless, wild and quite possibly wilderness.

Adjacent to the compact rock pile are several large slabs of granite, their origin the subject of Dartmoor's legends. Walter Branscombe (or Bronescome), the 13th century Bishop of Exeter, was riding home across Corn Ridge with his chaplain (or servant) when a stranger approached offering them bread and

Sourton Church

cheese. Branscombe was hungry and was just about to eat the gift when his chaplain knocked it out of his hand. The chaplain had spotted that beneath the stranger's cloak was the cloven hoof of the Devil. Had Branscombe eaten the food his soul would have been lost to Satan. The loaf and cheese were turned to stone as they fell to the ground where they still lie and the Devil promptly vanished.

With limited daylight today wasn't the time to venture further into the moor, so I retraced my steps down Corn Ridge to the stone circle, then making a circular walk, turned left following a track around the other side of Sourton Tors. A small boundary stone inscribed 'B' for Bridestowe on one side and 'SP' for Sourton Parish on the other was soon reached. This is the starting point for the 'Beating of the Bounds' which takes place every seven years.

The path runs along a steep-sided valley with Lake Viaduct on the old railway visible below. On the far side a tiny stream, swelled by recent rain, tumbled down the side of Lake Down. Bearing right I followed the wall at the foot of Sourton Tors back to the strole and hence the church, which in failing light I popped in to view. No doubt there are many tales associated with the 14th century church of St Thomas à Becket but I particularly like one which is definitely true and as recent as 2018. On this occasion the church was closed to visitors for the unlikely reason that a pair of bluetits were found to be raising their brood of eight chicks inside the lectern. To avoid disturbing them hymns were sung without the organ and after each service the birds received a blessing from the vicar.

Chapter Thirty

POWDERMILLS

I wonder how many people driving from Moretonhampstead towards Princetown notice a tall chimney on the moor beyond Postbridge and speculate as to its origin? Some may think it was once part of a tin mine, or perhaps a pottery. It does bear similarities to the old pottery at Bovey Tracey, now the House of Marbles glassworks. It would probably take quite a few attempts before the origin of the chimney is correctly guessed. It was part of a nineteenth century gunpowder factory.

With Dartmoor's extensive tin mining and quarrying operations requiring supplies of gunpowder, Plymouth alderman George Frean opened the factory to provide a local source of explosive in 1844. The site, halfway between Postbridge and Two Bridges, was ideal for such an enterprise, being remote but on a turnpike road and with a ready source of water from the Cherry Brook. It however lasted for only fifty-three years, closing in 1897 after the invention of dynamite and a reduction in mining activity caused demand to slump.

Extensive remains of the factory buildings can be seen on the moor and a line of workers' cottages are still in use, housing a bunkhouse, as well as residents. A pottery and café are in an adjacent building.

Back in the 19th century it was a very different community, employing not only those who made the gunpowder, but also blacksmiths, carpenters, coopers, waggoners, wheelwrights, plus staff managing and administering the operation. It seems hard to believe that only seventy years before I started walking on Dartmoor up to a hundred and fifty people were working in this dangerous place on what must have been and maybe still is, wild Dartmoor.

Deb and I visited on a sunny Sunday in August, enjoying an excellent cream

Powdermills

tea and a chat with Joss Hibbs, resident potter since 1999. Her range of rustic pots are made from clay and other materials found on the moor, then fired in a wood-fuelled kiln. With our purchase of a small jug we were taking a little bit of Dartmoor home with us.

The factory's buildings are widely spaced so that an explosion in one would not affect the whole site and it was a very pleasant walk of about a mile to view them. Passing the cottages, we followed the track beside the Cherry Brook with the remains of buildings to our left. A footbridge took us over the river and to one of the factory buildings, with a tall chimney behind it.

Further upstream are the well-preserved remains of three incorporating mills which consisted of two buildings with a waterwheel shared between them. The sites of the waterwheels can clearly be seen, as can channels which brought water from the leats which fed the site. Two leats came from the nearby Cherry Brook and a third, which was constructed later, from the East Dart, taking water from just below the beehive hut which we had walked past on our way to the Grey Wethers.

Gunpowder was manufactured in the mills, where a mixture of saltpetre (potassium nitrate), charcoal and sulphur was ground in stone troughs by huge water-powered stone wheels, the proportion being varied according to the type of application for which it was intended. Whilst the main market was mining and quarrying, the factory also supplied gunpowder for naval artillery and sporting rifles.

The process was highly dangerous and stringent safety measures were taken to minimise the risk or impact of explosions. To prevent sparks only wooden and copper tools were used, workers wore soft-soled boots and in the most sensitive areas the floors were covered with tanned leather. The incorporation mills were built from huge granite blocks to contain an explosion, whilst their roofs were constructed from light wood and tar, so they would be blown off rather than collapse onto workers below. Despite the safety measures,

Lych Way – Powdermills

accidents did happen, two fatal incidents occurring within weeks in 1858. One man died in the first and two in the second, which was thought to have been caused by a worker using an iron shovel which emitted a spark when in contact with stone.

Just below the mills we picked up the Lych Way, which crosses the Cherry Brook and took us to more factory buildings in the shadow of Higher White Tor. This famous path starts at Bellever and runs across the moor to Lydford. Also known as 'The Way of the Dead' or the 'Corpse Way', in medieval times it was used to carry the dead for burial at Lydford Church.

We thoroughly enjoyed our visit to Powdermills – the history, the pottery, the moors and of course the cream tea. This could so easily be an English Heritage or National Trust property, with a shop, visitor centre and interpretation boards, where one pays ten pounds or so to get in. It is far better as it is, free to visit and free to wander on unenclosed moorland.

PART 12

THREE DARTMOOR RAILWAYS

Despite its difficult terrain, over the last two centuries railways of various types have been built on and around Dartmoor. These range from the granite rails of the Haytor Tramway, to the double track main lines that skirted the moor – Great Western to the south and Southern to the north. Most of those on the actual moorland were mineral lines, concerned with extraction of china clay, stone or peat, the exception being the spectacular GWR branch line from Yelverton to Princetown. Finally there were military railways built to carry neither goods nor passengers, but to be shot at!

Whilst most of Dartmoor's railways get a mention somewhere in the book, for these chapters I visited one of each type; the Haytor Granite Tramway, the Princetown Line and the Rowtor Target Railway. The last of these was the most recently constructed and this along with the oldest, the Haytor Tramway, are the only two to retain their rails.

Ingra Tor Halt (*undated photo 123tony-tony eBay*)

Chapter Thirty-One

HAYTOR GRANITE TRAMWAY

Today I was to repeat my very first walk on Dartmoor. I was six and Dad's notebook records:

June 23rd 1967 with Peter.

Bus to Haytor. Walked via stone railway to Holwell Tor then to Beehive Hut. Then to Grea Tor. Then to Haytor. Had lunch (fried on stove) in natural cave. Mist & rain came down. Walked round rocks down to road & bus.

The beehive hut is the quarrymen's shelter below Holwell Quarry. Grea Tor was a name sometimes incorrectly used for Smallacombe Rocks and didn't refer to Greator Rocks which are close to Hound Tor on the opposite side of the Becka Brook. The stove was a little spirit burner that we took on the moors to cook our lunch. That was very exciting for a six-year-old and I still vaguely remember Dad frying the bacon by Haytor. My only other memories from the day are being a bit scared when the mist rolled in towards us and excited when the bus had to reverse to pass a coach on the road up from Bovey Tracey.

I wanted to take the bus to Haytor and hope it met a coach on the way but with a very limited service it was far simpler to take the car. I stopped on the way for a late breakfast at Ullacombe Farm. Like many on the moor, this has diversified and now includes an excellent café, butchers and farm shop. It is hard to make a living solely from farming on Dartmoor.

Paying for parking at Haytor proved problematic. Three times I put my card to the reader, three times it said payment had been accepted and three times it then decided it hadn't. I gave up, left a note on the windscreen and had to wait to check my bank account to see whether I'd paid for three tickets or none. It was none.

Turning right from the car park, I passed the Moorland Hotel in the small village of Haytor Vale. Back in the 1980s Deb and I often called in at the craft centre by the hotel, reminiscing with the chap running it who was brought up near our Essex home and used to play in the fields behind our house. The village grew up in the early 19th century when an inn and row of cottages were built for quarry workers. Each housed two men and the tenants at the front paid an extra threepence in rent.

Bearing left onto the lane towards Manaton, I soon met the tramway as it crosses the road and leaves the open moor. Turning left, I walked between granite rails that were laid more than 200 years ago. Several of the quarries around Haytor were leased by the Devon landowner George Templar but transporting the rock ten miles by horse and cart to the Stover Canal was slow and uneconomic. Hence he built the 8½ mile tramway, linking with the canal which had been constructed by his father.

Granite Tramway

With granite so readily available this was chosen for the rails, lengths varying from 3 to 8 feet, the shorter lengths skilfully engineered to form curves. Points were constructed where the lines divided and check plates made from metal or oak (sources vary) used to guide the trains along the required routes. The gauge was roughly 4 foot 3 inches, with flanges cut on the outside and unusually wheels ran outside the rails. They were not flanged and the trucks could be shunted when away from the rails if required. The flat-topped trucks were usually run in trains of twelve wagons, probably using gravity regulated by crude brakes to descend, the track having been engineered with a gentle gradient to the canal, and with around eighteen horses in single line pulling on the ascent.

After half a mile the tramway divides, a branch curving left on an embankment to Haytor Quarry. This is one of several sidings constructed to serve the various quarries. A stone here marks the start of the Templar Way, an 18 mile path which follows the route taken by granite from the quarries, along the tramway, the Stover Canal to Newton Abbot, then the River Teign to the docks at Teignmouth.

I continued on the main track, passing a small pool and through a cutting, then just before it divided again left the tramway taking a path north to Smallacombe Rocks. It was well worth the diversion to take in the extensive views from the rocks and a quick exploration of the adjacent hut circles.

Returning to the tramway, at a set of points I took the right branch which descends towards Holwell Quarry. With a reverse gradient to the rest of the line, horses were attached at the front when leaving the quarry but it must have been a hard job for them to haul granite-laden trucks up the slope. Close to the track, by a small tree, is a broken or unused rail which will have lain here for the best part of two centuries. Soon after this, on the left is an abandoned broken apple crusher.

The track bends to the right, passing through the main part of Holwell Quarry with a massive granite rock face to the left and a rocky plateau to the right. After a few yards of narrow path there is another, smaller, promontory. Below this, located amidst the spoil, is the small beehive-shaped Quarrymen's Hut.

Beehive Hut

The exact purpose of the remarkably well-preserved hut is unclear. Its sheltered position under large granite slabs suggests that the hut may have been a refuge for quarrymen when blasting took place, a view held by the prolific Dartmoor writer F.H. Starkey, although it would not have held many workers. Other sources however say that it was an explosives store, the solid roof making it reasonably blast proof, but it may have been simply a tool store, or place to eat lunch out of the rain. Whatever the hut was used for the quarrymen would have enjoyed a magnificent view across the Becka Brook valley to Hound Tor as they sheltered from rain, explosions or simply ate their sandwiches.

I walked back to the tramway junction, this time turning right to follow the rails to their furthest extent. A branch departed to the left, serving Rubble Heap or Middle Quarry, then close to a shallow pool the line petered out. There were once branches to Emsworthy and Horra Burrow Quarries but the track to these has been removed. Heading south, I walked almost

Hut circle near Smallacombe Rocks

to Emsworthy Rocks, a picturesque collection of granite outcrops which strangely is not named on OS maps, then followed a path to Haytor, the best known and most visited of Dartmoor's tors.

It was some years since I'd actually touched the mighty rocks and on a clear afternoon was looking forward to enjoying the extensive views to the Devon coast in one direction and across Dartmoor in the other. Approaching from the quieter eastern side there were plenty of recesses in which one could fry bacon should they so wish. The views didn't disappoint and I stopped a while to take it in, sitting by the more easterly of the two granite stacks. Standing near to the road and as the closest part of moor to the holiday area of Torbay, Haytor has been on the tourist route since the 19th century. Coaches stop here and in summer a procession of visitors can be seen walking to the tor. Many scramble over the rocks while some just enjoy the views and ice creams in the car park.

With huge tors and superb views this is a spectacular part of the moor but although little changed since the quarries closed more than a hundred years ago, it would seem to be best described as majestic or picturesque rather than wilderness.

My walk completed I too joined the tourist route, driving along the spectacular road to Widecombe, which was far more enjoyable to visit on a December afternoon than when the hoards descend in summer. Obviously I had to purchase a cream tea in the Café on the Green before delivering copies of *Walks Discovering Lesser Known Dartmoor*.

Chapter Thirty-Two

ROWTOR TARGET RAILWAY

With rain absolutely pouring down as my train pulled into Okehampton it seemed a good opportunity to support the station's newly opened Bulleid Buffet and enjoy a late breakfast before setting off for the moor. It looked as if I was the only customer but just as I got up from my table to order four motorcyclists walked in and beat me to the counter, then took an age pondering their choice of food and drink, paying separately of course. All four men were of mature years and could easily have escaped from a 1980s sitcom.

The breakfast was excellent but with heavy rain still falling it appeared to have merely delayed my soaking. Donning full waterproof gear I crossed the footbridge and set off into Station Wood, taking the same route to the moor that I described in Chapter 5 when my walk took me along the track of another military railway. With one of Dartmoor's rapid weather changes, by the time I reached the A30 bridge a few minutes later the sun was shining and a rainbow arced over Okehampton. Wisely I retained full waterproofs as on the side of East Hill the strong wind dislodged large droplets of water that had been hiding in the trees, falling onto me as even heavier 'rain'. The sun still shone as I passed Fitz's Well but once over the cattle grid swirling low clouds suggested that it wouldn't be dry for long.

Turning right, I followed the military road as far as the first parking area, then took a track on the left, soon reaching a ford on the Moor Brook. After a wet month this was wide and deep, fordable for army vehicles but wet feet for walkers, so I spent a while finding an easy place to step across the stream. Five men, all in red jackets, watched as they stood by their cars.

Branching right, the track took me below the summit of Rowtor, then to a vague grassy path (more like a stream today), past a bullet-marked metal target and on to the railway. I'd walked close by many times on the High Willhays track but never diverted for a proper look. I explored in pouring rain and was impressed.

More properly known as H1 Battalion Anti-Tank Range and Medium Anti-Tank Range, the 30 inch gauge railway was constructed in 1959. It used part of an older target railway which was V-shaped, with a limestone block shed at the intersection of the tracks that was destroyed by gunfire. The newer line is 450 metres long, consisting of loops at each end to enable continuous running and a long straight section beneath a low embankment. Wooden targets in the shape of running men or tanks mounted on trolleys were hauled along the track and soldiers would practice shooting at them from firing points.

The track remains in place and I followed it along the straight section which is protected by an embankment, around the loop and back to the engine shed. Inside the shed, but out of site, is a restored powered trolley. Many people see the sturdy granite building as they walk along the track towards Yes Tor but how many know what it holds?

Rowtor Target Railway & engine shed looking to West Mill Tor

Rowtor Target Railway

Rowtor Military Railway engine shed

The railway was heavily used in the 1960s and to a lesser extent in later years, but moving targets on the Willsworthy range have now rendered it redundant. The track is however still maintained by a group of railway enthusiasts, who also look after the trolley. It was assessed by Historic England in 2015 and considered to be of strong local interest but to fall short of the level of national importance required to merit scheduling.

Looking into the moor, with cloud swirling around the hilltops it felt as if this could be wilderness, however putting aside influence of the wild weather, military activity probably meant it wasn't. It could perhaps be argued that the disused target railway can be disregarded as historic but the military roads with cars parked just 250 yards away were either an incursion into wilderness, or detracted from its characteristics such that it longer qualified.

My objective for the day having been met, with heavy rain still falling, I opted not to extend my walk and to return by the outward route. Beneath

Rowtor I met a very wet gentleman who asked if the large tor he was heading for was East Mill Tor. He'd walked up from Belstone and was planning to wild camp on High Willhays but with such wind and rain thought the tor ahead would be more sheltered. I was able to advise that this was actually West Mill Tor and that he might find a more sheltered spot beyond the tor. It would be dark not long after five o'clock and I didn't envy him a long night alone in a tent but he said he had beer and gin and would be fine. Rather him than me!

Back at the station I had five minutes before the train left; just time to pop into the buffet and purchase a scone to eat on my way to Exeter. First job on the train however was to remove waterproofs and spread them out to dry. My boots on the other hand required two days in the airing cupboard.

I went back to Rowtor for a brief walk one afternoon after dropping off my father's collection of 168 railway books at the Dartmoor Railway Association shop on Okehampton station, this time walking directly from the Camp cattlegrid. As I walked I listed things passed that people had left by accident or design, detracting from wilderness characteristics and perhaps pushing the boundary of any wilderness further into the moor.

- Three Lydford boundary stones.
- Numerous grassy tracks.
- Paved military roads.
- Cars parked at various points along the roads.
- Red and white range marker poles.
- Two spent gun cartridges.
- Long disused quarry.
- Military flagpole.
- A bag of dog poo.
- A partly decomposed banana skin.
- A pair of black boxer shorts.
- Various small items of litter.

Adding to the human activity were about thirty soldiers donning camouflage paint (perhaps soon to become invisible) and several people on Rowtor or walking between the tor and nearby 'car parks'.

Such extent of human activity would appear to disqualify the area between Rowtor and the edge of the moor from being classed as wilderness. Looking into the moor from the top of the tor the view was wilder. Steeperton Tor and Hangingstone Hill stood out on the skyline but on both could be seen military huts. The metal target and engine shed of the target railway were clearly visible below the tor. Military roads could be seen extending into the moor with cars parked to the left and right. Whether I was looking into wilderness is debatable but it is clear that military activity has a considerable impact on this part of Dartmoor.

Chapter Thirty-Three

THE PRINCETOWN RAILWAY

One of the most scenic and wildest of all England's railway lines, the Yelverton to Princetown Railway opened in 1883. Much of its traffic involved carrying prisoners, officers and supplies to Dartmoor Prison, as well as serving quarries, locals and walkers. The line closed in 1956 but the moorland trackbed survives, making an excellent walking and cycle route.

My father travelled on it several times and was pleased to share his memories:

'I was fortunate in being able to travel on the line on four occasions. I first saw the train when walking on the slopes of North Hessary Tor west of Princetown, an excellent vantage point to see the railway in action. I saw the little one coach train ascending towards Princetown as it wound round the tors by its circuitous route and ran down the hillside to take a photograph with my Agfa Standard camera.'

On a cold February morning some pre-walk sustenance seemed justified, so a bacon sandwich with accompanying bowl of chips was enjoyed in the Old Police Station Café, before setting out from Princetown. Following the lane past the fire station, I turned left by the only part of the station that still remains; a GWR stable building that dates from around 1909 and housed the horses who hauled carts around the town carrying goods arriving by train. The station master's house and railway cottages still stand on the right.

A path runs between fences, then onto the old railway line as it makes its way across the open moor. The excellent views made up for the slight disappointment of opening the little packet of biscuits I'd bought in the café and finding they were ginger nuts and not the jammy dodgers I'd expected.

After ¾ mile the line passes through a cutting above which on each side of the track are granite boundary stones. Their inscription 'PCWW 1917' denotes Plymouth Corporation Water Works and the year the stones were erected. They are two of a series of posts marking the thirteen mile boundary of the water catchment area for Burrator Reservoir.

The line runs above the road from Yelverton to Princetown and out of the corner of my eye I noticed a blue light flashing. Soon a helicopter appeared, hovered briefly, then landed on Hart Tor. Figures could just be made out approaching it and I hoped this was an exercise or nothing too serious. The next day I read that very sadly this was not the case. A man in his seventies had been found collapsed and could not be revived. Ambulance personnel were unable to carry him over the rough terrain so the Tavistock Dartmoor Search and Rescue Team were called out to recover the body.

After crossing a bridge the railway bends sharp right, soon reaching the site of what was once one of the most remote stations in England. King Tor Halt, named after the nearby tor, although that is King's, was only open for 28 years. It served Foggintor and Swelltor Quarries but once these closed in the 1930s its few passengers were walkers. The wooden platform is long gone and just the concrete base of a shelter remains.

Princetown Railway near Kings Tor

Ingra Tor, where the next station stood, could be seen just under a mile away, although the track heads off in completely the wrong direction towards the rocky outcrop of King's Tor. It rounds the tor then reappears a few hundred yards below the halt, having completed a loop of 1¾ miles. A further loop around the side of the valley requires another mile to reach Ingra Tor Halt, meaning that in order for the railway to gain height at a workable gradient the distance between the halts is five times that a crow would cover, assuming of course that it wished to fly in its traditional manner.

One day in 1955 the geography of the line provided a challenge to three young National Servicemen who were travelling to Princetown. Jumping from the train at Ingra Tor Halt, they set out across the moor with the aim to rejoin it at King Tor Halt. The Princetown train never hurried but as the three men tore down the valley the fireman rose to the challenge, stoking the fire to encourage the locomotive up the gradient. His efforts however weren't sufficient to beat two of the servicemen who boarded the train to applause from fellow passengers. The third would have had a lonely walk across the moor to reach Princetown.

Almost sixty years later, on 9th August 2014, four men, including Michael Heaton, son of one of the servicemen, decided to repeat the challenge to raise

Ingra Tor Halt

money for charity. This time they raced a Land Rover driven along the track by a local farmer at the railway's average speed of 18mph and all three men arrived at the King Tor Halt before the 'train'.

I'd passed quite a few people on the track but it was quiet on the loop around King's Tor, although there is much of interest to see: the extensive remains of Foggintor Quarry and its ruined buildings, the forbidden Vixen Tor, Four Winds, Merrivale Quarry and antiquities and the ridge of tors beyond. I could just make out a red flag flying on Great Mis Tor and a vehicle by Little Mis Tor. I wondered if the chap I'd met there would be in the little hut with his dog today. It was perfect walking weather but the flag meant that access to this wild area of moor was not permitted.

The line bends sharp left through a cutting after which the vista changed again, Plymouth Sound, Cornwall and Bodmin Moor now in view. The railway crosses a bridge then runs along an embankment at the end of which a branch to Swelltor Quarry leaves on the left. I followed this grassy track, on which the remains of wooden sleepers can still be seen, soon passing some interesting stones. These are twelve abandoned bridge corbels which were cut for use in widening the old London Bridge in 1903. They were either seconds or surplus to requirements and were never collected, so have lain on the moor for over a century. In 1967 the bridge was purchased by an American businessman and shipped to Arizona but sustained some damage on the way. It is said that unused corbels were sent from Dartmoor as replacements, although opinions vary as to the story's validity.

Approaching Swelltor Quarry there is much of interest. Three granite blocks, two rectangular and one triangular, lay on the trackbed, so must have been placed here after the branch to the quarry closed. Close to the entrance are the remains of several stone buildings, one of which was a blacksmith's workshop and a stone platform from which trucks were loaded. Granite from here was used in the construction of the Thames Embankment.

The quarry is one of my favourite man-made places on the moor and unlike Foggintor or Haytor it's rare to find another person here. It was one of the points of interest I included in *Walks Discovering Lesser Known Dartmoor*, a sense that these places should be shared marginally exceeding a desire to keep them secret.

I entered with appropriate care using a narrow path on the bank to the left of the entrance, as ground level is very wet. The cavernous quarry cut out of the hillside is an atmospheric and awe-inspiring sight but in a very different way to the natural wild moor. Now reclaimed by nature, it has become a place of beauty, with trees perched on tiny ledges on the granite faces. There is another loading platform in the quarry and various other relics can be spotted if one looks around.

As I sat quietly on a rock enjoying sunshine in the sheltered quarry I heard the sound of children's voices and on emerging found a mother with her two daughters exploring the ruined buildings. They lived locally but knew nothing about the quarry or railway. If only someone had written a book with routes and information. They'd climbed over the hill but were walking back on the railway. I told them to look for the corbels and of their history.

Descending down to the main railway track I continued on my way as it looped towards Ingra Tor, passing under a bridge built to allow livestock to cross. A lady running with her dog was approaching and on seeing me stopped to put the dog on its lead. We exchanged greetings, then once past me she let the dog loose again. If only all owners were so considerate.

Soon I was at the site of Ingra Tor Halt. Like King Tor Halt there is little to show that there was once a railway station on the moors. The concrete base of a wooden hut on a raised bank and a few bits of wood by the trackbed are its only remnants. The wooden platform is long gone, as is the sign that famously warned passengers to beware of snakes. The station was open for only 19 years, being built in 1937 when granite waste from the adjacent quarry was taken away for road dressing but then kept to serve walkers and a farm in the valley below. My father was one of the walkers to make use of the halt:

> 'In the summer of 1955, Margaret, my wife to be and I used the train to the remote Ingra Tor Halt. It really was in the middle of nowhere. We boarded the train at Princetown having arrived there by Devon General

Swelltor abandoned corbels

> bus from Newton Abbot via Moretonhampstead, and alighted for our walk at Ingra Tor Halt. The train was quite busy with 34 passengers. The moor was covered with thick mist and when we stepped out on the little halt we could barely see one end of the platform from the other. I remember the guard getting out in the mist to collect our tickets then the train disappearing out of sight.'

I diverted into Ingra Tor Quarry, which is smaller than Foggintor and Swelltor but notable for two stone circular crane platforms which remain on the ground, then continued down the railway towards Burrator where Deb was due to pick me up. There was another halt here which Dad used shortly before the line closed:

> 'My other walk when I used the Princetown train was on 5th January 1956 when I started out from Cornwood station. I walked from here across the moorland heights of Penn Beacon and Shell Top to Cadover Bridge, across Ringmoor Down and through Sheepstor. I concluded by walking to the Burrator Dam, which I crossed then ascended the short

path to Burrator Halt. It was a delightful sight to see the little train emerge from the trees. I was the only person to board here but there were eleven passengers in the single coach. Interestingly, although the halt was named Burrator Halt in the timetable, the name on the station was Sheepstor and Burrator Platform.'

Realising that I was going to arrive well after the agreed rendezvous with Deb I changed my plans, picking up a path by the ancient enclosures at Routrundle that took me to the main road below Sharpitor. What did we do without mobile phones to keep in touch?

I shall leave the last words on the Princetown Railway to my father:

'My third visit to the railway was three weeks before closure when the train was made up of three coaches to cater for the large number of passengers saying farewell. Lastly I travelled on the final day in March when there were as many as six coaches to accommodate the even greater number of people paying their last respects to this piece of Dartmoor and railway history. This was another misty day on the moor and Princetown was grey and dreary. Motorists on the nearby road sounded their horns which added atmosphere to the occasion. A sad day indeed.'

PART 13

DARTMOOR GORGES & WATERFALLS

Whilst generally mild, the climate of South West England is heavily influenced by the Atlantic Ocean, the prevailing winds bringing warm moist air, which cools when forced up over the high land of Dartmoor. As the temperature drops the air can hold less water, so precipitates rain. Hence Dartmoor is one of the wettest places in England, receiving twice the rainfall as parts of Devon's south coast.

Much of the rain is absorbed by Dartmoor's peat, then gradually released into streams and rivers which slowly cut its valleys. Narrow streams high on the moor run through V-shaped valleys, often with water cascading over rocks and rocky gorges have been gouged where they leave the moor. These often steep-sided valleys or gorges are an integral part of Dartmoor's beauty and for some their favourite places.

Dartmoor isn't particularly known for spectacular waterfalls but with streams and rivers draining in all directions from the high moorland there are many falls that are worth visiting. Some are rocky cascades, like Broadafalls where the River Avon tumbles over rocks as the stream leaves the miry central plateau and enters the valley that takes it off the moors. Others, such as East Dart Falls and Black Tor Falls have a more significant drop where water falls into a pool below.

The most famous waterfalls are on the edge of Dartmoor. Becky Falls a tourist attraction for over a hundred years and the White Lady Falls in Lydford Gorge are probably the best known. Canonteign Falls with a drop of 70 metres that was formed artificially by diverting a leat over a rocky outcrop, opened to the public more recently. These three are all charged attractions whereas of course the vast majority of Dartmoor is free to visit.

I chose to visit two gorges and two waterfalls, contrasting in geography and management. Both gorges were in the north of the moor; Steeperton Gorge, remote and little-visited, high up on the River Taw and Lydford Gorge where the River Lyd has cut a deep path through rocks, the most famous of Dartmoor's gorges. My two contrasting waterfalls were the well-known Becky Falls on the eastern edge of Dartmoor and Shavercombe Waterfall, a very pretty hidden falls on a tributary of the Plym in the south-west corner of the moor.

Chapter Thirty-Four

STEEPERTON GORGE

Belstone is an excellent starting point for walks into Northern Dartmoor, with a good-sized car park (although it soon fills on busy days), a pleasant walk through the village where there's a pub and café (open Friday - Monday) and mostly gentle slopes rather than steep hills to reach well into the moor. As I arrived a group of youngsters were getting a lesson on use of the compass before setting off on their walk. With fine weather mine was to stay in the rucksack all day.

Walking through the village without stopping and taking the no through road, left by the old telegraph building, I was soon on the short climb up to the moor. The lane ends just beyond Belstone Water Works and with a right turn after the moor gate I was on the old track to Knack Tin Mine.

A diversion left took me to the Nine Maidens, one of Dartmoor's smaller stone circles. Consisting of 16 or 17 stones, it is also known as the Seventeen Brothers. The circle, which once surrounded a burial cairn, is of Bronze Age origin, although legend suggests that it is formed of nine maidens who were turned to stone for dancing on a Sunday. Petrification alone being considered an inadequate punishment, the maidens were also made to dance every day at noon. If one looks very carefully at midday it is said that the stones can be seen to sway.

Back on the track I met a most interesting couple, Julia and Chris from Chard. We walked together for a mile sharing tales of walks across Britain, before they departed by Winter Tor, heading for a ford on the River Taw and I continued towards Oke Tor. Deep in conversation, we'd missed the Irishman's Wall which crosses the track but I was able to tell them the story.

The wall, which runs for nearly a mile from close to the East Okement river, across the ridge of Belstone Tors to the River Taw, was constructed in the early 19th century, however never served its intended purpose. It was built by an Irishman who employed a number of his countrymen, with the aim to enclose an area of moor. Showing their contempt for the rough ground the workers walked barefooted but their labours would never come to fruition. The people of Belstone and Okehampton were not prepared to allow the wall to affect their access for grazing the moor but chose to bide their time. Once it had been almost completed, men from the villages turned out in force one night and armed with poles pushed over enough sections of the wall as to render it useless. Realising that to effect repairs would have been futile, the Irishmen quickly left but the remains of their hard work can still be seen on the hillside.

Beyond Knattaborough Tor, a collection of partly grass-covered rocks, was a large herd of noisy cows. Conscious that this included a number of calves I slowed, allowing them to walk ahead. Suddenly they turned and started heading towards me, prompting my quick diversion to the rock, rejoining the track to Oke Tor ahead of the herd.

As you will have gathered, I'm wary of cows. They're bigger than me, can run faster and you just can't reason with them. Ramblers have been trampled and seriously hurt on Dartmoor. I try to walk round them, especially if there are calves but if there's no alternative I walk quickly, talking to them quietly. I'm not sure if that reassures them or me but I haven't been eaten yet. I have however occasionally terminated, or changed the course of a walk because I didn't like the look of a herd ahead, especially in a confined area.

Approaching Oke Tor I heard a shout and looking back the cows were coming my way once more, this time being herded by a man on a quadbike with three dogs. Once more I diverted to rocks, finding a stone military hut and an interesting rock arch on the tor. In a cow avoiding tactic I decided to stop here for lunch, surveying the view whilst keeping an eye on the livestock. As I sat down the farmer rode off taking the dogs but leaving the cows. I don't know what he promised them for good behaviour but for twenty minutes the whole herd stood dead still until he returned and took them off into the moor.

The track descends for a mile beyond Oke Tor, crossing an ancient earth and stone wall and reaching the River Taw at Knack Mine Ford. Also known as Steeperton Tor Mine and as Wheal Virgin, Knack Mine was one of the most remote on Dartmoor. It was first documented in 1799 and ceased operation in 1881. Various remains of the mine and of earlier tinning activity can be seen in the area.

To my left was Steeperton Tor and 1½ miles ahead, reached by a military track, Hangingstone Hill. Both are fine viewpoints but their summits disfigured by military huts and flagpoles which are visible from miles away.

An article on Hangingstone Hill in *Dartmoor News* contains some strong words on subject. John Bainbridge, describes the observation hut as, *'dreadfully distracting'* and *'ghastly'*, adding, *'I have tried to keep my back to it and just contemplate the wilderness.'* Hugh Farrer talks of, *'the atmosphere of wilderness'*, but that the impact of what is the joint third highest hill on Dartmoor is, *'spoilt only by the ugly military flagpole that has been erected near the summit and the military shelter built into the side of a cairn'*.

The ford is a lovely spot. A partial dam forms a shallow pool, beneath which is a hard surface laid to allow military vehicles to cross. Little fishes jumped out the water to take a look at the walker who'd come to visit. Beyond the pool are the remains of a clapper bridge which collapsed many years ago and now lies beneath the water. Prior to the diversion for cows I'd planned to stop here for lunch but after a few minutes taking in the scene I turned left, downstream into Steeperton Gorge. I was heading away from the wild centre of the moor but out of sight of military installations felt that I was in a little oasis that had barely changed in centuries.

A narrow path runs through the gorge, although some sections are rough and diversions were needed to avoid boggy areas near the start. Having been told by Chris Cook earlier that he'd once sunk to his waist in a bog near Yes Tor I was being particularly careful. This isn't a path that many walk and it might have been a long wait for someone to pull me out. Sadly, in one of the bogs were the remains of a sheep that had ended its days here.

After a while the path reaches a stone wall which links with the old wall

Steeperton Gorge

I'd crossed on the track from Oke Tor and would once have bounded a large enclosure. The easiest route down the gorge is to stay close to a wall which runs along a reasonably flat plateau at the base of the valley. Whilst Steeperton Tor rises steeply directly above the right bank of the river, much of the left bank is less steep and the valley floor flatter (hence the bogs), so not quite the traditional V-shape.

Descending, the gorge becomes more spectacular with the stream tumbling over small waterfalls, a few trees carefully placed by nature adding to the scene - a scene that was being enjoyed by just me and an unseen cuckoo. A deep pool by a lone tree would make an ideal spot for an intrepid wild swimmer.

The gorge emerges onto Taw Plain, a broad, flat, boggy area through which the river meanders. Bounded by high ground on three sides, this spectacular natural amphitheatre may have once been the bed of a lake behind a dam formed either by build-up of material brought downstream by the river, or of glacial moraine. Whilst Dartmoor was outside the range of Ice Age glaciation and assumed to have been shaped by water, more recent studies suggest that icefields covered the high northern plateaus and that their melt-waters with associated moraine deposits influenced the geography of the moor.

On the right is a ford and beside it a boundary stone. I wondered if another stone lying flat on the ground beside it was also an old boundary marker. The ground ahead is boggy but a good path bends to the left and with only a few wet patches took me to the well heads of Taw Marsh Water Works.

This part of Dartmoor has been of interest to water companies for many years. As long ago as 1878 the Dartmoor and Exeter Water Company proposed to build two dams to supply Exeter with drinking water. This plan was dropped but in 1919 the Dartmoor & District Hydro Electric Company proposed Taw Marsh for one of twelve hydroelectric power stations around Dartmoor. A 439 yard dam close to the Irishman's Wall would have formed a 1¼-mile-long reservoir, feeding a power station above Sticklepath Bridge. Other dams, reservoirs, leats and pipelines on all Dartmoor's major rivers would have ruined the moor and there was opposition from conservationists, as well as those concerned that one company would gain control of all

Devon's water supply. The Private Members Bill was withdrawn in 1920, although a hydroelectric power station was built in the 1930s on the site that had been proposed at Mary Tavy and still generates electricity for 1,700 homes.

In 1936 South West Utilities Ltd applied for permission to build a 385 acre reservoir and hydroelectric scheme but this was rejected by the House of Lords. A scheme finally received approval in 1959, but this was for less damaging underground extraction by North Devon Water Board. Nine wells were sunk but as objectors had warned, the presence of radon meant that the water was radioactive. A huge underground treatment works had to be built near Belstone to make it safe. In the 1990s it was found that the water contained high levels of aluminium and that extraction was causing Taw Marsh to dry out, so South West Water agreed to cease taking from here in exchange for permission to extract from the River Exe. The licence for Taw Marsh was finally revoked in 2011 but it was considered more damaging to remove the wells than to leave them, so they remain intact, their access covers a reminder of relatively recent industrial activity on the moor.

The path through the mire meets the water works track, a very pleasant way off the moor. I met a chap with his collie dog, who if he was lucky would get a swim in the river. The man recommended that I climbed Steeperton Tor for the views, telling me that his mother's ashes were scattered there.

The track ends at a moor gate from where a lane runs into Belstone. This affords superb views across the Taw Valley to Cosdon Beacon and I stopped to chat to a lady who was painting the scene. We agreed that it was a lovely view. I said it changes from day to day but she corrected me – hour to hour. The light had been quite different when she started in the morning. I suggested that it would be nice if a couple of the ponies in the valley would pose for inclusion in the painting but she said they'd come earlier and got in the way so she'd made a separate sketch of them.

Resisting the burgers on offer from the counter outside The Tors, I completed my walk with a wander through the village, thinking again what a lovely place it is and a great starting point for Dartmoor walks.

Chapter Thirty-Five

LYDFORD GORGE

Lydford Gorge is very different to Steeperton. Whilst the latter is a little-visited, steep-sided valley on the open moor, Lydford Gorge, on the edge of the National Park, is one of Dartmoor's best known tourist attractions. Owned by the National Trust, it is a deep, narrow and dramatic rocky gorge, with the Whitelady Waterfall at one end and the Devil's Cauldon pothole at the other.

I arrived with Deb on a windy August afternoon to find that access was restricted as a result of a landslide and that the gorge was to close early to allow staff time to prepare for an imminent storm. We were told that it shuts for safety reasons if winds exceed 40mph. There are entrances at both ends and a path along the gorge but with limited time we had to chose to visit either the waterfall or cauldron. We opted for the Devil's Cauldron.

A path descends to the River Lyd which tumbles its way through the wooded gorge where ancient oaks cling to the rocky sides. This is temperate rainforest, a globally rare habitat. A path cut into the rock allows visitors to reach the Cauldron but is not for the faint-hearted and it seemed that the many children here were braver than a lot of the adults. The last section, with no fence, leads to a metal walkway over the pothole where water swirls violently surrounded by vertical rock walls covered with lush greenery. It is an awe-inspiring sight but also somewhat scary. Like other smaller potholes in the gorge, the Devil's Cauldron was ground out by huge rocks thrown around by the force of the water.

Even with the power of the gushing water it is hard to believe that the gorge, sections of which are twenty metres deep, was cut by the River Lyd but one has to consider the immense timescale. Fossils of bryozoans, tiny filter feeding sea creatures, show that rocks in the gorge date back to the

Lydford Gorge

Devonian Period, around 400 million years ago. About 300 million years ago dramatic movements in the Earth's crust caused twists and folds that brought the rocks to the surface. The river was once far larger than it is today and around 450,000 years ago captured the smaller River Burn, which changed its course. The difference in size between the Lyd and what remained of the Burn meant that the former eroded rock more effectively, resulting in the height differential that formed the Whitelady Waterfall. Meltwater at the end of the last ice age swelled the Lyd, creating the gorge which we see today.

Whilst Steeperton Gorge has been little-used by humans, the main changes to the natural valley being prehistoric felling of trees, construction of a few walls, some of which are ruined and centuries of sheep grazing, Lydford Gorge and its surrounds have been used by humans for over a thousand years. Anglo-Saxons reinforced the natural defences with ramparts and enclosed the whole area to keep out Vikings, and Normans built a castle nearby. In the 18th and 19th centuries tunnels were dug to try to extract minerals, the longest of which is 200 metres long and home to bats, moths and rare lichens.

The gorge has been owned by the National Trust since 1943, bequeathed by the Radford family, with the aim for it to be preserved for the nation and open to the public. Three rangers and a team of volunteers work to keep the gorge safe and accessible and look after the wildlife. Much of the heavy work is done in winter when most of the paths and the Devil's Cauldron are closed, although the Whitelady can still be visited. All this costs money, hence other than in winter months the gorge is a paid attraction, although as it was partly closed admission today was half price. Our visit was brief but the Lydford Gorge certainly merits half a day, which should of course include a cake in the tearoom.

Chapter Thirty-Six

SHAVERCOMBE WATERFALL

Like most falls on Dartmoor, Shavercombe Waterfall is notable neither for its drop nor volume, but it is simply a very pretty spot in a remote location. It can be reached from the Burrator area but that requires a crossing of the Plym which isn't always easy, so I chose to approach from Trowlesworthy Warren, passing various points of interest on the way, a route included in *Walks Discovering Lesser Known Dartmoor*.

I left the car in the parking area by the confluence of the Blacka Brook and River Plym, an attractive spot and quieter than nearby Cadover Bridge, then followed the stony track over the Blacka Brook bridge towards Trowlesworthy Warren house.

Trowlesworthy was probably the first of the many warrens on Dartmoor, the earliest reference to rabbits being farmed here being in a lease dated 1651 to John Hamblin, a skinner from Plymouth. It continued to operate as a warren until 1956 when Devon was declared a rabbit clearance area. Trowlesworthy was owned by the Woollcombe family from 1560 until 1969, when it was left to the National Trust. The present house probably dates from the early 19th century and contains stone from the former warren house. It now operates as Trowlesworthy Warren Farm.

A path took me above the house to the 3-mile-long Lee Moor Leat which takes water from the River Plym close to Ditsworthy Warren. It was originally constructed to provide power for Bottle Hill Tin Mine at Plympton but later adapted to serve the extensive china clay works, where it feeds into a lake known as Big Pond.

A concrete bridge crosses the leat, from where I ascended Little Trowlesworthy Tor. Looking ahead from the tor there are good views into

Shavercombe Waterfall

the moor but looking back the outlook is marred by Lee Moor china clay workings.

To the right of the tor is a large cylinder of granite known colloquially as 'The Bandstand'. It was cut in the 19th century from a particularly fine grade of pink granite and intended for use as the base of a flagpole in Devonport Dockyard to celebrate its independence from Plymouth in 1825, however was never moved from the moor. There are two theories; the first that it was considered too difficult to transport the rock to the coast and the second that funding did not materialise.

Heading into the moor, I descended to a ford across Spanish Lake then climbed to the second of two reaves which curve around the lower western slopes of Lee Moor. Ditsworthy Warren soon came into view on the opposite side of the Plym Valley. The house still stands and was used as a filming location for the film *War Horse*.

After crossing Hen Tor Brook, I continued on the hillside below the extensive clitter of Hen Tor and above the enclosures of Hen Tor Warren. One of Dartmoor's more remote warrens, this originates from the late 18th or early 19th century and occupied the area of the former Hen Tor Farm. It was operated as part of Ditsworthy Warren until the 1930s. Nothing remains of the house but fifty-eight pillow mounds (artificial earth mounds in which the rabbits made their burrows) and four vermin traps have been recorded. Whilst the land here is hardly conducive to cultivation and it is said that thirteen horses (or oxen according to the source) were needed to haul a plough, crops were grown within the warren's enclosures.

The land here and almost as far as Plym Head is also owned by the National Trust, purchased in 1966 with the help of bequests, donations and a grant from the DPA, to protect it from china clay working. What a tragedy it would have been to have lost the beautiful Plym Valley with its many prehistoric and industrial remains.

After negotiating a boggy area the tops of trees in a valley could be seen ahead. This is the valley of the Shavercombe Brook and the small copse surrounds the falls. The brook falling into a pool amongst trees in a steep-sided gorge is one of the most delightful places on the moor, yet as on every previous visit I was the only person here. I've never seen much water in the falls but the stream dropping over moss-covered rocks into a shallow pool overhung by a partly fallen tree, is as picturesque as anywhere on Dartmoor.

The falls lie at a junction between granite and softer sedimentary rocks and were formed by differential rates of erosion, accelerated by joints in the latter rock. Whether this beautiful oasis surrounded by rugged and boggy moorland is wilderness is of course a matter of opinion. Some distance from a road, it is remote and not obviously altered by humans but once again I felt it was just too pretty to be wilderness. Perhaps now is the time to reveal the three words I that submitted – *'Untamed, remote, wild'*. I had in mind the rugged hills of central Dartmoor, the atmosphere of Fox Tor mire and granite tors looming out of the mist. As I have read and thought more maybe my views are changing but I still find it hard not to allow beauty and weather to impact on my view of wilderness character.

Chapter Thirty-Seven

BECKY FALLS

'No visit to Devon would be complete without a visit to Dartmoor's iconic landmark. Come and breathe some of the purest air in England, explore fifty acres of stunning woodlands and enjoy a very, very warm welcome!'

Generally preferring to walk freely on the open moor, it was more than thirty years since I'd last visited what is now marketed as 'Becky Falls Woodland Park', a 'visitor attraction' near Manaton but with such promises how could I not include this as one of my Dartmoor waterfalls? If their website is to be believed I've had something like five hundred incomplete visits, so it was something of a relief when Deb and I drove along the picturesque road from Bovey Tracey, knowing that we could return from this trip to Devon feeling suitably fulfilled.

With a welcome that I'd classify as warm, but probably not justifying one 'very' let alone two, the chap at the car park took our nine pounds entry fee, giving us in return a red sticker, a map of the 'park' and '*A Complete Guide to Devon's Top Attractions*'. Becky Falls makes the list as number 25, under '*Animals & Nature*' but a cynic might suggest that the brochure might better be named '*A Complete Guide to Devon's Paid Attractions who have Chosen to Advertise in this Leaflet*'.

We followed a path into the woods, walking beside a leat which was built by in 1850 by convicts from Princetown Prison to take water to potteries in Bovey Tracey and also powered two waterwheels at a copper mine. It closed in 1957 but a short section was reopened in 2016 to supply water to hydroelectric turbines which generate electricity for the Becky Falls site.

The falls are on the Becka Brook which rises near Emsworthy, close to the

Haytor to Widecombe Road and flows into the River Bovey. They used to be called Becka Falls but the name was changed when it became a tourist attraction.

The first attraction reached is the meerkats, who we viewed in their small enclosure before setting off for the falls. The map gave us three options for trails:

- *The Blue Trail – 'Reasonably flat, some steep steps and trip hazards.'*
- *The Red Trail – 'Demanding, steep descents and rocky climbs.'*
- *The Purple Trail – 'Very demanding, must be fit and have good footwear.'*

We chose the red which would take us to Main Falls, then beside the river to Log Bridge, returning on the opposite bank via Boulder Scramble. Steps took us to the base of the falls which are about 20 metres high and quite spectacular, although more for the huge boulders over which the stream divides and falls than the water. It would be more spectacular in winter but the 'park' generally closes between the autumn and spring half terms.

Becky Falls

I did however learn some geography which answered a mystery. For many years I've wondered how even in flood Dartmoor's rivers are powerful enough to carry huge granite boulders off the moor. The answer, an information board tells us, is that huge rivers were formed when permafrost on the central moor melted after the last ice age and it was these that had the strength and depth to carry the rocks to more or less where they now lie.

The path continues through the wooded valley, which was at its best in late autumn, then crosses the river on a clam bridge. This is one of many such simple wooden bridges that span Dartmoor's rivers but is unusual being built over a fallen tree. The path on the right bank is steeper and sections require clambering over rocks. Views of the tumbling river are just as good and in warmer weather many visitors take off shoes and socks for a paddle.

Leaving the falls we diverted into the shop, which is very much aimed at the family market, then the café where a good lunch was enjoyed. Seeking full value for our nine pounds we visited the various animal enclosures, chatting for a while to the lady in charge of the skunk. It had only sprayed her once but the noxious odour persisted for days. The Animal Discovery Zone was disappointing, with only a couple of lizards showing their faces, the other inhabitants either hiding or non-existent and the Halloween displays didn't really interest us.

The falls were well worth seeing but without much water didn't really have a 'wow factor' and were more like a larger version of waterfalls on other Dartmoor rivers than an outstanding feature that stands apart.

The blog *world-of-waterfalls.com*, who have visited waterfalls across the world shared my view:

> 'the waterfall itself wasn't particularly impressive.' 'Unfortunately, both of the waterfalls were bouldery, and the stream flow during our visit was low enough that most of the water was hidden beneath or in the cracks of these boulders. I'm sure when it's raining heavily or the stream has had a chance to accumulate a lot of water from continued rains the falls would be more impressive than what we were able to show you.'

Becky Falls

So were they worth nine pounds? Online reviews are generally good, with families having enjoyed it but a general view of those without children is that it is expensive. So should one have to pay to visit a natural feature? Some refuse and don't get to see the falls. Others don't mind if it's good value. Plenty of places do charge but this is in a National Park. The National Trust charge to enter Lydford Gorge but perhaps that is more justifiable for falls and a gorge that is unique in Devon. Becky Falls is privately owned and the entry fee covers maintenance of the 'park', the other attractions and a living for the owners. They could close it to the public then none of us would see the falls. I'd rather have the choice to pay than not be able to access a part of Dartmoor at all.

I've concluded that you can't really compare Becky Falls with places like Broadafalls on the open moor. Visitors are paying for a package of attractions, even if some, like the woodland walks, are little different to many that are freely accessed around the moor. It however makes a good half-day out, particularly for families. I'm glad we went but I'd rather pay half the price and do without the meerkats.

Almost a year later, keen to see the waterfall with more water flowing, I went back to Becky Falls on a very wet September morning, two days after a month of Devon rainfall had fallen in 24 hours. The falls were more spectacular with the higher volume of water but I still preferred some of the smaller but prettier falls on the open moor.

The chap who had emerged from his hut in pouring rain to collect my now £9.75 entrance money and provide another warm welcome, agreed that the falls are at their best when closed in winter. He said the previous owners had tried winter opening but with little success and they'd considered Christmas opening but people now expect that to include some kind of 'event'. It is a shame that the public are unable to view these 'iconic' falls, inside a National Park, when they are often at their most spectacular, although as I found they are definitely worth visiting after heavy rain in spring and autumn.

PART 14

IN SEARCH OF WILDERNESS

The walks I've described so far have visited destinations with various themes and found plenty of interest on the way. Whilst I have often mentioned wilderness this has not been the main focus of the walks, however before considering the 'last wilderness' question in detail I felt that more investigation was necessary. Hence the following series of walks which took me into the remote central areas of North and South Dartmoor and to various viewpoints where I could consider whether I was amongst or looking into wilderness.

From Fox Tor looking across Fox Tor Mire to Whiteworks & North Hessary Tor

Chapter Thirty-Eight

BLACK LANE & CRANE HILL

My aim today was to consider the wilderness characteristics of the central plateau of Southern Dartmoor. As with the walk to Goldsmith's Cross, I set out from near Whiteworks and followed the Devonport Leat towards Nun's Cross Farm. Progress was at cow pace, a herd ambling gently along the path ahead of me who I had no wish to overtake. Turning left at Sunny Corner, I again followed the undulating path below the wall but this time continuing for a mile to Childe's Tomb, subject of one of Dartmoor's most famous legends.

The cross, which stands on a substantial base of granite blocks, marks the spot where Amyas Childe of Plymstock, known as Childe the Hunter, died in the 14th century. In stormy weather Childe became lost and realising he was in danger of freezing to death, killed his horse, disembowelled it and crawled inside. This was however to no avail and he died from the cold but not before writing a note in blood leaving his estate of Plymstock to whichever church buried his body. The legend however did not end here, as a battle to claim his body ensued. It was found by men (possibly monks) from Tavistock but as they carried it to the abbey news reached them of a plot by residents of Plymstock to ambush them at a bridge over the Tavy. Thwarting the ambush, the monks quickly erected a new bridge outside Tavistock and smuggled Childe into the abbey, which then inherited his lands.

Childe's Tomb may be based on a prehistoric kistvaen, although most of the structure is relatively recent as the monument was largely destroyed in the 1812 when its stones were used in the building of Fox Tor farmhouse. It was repaired in the 1880s by Mr Fearnley Tanner and the DPA, who recovered nine of the original twelve blocks forming the pedestal and had a new cross made in Holne.

I stopped here only briefly as a couple were sitting on the stones eating their lunch and didn't seem to want to talk. I had mine on Fox Tor, enjoying the view across Fox Tor Mire to Whiteworks, one of the most atmospheric on Dartmoor but which was so nearly lost to Swincombe Reservoir in the 1970s.

Heading south I descended into Fox Tor Girt, a relic of tin mining, then to Black Lane, an ancient peat pass cut to enable cattle to be driven from the Erme to Swincombe valleys, which leads to the centre of the southern moor.

The pass is in two parts. The northern section runs from Fox Tor Girt to a shallow dip between the wild and desolate Nakers Hill and Crane Hill, and is marked by an old railway sleeper known as Cater's Beam, although this is actually the adjacent hill. This is the watershed between the Dart and Erme, a significant, wild and remote spot. The southern part starts a few yards south-east of the post and runs down the shallow valley of Blacklane Brook, to another wooden post. The first post was placed here in 1922 when the local hunt paid two men to maintain Black Lane and the current dates from 2016. Its rotting predecessor had '69' carved on it, so is assumed to have stood on this wild spot guiding walkers for almost fifty years.

In another of Dartmoor's controversies, there is some disagreement as to whether both sections are classed as Black Lane. Ordnance Survey maps show it as the northern section and don't mark a path on the southern part, whereas Harvey's Map marks it as just the southern part. Dartmoor author Max Piper says, '*Given that the Harvey Map was influenced by Eric Hemery, a person who knew his ancient tracks, I'd be obliged to favour that*'. Hemery states in *Walking Dartmoor's Ancient Tracks : A Guide to 28 Routes* that the posts indicate Black Lane Peat Pass and I too have always considered that it runs between the railway sleepers.

What isn't in doubt is that this is a wild, remote and boggy place. Whether cattle could still be driven through here must be doubtful as most of the pass is miry and even the narrow path at the edge often very wet. Richard Knights on his excellent website (*richkni.co.uk*) describes it as, '*just about the most isolated part of the southern moor*' and the very helpful *holidayindartmoor. co.uk* as, '*an uneven, sunken stretch of moorland that's boggy and tussocky*'. They were right! Although I was walking in August, the summer had been

Cater's Beam (the original – photo 2015)

wet and the going was far from easy. Black Lane seemed to be wilderness – but it was shaped by man.

Progress was slow with frequent diversions, especially as I was taking extra care having the night before read Paul Rendell's article in *Dartmoor News* about bogs. He describes at the age of about sixteen sinking to his waist in Raybarrow Pool, one of Dartmoor's most fearsome mires. Also in the article and even more worrying, was a photo of a lady sunk up to her chest in blanket bog near Cut Hill. I thought of the advice my father was given which he used to tell me – '*if you feel yourself sinking put your arms outstretched'*. This is what he did when crossing bogs but I'm not sure it would have done any more than perhaps stopping you going in above the shoulders.

In the end, delayed by bogs, with rain forecast and with Deb picking me up at Whiteworks, I decided to turn back rather than follow my original plan to continue to Duck's Pool, home to one of Dartmoor's iconic letterboxes The letterbox was constructed in 1938 and forms part of a memorial to William Crossing. The 'pool' which lies in the centre of the southern moor, holds virtually no water. It may have always been just a depression or could have been drained by tinners, there being many remains of their activity in the vicinity.

It was a good decision to curtain the walk as even if I hadn't been swallowed up by a bog, I'd have been very late for our rendezvous. Either way I'd have got a telling off. Instead I took a wander onto Crane Hill, which more exposed, without the extensive tinning remains and with fewer visitors, holds greater wilderness value.

My notebook recorded, *'featureless, inhospitable – wilderness'*. There is no obvious summit to the hill. It's more a vast plateau out of which rise the Plym, Erme and tributaries of the Dart. The ground was wet, the grass tussocky and paths non-existent. As I wandered around the boggy hill I thought, if there is wilderness on Dartmoor then this is part of it. This is the wild and remote Dartmoor landscape that I love most and have always considered to be wilderness. It is not what one would traditionally call pretty but it is remote, rugged and wild. It can be immensely peaceful but also be slightly scary.

Writing in *Dartmoor News*, in an article entitled *'Crane Hill – A Journey into Desolation'*, John Bainbridge shares similar sentiments:

> *'Once south of Fox Tor I always feel the greatest sense of Wilderness'.*
> *'It is the kind of landscape that defines Dartmoor and led to the Moor's*

Childe's Tomb

designation as a National Park.' 'Crane Hill is for me, the hill that demonstrates the very ideal of wild country as a precious asset and one we mustn't lose'.

There seems little sign of human activity, but analysis shows there is some. Dartefacts, a data base that catalogues most items of interest on Dartmoor, lists only a former trig point, a cairn and some benchmarks in the summit area, but the plateau extends to include Black Lane, Duck's Pool and various tin workings. Heritage Gateway lists ten items of interest, although some are on the lower slopes, including Goldsmith's Cross, so whilst this wild moor appears untouched, it has actually been used by humans for millennia and a variety of permanent marks left behind.

As always, on making my way back up Black Lane it was good to see the railway sleeper, which whilst an intrusion into the wilderness, is a welcome sign for walkers as they negotiate this featureless part of the moor, as is Fox Tor peeping over the horizon when one heads north.

The view from Fox Tor, which had seemed so wild on the way out, now seemed less so in comparison to Black Lane and Crane Hill. There I could see nothing but wild moor, however the plantations, roads and occasional houses detracted from the wilderness characteristics of the expansive panorama from the tor. There seemed little doubt however that the depression of Fox Tor Mire, despite its specks of human influence, was a wilderness.

I took a higher route back from Fox Tor, following the path on the northern slope of Crane Hill but losing it soon after Little Fox Tor. Nun's Cross Farm could be seen ahead so navigation was no problem but the ground wasn't ideal, with long and wet grass.

In order to avoid bits of bog or turning an ankle I tend to look downwards when negotiating such terrain. On this occasion it was a good thing that I was. As I made my way through clumpy grass my foot came down inches from a coiled adder. It's quite common to see adders on the moor and I'm always pleased to do so but generally they are in dryer areas and don't hang around when they detect footsteps. So much for them sensing a human approaching and slithering off. On this occasion it was me who leapt, somewhat rapidly, to the side, another mishap on the moor avoided.

I have often wondered what one should do if bitten by an adder when alone on Dartmoor. NHS advice is to call 999 or go to A&E immediately and whilst waiting keep the part of the body that was bitten as still as possible, lying in the recovery position if you can. Conscious that not all of these may be possible I asked Dartmoor Rescue for their advice. This was to where possible follow NHS advice and that the controller, police or ambulance would call out Rescue if necessary. If a mobile phone cannot be used shout or use a whistle to attract attention. As they said, the reality is that each situation would be different.

Chapter Thirty-Nine

KNATTABARROW POOL

In search of wilderness I set out to visit one of my favourite wild places on the moor. I usually try to choose walking days when the weather is reasonable but today was an exception - thick mist. Would such weather mean a greater 'wilderness experience'?

My starting point was Shipley Bridge, a picturesque spot on the River Avon. High stone walls bordering the car park were once part of 19th century naptha works, processing peat brought from Red Lake along the Zeal Tor Tramway, then later for drying china clay from Bala Brook Head. I took the Avon Dam road, then the branch to the Avon Filtration Works, where the Zeal Tor Tramway can be picked up. Constructed to carry peat from Red Lake Mires to the works near Shipley Bridge and opened in the late 1840s, this was a most unusual railway, with five foot gauge wooden rails spiked to granite sets. Trains were horse-drawn with the horses probably hitched at the rear to slow it on the steep descent towards Shipley Bridge.

After two miles of steady ascent, passing various railway relics and a green tent in a misty hollow above the Bala Brook, I reached a path heading south to Three Barrows. This tends to be wet at all times of the year but on a misty autumn afternoon many diversions were required around bogs. I left it after ⅓ mile, turning left by a boundary stone and heading across rough ground towards grassy mounds which I could just make out in the mist. Beyond the mounds appeared one of Dartmoor's lesser-known but mysterious pools.

The dark peaty waters of Knattabarrow Pool, a former china clay pit, are rarely visited but can be one of the most atmospheric places on the moor, especially in weather like today's. Crossing (who calls it both Knattleborough and Knattaburrow in his *Guide to Dartmoor*) suggests that the pool is perhaps more deserving of notice than any other on the moor, noting that its

Knattabarrow Pool

outline appears more like a natural tarn than other artificial pools such as Crazy Well. Dartefacts describe it as '*a truly desolate spot*'.

The pools (there are actually three, one much larger than the others) are not far below the flattish summit of Quickbeam Hill above the Erme Valley and are also known as Quickbeam Pools. As I stood on a mound there was no view today, just the main pool, wild grassy moor and mist. This isolated pool always feels like it is in wilderness but today there seemed no doubt. The weather was wild, the moor wild, I had seen no one and not even sheep had ventured across the rough terrain to stand by a dark, still pool.

But who put the mounds here, who made the pool, who had erected the boundary stones, formed the path and built the tramway? Human influence was literally beneath my feet. Could this be wilderness when people had altered the land and left their marks?

Milestone, Zeal Tor Tramway

Of course mist doesn't make somewhere more of a wilderness but as with green hills and prettiness, human perception can be influenced by the weather. At Leighon Tor the weather was wild but with good visibility I could see that I wasn't in a wilderness. The remote Knattabarrow Pool I have felt was wild every time I've been there and in an eerie Dartmoor mist it seemed even more so.

Chapter Forty

NORTH HESSARY TOR

Standing centrally, adjacent to Princetown, North Hessary Tor is probably the point on Dartmoor most visible from across the moor and indeed much of Devon, however I'd never previously climbed the hill. It's not really on the way to anywhere and I'd avoided it for the very reason of its visibility – a 196-metre-high mast – the highest man-made structure in the south west.

Originally a television mast and still often referred to as such, in the digital age it is now primarily used for radio. Construction of the huge mast was controversial and opposed by both the DPA and Campaign for Rural England but permission was granted after appeal and it was erected in 1954, becoming fully operational two years later. There have been suggestions that it could be removed and whilst those who don't wish to see such intrusions on the moor would be delighted, some in the letterboxing community voiced concern that they would lose a useful direction marker. It was however shortened by 50 feet in 1987.

I was staying at the excellent Duchy House bed & breakfast and after a large dinner at the Prince of Wales, followed the path from opposite the fire station, through a small wood, then a gate to open moor. From here it's a straightforward climb to the tor. Whilst unlikely to be wilderness itself, standing relatively alone in a central position the hill promised views right across the moor.

I started at a gentle pace, quickening slightly when three cows, two brown, one black, started following me, the rest of the herd not far behind. Then as I looked back the black cow decided to mount one of the brown ones, while the other looked on. Thinking that with their minds on procreation of the species, or whatever cows think of when engaging in (or indeed watching) such activity, I slowed down. After a minute it dawned on me that bonking

North Hessary Tor Mast

cows presumably meant that (although one must never assume), one was a bull. I accelerated once more but the cows' interest remained in romantic liaison and not chasing a lone walker.

Two things struck me on climbing to the top of the small tor; the size of the mast which protrudes from the transmitter building and the panoramic view. I could see well into Cornwall with Bodmin Moor standing out, Plymouth Sound and the coast, a huge swathe of Southern Dartmoor – Trowlesworthy Tors, Hen Tor, the Plym Valley, Crane Hill, Burrator and the tors which surround it. Looking to the northern moor, the massive Great Mis Tor was prominent, with Roos Tor and Cox Tor to the left. Fur Tor and Cut Hill could be picked out further into the moor. The tors in this 360-degree panorama were far too numerous to count.

In his *Guide to Dartmoor* William Crossing refers to the tor as '*North Hisworthy*' but notes that it is known locally as '*North Hessary*'. He writes that, '*no less than about sixty tors are to be seen*' and describes the view:

'*Northward and southward are the untamed hills, rising grim and bare ; vast solitudes where nothing of man's work is seen.*'

Great Mis Tor from below North Hessary Tor

As I stood on the tor and looked from afar, like Crossing I saw wild and remote moor. On a clear summer evening with the sun starting to go down it was immensely beautiful. Was it wilderness? From afar I had to say yes, although the huge mast and building next to me meant that the tor on which I was standing was definitely not. I wondered, does this gigantic mast, that is visible from much of Dartmoor, diminish the wilderness value of the whole moor, or just the tor on which it stands?

Chapter Forty-One

EYLESBARROW & PLYM FORD

After another night in the Duchy House B&B with the usual friendly welcome and excellent breakfast, I started from Princetown, following the Devonport Leat through Peat Cot. This tiny settlement was founded not long after the leat was constructed and comprises little more than a couple of farms linked by a clapper bridge, and a former Wesleyan Chapel. This opened in 1912 and was still holding monthly services when I first walked by with my father in 1975 but closed ten years later.

Near Whiteworks I met a lovely couple with a little white dog and a teenage boy wearing an Arsenal shirt. We talked for some time, the lady having a great interest in Sherlock Holmes was very excited to see Fox Tor Mire, the inspiration for Sir Arthur Conan Doyle's Grimpen Mire, haunt of the terrifying beast in *Hound of the Baskervilles*. I dissuaded them from trying to cross it and suggested following the leat to Nun's Cross. The lad was less interested, sitting a little distance away playing with his phone. It was however the dog who ran out of patience first, announcing with sudden woofing that it was time to get walking.

A cow cooling its feet in the leat seemed to have the right idea on what was a very hot day. Walking past Nun's Cross Farm, I picked up the bridlepath known as Ivybridge Lane that runs from Princetown through Eylesbarrow Mine to the lane leading to Sheepstor village. The gravel track makes for easy walking but can be seen from miles around – another intrusion into the wild landscape.

My initial destination was not the mine, but the hill Eylesbarrow which affords fine views. Once again I wanted to consider whether I was looking into wilderness. There are indeed excellent views into the centre of Southern Dartmoor, notably towards Plym Head and the desolate Crane Hill. I may well have been looking at wilderness but felt that the very path which had brought me close to the summit reduced the wilderness characteristic of my immediate surroundings.

It is an ancient track and a popular route for walkers and cyclists, hence to prevent erosion it needs a good surface. In the late 1990s DNPA repaired the eroded track between Princetown and Nun's Cross, using decomposing granite which was a light-yellow colour. It was highly visible and the track became known locally as The Yellow Brick Road. On reaching Nun's Cross the workers mistakenly started to repair the path up Eylesbarrow, not the bridleway, resulting in further erosion when mountain bikers started to use this route. By 2014 the new surface on the most popular sections had been badly eroded and it was repaired again, this time using imported stone which had been crushed and rolled to form gravel. Not being granite this is not only highly visible as it crosses the moor but an alien stone.

It is a difficult issue. People want to walk and ride in the National Park to experience 'wilderness' but in order to accommodate them we have to impact on the wildness they've come to see. Is it better that visitors are encouraged to go to certain well-managed places, or that they spread out across the moor? In this case it is a bridleway so cycling is permitted. Cycles tend to cause more damage than feet but they have a right to use the track and if they are to be encouraged not to erode open moor elsewhere then it seems reasonable to provide some well maintained routes.

Access versus wilderness is a conflict that has to be considered in all our National Parks and indeed in many wild places across the world. The popularity of the Coast to Coast Walk from St Bees to Robin Hood's Bay has led to flagstones being laid on some sections to combat erosion. It makes walking easier but as Mark Allen, a serious rambler, told me after completing the walk, *'it detracts from the wilderness'*. There is no easy answer.

My intention had been to cross the Plym and walk to Broad Rock, an ancient boundary marker in a remote spot between the heads of the Plym, Erme and Langcombe but decided that today it was too hot to continue further into the central moor.

Plym Ford

Two months later, on a very wet and windy day I set out from the other end of the track, starting from the Scout Hut below Gutter Tor. Again the path stood out as a man-made scar across the hillside but this time showing a way through the mist rather than reflecting bright sunshine. After walking through the remains of Eylesbarrow tin mine, the largest on Dartmoor, I branched right, taking a path to Plym Ford, which was reached down a tinning gulley below Wheal Katherine wheal pit. Here I met the Abbot's Way. The intention had been to follow it to Broad Rock, however there was the small matter of crossing the Plym, which after days of rain was high and fast-flowing. Choices were to paddle through the ford or attempt a leap slightly upstream. I might not have got much wetter than I already was but safety coming first, I turned back.

On his website *www.rickkni.co.uk* (Dartmoor Walks) Richard Knight writes that, *'once you are past Plym Ford then you enter into the wilderness of the Southern Moor'*. As the Abbot's Way disappeared into the mist on the slopes of Great Gnats' Head, a remote and largely featureless hill, which I remember as a wild place when I first came here with my father, it certainly

Side wall of stamping mill, Eylesbarrow Mine

looked to be wilderness. I had seen no one since some soldiers training near the Scout Hut and surrounded by mist it seemed that I was in a wilderness but do the track and extensive remains of Wheal Katherine Mine negate this?

Wheel Pit, Wheal Katherine Mine

Chapter Forty-Two

CUT HILL

Looking into the centre of Northern Dartmoor I'd already picked out Cut Hill from various directions and suggested that this might be the wilderness. It is commonly said to be the most remote place on Dartmoor and the furthest from a road, although this is debatable. Cut Hill was the most remote when the public were permitted to drive around the full military loop road but now that (thankfully) they are not, according to the usually reliable source of Dartefacts, nearby Black Ridge is the furthest point from a road south of Northumberland. The exact point on the ridge depends on whether the military roads are included and the distance either 3.9 or 4.1 miles. Of course this is in a straight line and realistically most walkers would cover a significantly longer distance.

Sitting in the central area of the northern moor, Cut Hill can be reached from all directions, some easier than others and on a sunny August day I chose the picturesque walk along the East Dart from Postbridge.

The first part is easy, following a gravel path from behind the Visitor Centre, soon crossing a double-span clapper bridge over the Galler (or Gawler) Brook, a small tributary of the Dart. This is Drift Lane, an ancient route onto the moor. Passing through a gate onto open moor, with the East Dart to the right and Hartland Tor beyond, the path follows the newtake wall as it bends left away from the river.

I shared brief greetings with a farmer rounding up his sheep; one dog working and three others in a cage on the back of his quadbike. I wondered if they were youngsters being shown the ropes.

Roundy Park, a circular walled Bronze Age pound was passed in the field on the right. Usually I divert to view one of Dartmoor's largest kistvaens which stands in the field just outside the pound, but with cows surrounding it chose not to bother today.

I stopped to talk to a man walking down the hill. He had been camping overnight near East Dart Waterfall and was heading to Postbridge for supplies. He'd walked across the moor from Gidleigh and planned to camp another night but had no idea what weather was forecast. It wasn't good I had to tell him.

After crossing the pretty Braddon Lake stream, then the dry Powdermills Leat, I ascended Broad Down, stopping at Broadun Rocks on the summit to take in the view up the East Dart Valley and my route ahead: Waterfall, Sandy Hole Pass and the dome of Cut Hill.

I walked down to the falls and said hi to the only person there, a lady surrounded by camping gear and dirty pots. There followed a slightly awkward conversation. I said I'd met her partner on his way to Postbridge and she looked a bit confused. Her partner, she explained, was fishing further up the Dart. Whether she wondered if she'd been abandoned on the moors I'll never know but the misunderstanding was resolved when she told me a family had been camping near the falls.

Lingering no longer, I followed the path above the river towards Sandy Hole Pass, a narrow gorge formed when tinners straightened, deepened and narrowed the river, increasing its rate of flow. This helped take away the mining waste but resulted in problems downstream at Dartmouth where sand caused the harbour to silt up.

Progress was then delayed by a herd of cows. Several stood on the higher path and a mother with her calf guarded the lower path that enters the pass. There were more the other side of the river and a couple standing in the water, making a good photograph but adding to the concern for a walker who has read of and watched too many tales of unprovoked bovine assaults necessitating helicopter rescues. I decided to eat my lunch and hope they moved on. It was a beautiful place to sit above the meandering Dart – just me, cows, and the chap fly fishing a little downstream.

Lunch eaten and cows moved on, I set off again, walking through the atmospheric Sandy Hole Pass, then picking my way along a narrow, somewhat boggy path diagonally left towards Broda Stones, a rocky outcrop just beyond a stream. The view from the rocks exceeded even that from Broad Down. The route to the top of Cut Hill was laid out before me – East Dart, Cut Hill Water, then peat passes almost to the summit. A line of red and white military range poles intruded into the wilderness but provided a useful guide to the route. I have always felt that Sandy Hole Pass is the gateway to Dartmoor's central wilderness and concur with John Bainbridge's words in *Dartmoor News*:

> 'The pass might be mostly artificial, but it always seems to me to be a magical frontier – like the Khyber Pass in miniature, with a strange and desolate territory beyond.'

After an easy section along the Dart the riverside path disappeared, dividing into several vague routes through a low-lying marshy area to the left. I made my way, with some difficulty, using the patchy paths and avoiding the worst of the bogs. On the return I found a better path but suspect that both would have been easier than staying by the Dart. Reaching what the OS map names as Cut Hill Water, but is commonly known as Hangman's Stream, I was on the edge of Cut Hill.

Before starting the ascent I stopped to visit a tinners' hut by the stream, a relic from industrial activity here centuries ago. Somewhat less old was a caterpillar tracked vehicle parked just above the stream. It was slow going dodging bogs but I soon picked up the North West Passage one of Dartmoor's Phillpotts Peat Passes. These were routes cut through the peat, mainly for the benefit of fox hunters. Frank Phillpotts had a great knowledge of the northern moor and areas where peat had been eroded down to the granite bedrock. He had the idea to remove the remaining peat and form a hard track through the rough and boggy ground. Small stone marker posts still stand at the ends of most of the passes, with bronze plaques explaining their origin:

'THIS STONE MARKS A CROSSING THROUGH THE PEAT, WHICH MAY BE OF USE TO HUNTING AND CATTLEMEN; THE CROSSING WAS MADE BY FRANK PHILLPOTTS, WHO

DIED OCTOBER 1909, IT IS KEPT UP IN HIS MEMORY BY HIS BROTHER AND SON.'

The North West Passage is thought to have been named by Mr Sam Adams, master of the Lamerton Hunt from 1896 to 1904. It is in two sections, a short length above Cut Hill Water and a longer one which runs south-east to north-west almost to the top of the hill. I missed the marker posts for the first, probably because the ground seemed as wet in the pass as around it and many deviations were required to avoid bogs. The main part is wider and I followed its whole length, grateful to Phillpotts for his help in aiding my ascent, a sentiment which was probably not shared by the foxes which it assisted huntsmen to catch.

The North West Passage Phillpotts Peat Pass

I was now in wildest Dartmoor which Richard Sale in *Dartmoor (Collins Ramblers Guide)* describes as, '*a wild hillside of peat hags*'. He goes on to mention that the path below the North West Passage is, '*soon lost in the difficult wilderness*' and mentions two range notice boards which have now thankfully been removed.

As I neared the end of the pass five figures appeared over the horizon. All were men, older than me, who had walked beyond Cut Hill to Fur Tor. We spoke briefly, discussing the state of the ground which was unusually wet for August, before parting in opposite directions. These were the only people I saw beyond Sandy Hole Pass.

A path continues towards nearby Fur Tor but it was Cut Hill that I'd come to see today, so I branched off to the summit, a very gentle dome covered in bogs and peat hags. It is a strange environment. Other than the hags, most of the peat has gone, either cut or eroded. Opinions are divided but the method of removal may impact on the hill's wilderness properties. In *Crossing's Guide To Dartmoor*, William Crossing, considered by many to be the greatest authority on Dartmoor, writes:

> '*On the N. side of the hill the rain has washed away vast quantities of peat, in one place to such an extent that at first glance the visitor might be inclined to imagine that it has been removed by manual labour.*'

Michael Hedges in *Dartmoor Captured* agrees saying:

> '*a great tract of peat has been washed away from the centre of the hilltop.*'

Steve Griggs' *dartmoorexplorations.co.uk* references Dr Tom Greeves in *Dartmoor Magazine* and considers that the peat has been cut by humans:

> '*On the top plateau of Cut Hill, there is a 100m-wide strip of ground (that) is lower than the surrounding peat which has been totally removed. The peat removal is said to have probably been done by "human agency" since medieval times when peat was cut for charcoal production, exposing an old, presumably prehistoric, land surface.*'

The summit plateau that I'd reached by a steady but not steep climb, belies that at 1978 feet (603 metres) it is the joint third highest on Dartmoor. The ground all around me was in keeping with the setting – the most remote in Southern England. Having described views all across the moor I have run out of superlatives but this was the best – a 360-degree panorama of Dartmoor.

The iconic Fur Tor was just under a mile away to the west and the massive Great Links Tor to the north-west. High Willhays, the highest point in Southern England, to the north, with Yes Tor close by. Hangingstone Hill, with a military hut on the summit, and Whitehorse Hill to the north-east. Sittaford Tor, where my brother and I had sat considering wilderness to the east. To the south were tors in the West Dart Valley that I'd visited on my Brown's House Walk – Rough, Higher White and Longaford. South the view to Postbridge and Two Bridges extended into Southern Dartmoor – Ryder's Hill and possibly Three Barrows. Whilst not the geographical centre of the National Park (that is around Bellever), it felt that I was at the true centre of Dartmoor. It is a simply wonderful place.

Simon Dell seems to agree, describing Cut Hill as, *'the most remote spot on Dartmoor'* in his walking guide *Dartmoor Wilderness Walks,* and commenting:

> *'The sense of achievement on reaching Cut Hill is certainly worth the effort and if you walk up to the very top of the hill and stand aloft on the highest of the peat hags you will achieve what must be one of the best views on the moors.'*

Cut Hill with range pole, looking to Fur Tor

Liz Miall's review of Dell's book in *Dartmoor News* agrees that he finds wilderness;

'takes the walker to some of Dartmoor's hardest to reach spots, such as Cranmere Pool, Fur Tor, Ryders Hill, Hangingstone and beyond – wilderness walks certainly.'

John Hayward writes of Cut Hill in *Dartmoor 365*:

'Cut Hill has an aura of bleakness and remoteness that acts as a magnet to those who like to penetrate the innermost recesses of any wilderness. There is no direct route from any road – at least not one that you would take twice.'

William Crossing describes the view as:

'such as can be obtained from no other point throughout the length and breadth of the moor', adding, 'We look upon desolation ; upon a vast wilderness, from which life is absent.'

He comments that other than the distant Princetown and enclosures of Teign Head Farm, hardly a sign of man's work is visible. Crossing was of course writing more than a hundred years ago, since which time Teign Head Farm has gone, although the walled enclosures remain, Princetown has grown in size and military range poles have been planted on the hillside.

There seemed little doubt that I was in a wild place. The terrain, the starkness, the remoteness but with beauty both raw and pretty. Peat up to 1.8 metres deep covers Cut Hill's granite base, the ground is boggy and the grass long. Cattle and sheep mainly stay away, although it's also a place where their bones can be found.

As I stood on this amazing spot in wildest Dartmoor, with a panorama of the moor around me, I considered the big question: is this wilderness?

My walk had started alongside walled enclosures holding sheep and cattle. Once over the summit of Broad Down, with views into the central moor it felt wilder but maybe not wilderness. Waterfall seemed too beautiful and visited by too many people. Beyond Sandy Hole Pass the land felt wilder and ascending the boggy slope of Cut Hill was certainly wild country. On a fine summer's day, surrounded by remote hills, it definitely felt as if I was in wilderness and in winter conditions I'm sure would seem even wilder, if indeed one could get here at all.

Perceptions were however clouding my analysis. It felt as if I was in a wilderness but was I? This is not land untouched by people. I'd walked though a peat pass cut by man and there is another (Cut Lane) on the opposite side. Also on that side is a prehistoric stone row, discovered as recently as 2004. A small cairn, the stones placed by persons unknown, marks the hill's summit and the invasive line of red and white range poles runs up and across the hill. Can it be wilderness if people have left their mark?

A paper published in 2009 by Ralph Fyfe and Tom Greeves, *The date and context of a stone row: Cut Hill, Dartmoor, south-west England*, provides information on the Cut Hill stone row. It tells us that the row consists of nine granite slabs over a distance of 215 metres, aligned ENE/WSW, the orientation of most of Dartmoor's stone rows. The stones are recumbent, and the paper suggests that some or all of them may have been placed in this way rather than upright. The paper contains some very technical detail with regard to pollen analysis and variables but concludes that the row was probably placed here between 3200 and 3700BC and that it, *'seems irrefutable that this particular row is of fourth-millennium BC date – and hence Neolithic rather than early Bronze Age'*. Interestingly this conclusion is contrary to the commonly held believe that all Dartmoor's stone rows date from the Bronze Age.

The paper comments on the stone row's location, describing Cut Hill as, *'a very striking, massive and gently rounded hill'*, *'at the heart of upland, at the head of the watersheds of the East Dart and the River Tavy'*. It suggests that the choice location for the stone row seems significant but without an understanding of the purpose of the monument it is not apparent why Cut Hill was chosen. The paper goes on to say:

'The location of the monument on Cut Hill is remarkable in a modern sense, as it lies in the most remote and inaccessible location within the

West Dart meanders below Sandy Hole Pass

region. It should be remembered, though, that this sense of remoteness and inaccessibility is a modern cultural construct and almost certainly does not reflect the views or approach to the landscape held by earlier Neolithic groups.'

Five thousand years ago Dartmoor (if indeed one could have called it a moor then) would have been largely wooded, with patches of heath and bog. Pollen analysis shows that the Cut Hill stone row was placed on one such open heath. It is likely that the Neolithic and Bronze Age people would have walked on paths within the mainly wooded country, so it may not have appeared so remote then as we see it now.

So here we have evidence of a stone monument constructed on Cut Hill around 5,500 years ago. Human activity. The paper also refers to later activity, stating that four of the stones lie in within a 100-metre-wide strip where the peat has been totally removed, probably for charcoal production. So as well as some extremely interesting history, this academic paper confirms that Cut Hill, the most remote and perhaps wildest place on Dartmoor, has been affected by historical human activity. So can it be a wilderness?

On my way back I paused at Waterfall for a cake, enquiring of the man I'd seen fishing as to his fortune in the matter. He'd caught several brown trout, small he said, but his indication of about nine inches looked a good size for high up a Dartmoor stream. He'd dutifully returned them to the river as the property of the Duchy of Cornwall. The chap I'd met on his way down for supplies was sitting on a rock below the main falls on the opposite bank with his partner and two young girls. Conversation was difficult over the roaring water but we established that I had made it to my target hill, he had obtained supplies and his daughters had swum in the clear pool below the waterfall.

Usually on a sunny August day one sees a number of people at or around Waterfall but these were the only two groups I met and the only other walkers seen all day the five gentlemen on Cut Hill. Back at the visitor centre I was told that they hadn't sent anyone up to Waterfall today and only one couple yesterday, adding that foreign visitors are reluctant to walk far when they find there aren't signed trails on the moor as they are used to. For many however it is the lack of such trails and the challenge of navigating one's own route through the wilderness that help to make Dartmoor unique.

Chapter Forty-Three

RYDER'S HILL, GREAT MIS TOR, EAST MILL TOR & UGBOROUGH BEACON

Finally short accounts of four more walks into the moor with the specific objective to consider its wilderness properties.

On a fine May morning I walked to Ryder's Hill, the highest point on Southern Dartmoor and an ideal place from which to consider the moor's wilderness potential. Starting from Combestone Tor, I followed the route described in my father's book, passing Horn's Cross and around Holne Ridge, where I picked up the Sandy Way, one of Dartmoor's ancient tracks. Turning right at the head of the Mardle Valley I was now walking through what the book describes as, *'rather wild country'* as I ascended the gentle slope to the summit of Ryder's Hill. Two boundary stones and a trig point stand on the summit. Its shallow dome shape betrays the hill's height but it provides a magnificent 360-degree view across the moor. On one side was a

Ryder's Hill summit

panorama of Northern Dartmoor and on the other Naker's Hill, Aune Head Mires and the central southern basin.

John Bainbridge chose Aune Head when asked to write about a wild place that defines Dartmoor and in *Dartmoor News* describes the source of the River Avon (known as the Aune on Dartmoor) as a *'great mire'*, *'unspoilt'*, *'vast'* and *'untouched'*. Interestingly, writing in *Call of the Wild*, Bainbridge reveals, *'I was first tempted to write about the north moor but felt that the military had diminished its sense of wildness'*.

Looking into this wild and perhaps desolate expanse the only signs of human activity were the pools and china clay spoil heap of Red Lake 1½ miles distant across rough and miry ground, a herd of cows on Green Hill and the altered Bronze Age cairn on Eastern White Barrow. There were no trees, no houses and no people. Dad was right that this is wild country and surely it is wilderness.

I went back to Great Mis Tor on a wild and windy summer's day. It was too windy to climb on the rocks but I returned to the military lookout, the objective of my walk being to decide whether what had seemed to be wilderness in winter would qualify in summer. The view was the same, just greener. Cows added the only additional evidence of human's use of the land but this time there were no red flags or men in lookout huts. The valleys, plains and tors of central Northern Dartmoor seemed less barren and not quite as foreboding in their summer green but I had no doubt that it was still wild. It still felt like a wilderness but perhaps one notch down on the scale compared to winter. But this was based purely on my view of the aesthetics. I was allowing my perception of wildness to cloud judgement. If it met the definition of wilderness in winter it still met it in summer. Seasons and weather are not a factor.

Whilst the likes of Cut Hill and Crane Hill may appear as wilderness, in order for Dartmoor to qualify these most remote areas need to be part of a wilderness area of significant size. Having already decided that Rowtor doesn't qualify I set out once again from Okehampton Camp, this time walking south with the objective to determine where any wilderness might start. On a late November day, for which the forecast had been dry, but in which I encountered rain, mist, sun and wind, sometimes all at the same time, the moor looked wild from the start. The summits of Yes Tor and High Willhays never emerged from the cloud and as I passed Rowtor the rocks of East Mill Tor were shrouded in mist. It lifted as I crossed New Bridge over the Black-a-ven Brook and on ascending the tor I was rewarded with one of Dartmoor's incredibly atmospheric views.

It wasn't the panoramic view of Central Dartmoor that I'd hoped for but a constantly changing vista of mist, moor and clouds. Tors and hilltops popped in and out of the mist, one moment with winter colours highlighted in sunshine and a minute later dark under foreboding clouds. It was enchanting, captivating, wild Dartmoor.

On the east side was Oke Tor and beyond it, sometimes visible but always with its head in the cloud, Cosdon Beacon. Steeperton Tor with its distinctive military hut stood out as it does from so many angles and just beyond it was Wild Tor, which I shall forever associate with the heart attack walk. Hangingstone Hill rarely revealed its summit but for a moment a ray of sunlight illuminated the military track that ascends the hill. It looked like a stream but I knew it to be a man-made blot on the moor. To the west Yes Tor and High Willhays remained in cloud but the lower Dinger Tor, which I remember walking past on my way to Cranmere Pool with my father in 1969, could be seen intermittently. Ahead was Okement Hill, also with a military road ascending it, and beneath the mist Dartmoor's wild central northern basin. In better weather I would have walked on further but cold

East Mill Tor

after half an hour in the wind enjoying this Dartmoor spectacle and with the cloud level falling, it seemed sensible to turn back. In any case my objective had been met – surely this was wilderness. Or was it?

I was some way beyond the last private car parked beside the military roads and the tor felt remote and distinctly wild. Just one factor provided doubt and much doubt at that. Military activity. There is an observation post on the tor, I'd found a field telephone point here and all around were their tracks and roads. East Mill Tor seems a reasonable point to mark the wilderness boundary but unless we are to discount the military's activities can there be any wilderness at all?

Finally, to consider the view from a hill on the edge of the moor I repeated the route of another childhood walk, taking the bus to Bittaford, crossing the Lud Brook, following Butterdon Hill Stone Row and returning past

Spurrell's Cross

Spurrell's Cross, then over Ugborough Beacon. As I sat on the beacon surveying the moor in her brown winter colours I looked for signs of human activity. Cairns on some of the hilltops and a reave running down Three Barrows dated from Bronze Age, tin workings in the Glaze Brook Valley from medieval times, while the Redlake tramway closed in 1933. That was all I could see as direct signs that humans had used the moor. Of course there is other evidence; the trees having been felled and the cattle, sheep and ponies whose grazing stop the growth of scrub and trees but does this mean that Dartmoor is no longer a wilderness? This it seems is going to be a key question.

There was one more walk which I wanted to do but was thwarted by a combination of weather, military firing and problems with my hip. Each of the squares covered in John Hayward's *Dartmoor 365* features a place or item of interest - bar one - *'The Wilderness Square'*. Situated on the southern end of Amicombe Hill, between the Amicombe and Rattle Brooks, even Dartefacts with its 17,704 items has failed to find anything of interest in the Wilderness Square. But that is the interest – it's a wilderness. Or is it? The massive Amicombe Hill is about as wild and featureless a place as one can find on Dartmoor. The ground is wet, rough and as I have found on previous excursions, doesn't make for pleasant walking. It lies within the frequently used Willsworthy Firing Range but whilst there is military paraphernalia at the northern end, the Wilderness Square is spared this intrusion. Again questions arise. How far from obvious human activity does somewhere have to be to qualify as wilderness and does just limited grazing and historic removal of trees count as natural and little-used? However, if anywhere on Dartmoor is wilderness then this wild area of the northern moor is part of it.

PART 15

WILDERNESS

This final section discusses wilderness, what I have seen and what others have said, and the big questions – is Dartmoor a wilderness and if so is it England's last?

First however a quick word on the subject of cows. You will have gathered that to put it mildly, I am not particularly happy in their company. Around five people are killed by cows each year in the UK, three quarters of whom are farm workers and of the walkers most had dogs with them. The chances of being killed when walking on Dartmoor, without a dog and avoiding cows with calves, is very slim, although walkers do sometimes get seriously injured.

Just before completing this book I had an experience which put cows in a different light. On a wet and windy day I walked from Hexworthy, along the River Swincombe to John Bishop's House, another abandoned Dartmoor dwelling. Coming back, as I crossed the footbridge I saw a man walking down the track, carrying what appeared to be a large black dog, with a cow following and a Land Rover behind. I caught them up by Gobbet Mine just as they stopped, laying the 'dog' on the grass. It was however not a dog they told me but a calf that had been born on the moor overnight. In such conditions it would not have survived and they were taking it to their dry barn at Sherberton Farm. The creature looked lifeless but moved a little as the mother (Caroline was her name) licked it. She mooed, calling to her herd down the track (boasting about her baby the farmer said) and they slowly wandered over to take a look, sniffing and licking the calf themselves. For me this was a new insight into bovine behaviour – kind, gentle and loving – not adjectives that I'd associated with cows. I felt privileged to have witnessed this little episode of Dartmoor life.

Having said hello to the new arrival the herd returned to the track, gathering just where I was about to walk. Not to worry the farmer said, as long as I didn't have a dog and they didn't have calves, I could walk right through them. And so I did, the cows moving just a little so I could get by, although only inches from their heads. I know that cows can be gentle and usually won't harm walkers but the difficulty is knowing which ones might.

Fox Tor

Chapter Forty-Four

REWILDING

It's easy to conflate rewilding, wild and wilderness, so I will consider the first of these, another of Dartmoor's controversies, in its own chapter.

Rewilding is already happening. Reduced numbers of grazing livestock is allowing more vegetation to grow, with broadleaf woods starting to extend and is leading to the spread of Molinia grass, which as the conservationist, rural social scientist and author Adrian Colston writes (*adriancolston.wordpress.com*), is a matter for concern:

> *'The spread of Molinia concerns farmers as this grass is relatively unpalatable to stock and it is of concern to conservationists as the 'rafia' fields of the grass produce monotonous species-poor landscapes which suppress other moorland species such as heather.'*

As long ago as 2004, in their annual report the Dartmoor Livestock Protection Society expressed concern about Holne Moor becoming overgrown with scrub as a result of reduced animal numbers, describing the land as, '*of little benefit to sheep or cattle and impenetrable to walkers*'.

Hence in some places rewilding by reduced grazing is contributing to more varied and biodiverse habitats but in others it is harming the natural diversity of the moor, as well as making the land more difficult for farmers and walkers.

Over centuries some of Dartmoor's peat bogs have been damaged by draining, overgrazing, fires (deliberate or 'wild'), removal of peat for fuel, erosion and now climate change. Opinions vary as to the extent but as I saw on the summit of Cut Hill, there are places where much of the peat has disappeared or dried out. This results in release of trapped carbon and potentially more flooding downstream as the land loses its ability to hold water. Work is being undertaken to restore the peatlands by blocking eroded channels and gullies, so that water is released more slowly. Is this rewilding? It is returning parts of the moor to their state of a few hundred years ago but not as it was before people felled the trees.

Moor Trees, a charity dedicated to restoring native woodland on Dartmoor, have a vision to create a *'wilder Dartmoor'* with restored broadleaf woodland, upland heath, blanket bog, mires and meadows. There would be woodland along the valleys, spreading up the hills, before giving way to scrub, then grass and heather on the tors. Grazing would be essential to limit growth of trees and scrub, allowing some grassland to remain, so livestock, particularly cattle and deer would play an important part in creating and maintaining this new Dartmoor. Species such as wild boar, beavers and even wild cats would

be reintroduced. (The controlled reintroduction of pine martins, who were hunted to extinction on Dartmoor in the 1880s, is already being considered for the Teign Valley.) Eagles, cranes and red squirrels would return to the moor, which would be a more biodiverse environment than the current grazed moorland, although of course significant areas of the National Park are already wooded. Perhaps a first step would be to replace the conifer plantations with native broadleaf trees.

Moor Trees are proposing what may be a more managed but more diverse Dartmoor, however whether this would be wilder is a matter of opinion. Whilst closer to the Dartmoor that existed before people arrived to change

Looking to Crow Tor from the edge of Wistman's Wood – an expanding woodland

it, the environment would be created by human intervention to manage nature. It would still be a wonderful place but we would lose much of the wild open moorland that for many is the very essence of Dartmoor. With human management could this rewilded moor be a wilderness?

Perhaps rewilding could be taken further and the moor left entirely to nature. As illustrated by the enclosure on the West Okement, if grazing animals are excluded trees and scrub will take over the lower parts of the moor. Even this however would require management. The increasing number of deer would need to be removed and perhaps the rabbits which the Normans and possibly the Romans before them brought to Britain. Predators could be reintroduced – lynx, wolves and maybe even bears, allowing Dartmoor to return to its pre-Bronze Age environment. This could be an inhospitable environment for people and a true wilderness but would be hard to achieve in isolation. There would still be conflict with the demands of people who visit, live and work on Dartmoor and perhaps the only way it could be truly wild is if people moved out, a big fence encircled the moor and nature, with its reintroduced predators, was left to it.

Writing in *Dartmoor Magazine,* farmer and author of *The Complete Bullocks*, Anton Coaker (who I later found out was the farmer I'd met at Gobbet Mine with Caroline the cow), provides some forthright views on rewilding:

> '*Apparently once released from the burden of human interference, whole landscapes will blossom into some kind of pre-industrialised Nirvana.*' '*The presence of tens of millions of people – all their cars, houses, supermarkets, concrete and tarmac – will fade away into the hazy distance.*'

Clearly he is a little cynical but makes the very valid point that rewilding in isolation will have limited benefit.

He talks about, '*the fixation on planting trees*' and that these are not the productive ones which would reduce our imports of timber but '*natural*' woodlands. Species reintroduction is described as, '*the fantasy that what Dartmoor is missing is its long-extinct animals*', with the question raised as to what lynx will eat once all the sheep are gone (household pets he suggests is what has been found elsewhere).

He writes of, '*purists evangelising on their crusade*' and the article ends, '*And I wouldn't care one jot ... until they come along and tell me how to farm my sheep, or that my cows' burps – which, like the cows themselves, are made of grass and rainwater – are somehow responsible for global warming*'.

Whilst some of his science is questionable there is certainly merit in some of Coaker's arguments and they illustrate the conflict that occurs between farmers and rewilders. Is the answer simply to subsidise farmers to change the way their land is managed, ending a way of life that has continued for generations but facilitating biodiversity and carbon capture?

Back in 2001 Paul Rendell, editor of *Dartmoor News*, considered the potential impact of reduced grazing which was thought to be a likely impact of the Foot and Mouth outbreak that had recently hit the UK.

'The Dartmoor landscape is man made, it is looked after by farmers and it is this landscape that visitors come to Dartmoor to see but this is about to change.'

He gives the example of Roborough Down where after fewer animals were let out to graze in the 1970s and vegetation was not managed, '*trees, gorse, bramble and bracken took over and it started to become no use to commoners or visitors*'.

Whilst farmers continued to graze stock on the moor after Foot and Mouth, other managing factors have intervened. In order to encourage new growth (rewilding?) Natural England reduced the numbers of livestock permitted to graze and there are considerably fewer animals than thirty years ago and far fewer than a century ago. At the start of the 1900s around 55,000 ponies grazed on Dartmoor but this had dropped to about 2,500 at the turn of the 21st century. When in 2023 Natural England proposed a further reduction in livestock numbers the outcry from farmers, landowners and those concerned that historic remains will become overgrown resulted in a government review – the *Independent Review of Protected Site Management on Dartmoor*.

The Dartmoor Society's September 2023 newsletter considers the issue, with articles from its editor Annabel Crowly and Dr Tom Greeves.

Wild / overgrown enclosure on West Okement

Greeves, correctly in my view, dismisses the views of former environmental Advisor to the Government Ben Goldsmith that Dartmoor is, *'grazed to death'*, *'utterly desolate, barren, sheep-wrecked, and largely devoid of wildflowers, birdsong or much wildlife at all'*. Those of us who walk on the moor know that every one of these claims is wrong. Greeves describes as, *'outrageously inaccurate'* statements in a *Guardian* article that Dartmoor's peat bogs are in a *'terrible state'*, *'mostly due to increased grazing'*, *'animals on the land stripping vegetation from the peat bogs'*. As Tom Greeves says, *'these are the least grazed of all vegetation types on Dartmoor'*.

Annabel Crowley asks if it is possible to reconcile the wide range of views on the management of Dartmoor, suggesting that a mosaic of habitats may be the ideal; *'some long vegetation, some grazed tight, some trees, some scrub, some water, some dry heath, some valley mire etc'*. As I thought as I read her article and she goes on to say, *'This sounds as if it could be a description of Dartmoor'*.

Dartmoor has never been a static landscape. It has been altered and maintained by human management and even if the most ambitious rewilders have their way, it will continue to be so, raising questions as to its wilderness characteristics. As humans change the planet's climate and pollute its air, more management is required even to maintain the status quo. Warming climate and nitrogen deposition from airborne pollution are thought to be stimulating growth of gorse, bracken and Molinia grass, stifling diversity of flora and fauna and altering Dartmoor's aesthetics and accessibility. Managed grazing can help to counter this but Natural England propose less, including a complete removal of livestock in winter.

As we face a climate emergency it is natural to want more trees but this is not necessarily always beneficial. The Woodland Trust are undertaking research in Wensleydale to determine whether the carbon captured by trees exceeds that released by the accelerated weathering to the limestone bedrock which their removal causes. Peat is more effective at carbon sequestration than trees and further research by the Woodland Trust will ensure that trees are not planted where the carbon they capture is less than that released from the ground.

In his submission to the Independent Review former Dartmoor Society Chair Alan Endacott states:

> *'In any case, peat is ten times more effective at carbon sequestration than trees so an active peat forming vegetation would have far greater environmental value than forest in this case and, from my personal observational experience, managed grazing and occasional swaling is an essential part of this.'*

It seems that on High Dartmoor controlled grazing and occasional swaling to encourage peat-forming vegetation would have greater environmental value than forest. A landscape that for millennia has held carbon and soaked up water would not seem to be a priority for planting trees when far greater environmental benefit can be gained elsewhere.

The Independent Review's report in December 2023 was generally received positively. Key amongst the forty-one recommendations were to, *'improve hydrological function and re-wet blanket bogs and peatlands*' and '*to control Molinia, using a combination of active management practices, including grazing*'. Both are essential to prevent deterioration of the moor and demonstrate that Dartmoor is indeed a managed environment.

At first glance rewilding sounds a great idea. Then one might need to consider that Dartmoor is already wild (or is it?). What are the reasons for changing it? Are the benefits really as claimed? Who will be affected by proposed changes to the landscape? What is the impact on historical sites? Many people have their views on future management of Dartmoor, most of which have some validity, some conflicting but with considerable overlap. Very careful consideration must be given to how the moor is to be managed for the benefit of all. Compromises and variety are required but 'rewilding' should not be allowed to prevail by stealth.

Chapter Forty-Five

WILDERNESS?

Back in Chapter Four we looked at the various definitions and after walks exploring the moor now it is time to consider whether Dartmoor really is, *'England's Last Wilderness'*.

First we can deal with the supplementary question; is only part of Dartmoor wilderness? This would seem straightforward. The National Park contains villages, farmland and woods that clearly don't meet the definition, so not all of Dartmoor can be considered wilderness.

In *Escape to Dartmoor* Michael Hedges agrees that the Dartmoor land used for agriculture and settlements is not wilderness but also considers that the open moor close to roads, such as around Haytor, Bellever and Kings Tor, does not have special wilderness characteristics.

Hedges suggests that once the areas enclosed for agriculture and the various settlements around the moor are excluded, only two areas of wilderness remain; the centres of the north and south of the moor. He estimates that the 'northern wilderness' occupies about 77 square miles and the southern about 49, so together they cover only around a third of the National Park's 368 square miles.

It would be useful to consider some more words that others have written.

On his website *www.rickkni.co.uk* (Dartmoor Walks) Richard Knight says:

> *'Dartmoor is one of the few real wildernesses left in England. Although it is not mountainous, the exposed moorland is primeval, bleak and remarkably free from human interference - although many have tried to tame it.'*

Brian Carter and Brian Skilton also include the designation in their book *Dartmoor The Threatened Wilderness*, their reference to *'England's last great wilderness'* adding an adjective that raises a further question. Are there other wildernesses in England but Dartmoor is the last 'great' one?

Writing in a *Dartmoor News* article celebrating fifty years of National Park status, Kate Ashbrook is another who describes the moor as wilderness:

'Dartmoor is still wild and free, I can still refresh my spirit among its silent hills.' 'Of course, the military have done their best to destroy the wilderness, with their roads, look-out huts, flagpoles and shellholes, and it is outrageous that they are still allowed to batter wild Dartmoor with live firing'. 'But we have seen off reservoir schemes and china clay expansion'. 'Even when I cannot be on Dartmoor, knowing it is there means a huge amount to me. May Dartmoor be forever a true wilderness.'

Author and former editor of *The Countryman* Crispin Gill includes in his book *Dartmoor* a chapter headed *'The Northern Wilderness'* and writes that, *'Dartmoor is not just the last wilderness in southern England, it is a territory that has only been lightly inhabited at any time in history'*.

Max Piper starts his introduction to *East Dartmoor's Lesser-Known Tors and Rocks*:

'Dartmoor is sometimes described as southern England's last great wilderness due to its seemingly endless hilly moorland terrain, remoteness, notorious mires and impressive tors, but in truth the land we all know and love today has been lived on and exploited for millennia and the landscape we see is far from natural.'

Adrian Colston is another who does not class Dartmoor as wilderness, writing in a blog on his website:

'Mention the word 'wild' or any of its derivatives in connection with Dartmoor and conflict and argument will swiftly follow. An oft – used phrase 'Dartmoor – the last Wilderness' is such an example as the farming

community will quickly remind you that Dartmoor is not a wilderness or wild – it is in fact a man created landscape.'

Dr Tom Greeves, perhaps the foremost expert on Dartmoor archaeology, commented when I told him the theme of my book:

'In my opinion, and that of many others, Dartmoor is definitely not 'the last wilderness'. I believe it to be one of the most vital human landscapes on earth.'

Writers are divided, some considering parts of Dartmoor to be wilderness, whilst others say that the activities of humans preclude it.

In his excellent BBC documentary *Wilderness* Simon Reeve ignored Dartmoor, instead choosing to visit the Congo Rainforest, Patagonia, Indonesia's Ocean's Coral Triangle and the Kalahari. Whilst all of these are undoubtedly wild and few would question their wilderness designation, they are all to an extent used and impacted by humans. When visiting Patagonia, Reeve gave us another definition, saying: *'Wild cats roaming free. This surely is the absolute definition of a real wilderness'*. So all we need to do to confirm Dartmoor as wilderness is find proof of the regular 'sightings' of big cats, then maybe the next series could feature Fur Tor or Crane Hill.

It would seem a good time to remind ourselves of our own definition:

A wilderness is an area that is natural, uncultivated, undeveloped, little used or modified by human activity, and uninhabited or sparsely populated. It is commonly considered to be wild, remote, untamed and of significant size.

There are nine key points to discuss and in doing so it may be necessary to consider in more detail the meaning of some of the definition's words. I shall start with the easiest.

- Uninhabited or Sparsely Populated
  In his documentary Simon Reeve set out to meet people who lived in the wilderness areas, mostly in commune with nature, telling viewers:

'Humans are actually an integral part of many remote areas.'

and

'Wildernesses are full of life and often people too.'

Whilst these comments may seem to go against the common definitions, the wildernesses he visited were vast and in comparison to their size the populations sparse, so there seems no need to consider modifying our definition.

Dartmoor National Park contains a number of towns, villages and smaller settlements and has a population of around 34,500. Dartmoor itself is therefore far from uninhabited but most of these settlements are around the edge or in the less rugged north-east corner of the moor. Other than Princetown and Widecombe there are no settlements of more than a few houses close to the middle of the National Park. Isolated houses and farms are found on or just off the roads but beyond these no one lives in the central areas of the north and south moor. People lived here in prehistoric times and more recently in remote farms and warrens, or temporarily while working on the moor, but whilst the remains of homes can still be seen, they are all empty now. In the potential 'wilderness area' away from roads only Nun's Cross Farm and Ditsworthy Warren are still habitable and neither are permanently occupied.

The wild areas of north and south Dartmoor are therefore not sparsely populated, they are uninhabited. Unlike parts of the definition, this clause clearly refers to the present, leaving no doubt that the criterion is met.

- Size
  This was a property which I was unsure about including in the definition but felt that on balance the research and common sense suggested that it is unlikely that a wilderness can be tiny and hence must be of significant size.

At 368 square miles Dartmoor is the seventh largest of England's ten National Parks. It is more than twice the area of the Isle of Wight, a third the size of Luxembourg but comprises only 14% of Devon. At roughly 20 miles north to south and east to west, it can be crossed in a day by a fit walker, although given the nature of the ground most prefer to stop overnight.

It would seem reasonable to say that Dartmoor is of significant size but large, huge or vast are more subjective and require a comparative point of reference.

Dartmoor is tiny in comparison to the world's greatest wildernesses such as the Australian deserts, the Amazon Rainforest, Alaskan tundra and Siberian forests, which can all truly be described as vast. Wildernesses in Europe are however more in the order of magnitude of Dartmoor. The Białowieża Forest, a World Heritage Site, on the border between Poland and Belarus, covers 547 square miles. The twelve areas designated as wilderness in Northern Lapland total 5,791 square miles, an average of 483 square miles. We have however established that the majority of Dartmoor is not wilderness but are its wild central areas large enough to qualify?

In *A Working Definition of European Wilderness and Wild Areas (2013)* the foundation Wild Europe, considers size and states:

'A minimum of 3,000 hectares is recommended for labelling any new core area as 'wilderness.'

'A minimum of 10,000 hectares for core wilderness areas is however recommended as an objective wherever feasible, particularly where larger areas are needed for effective functioning of natural processes.'

3,000 hectares is 11.6 square miles and 10,000 hectares is 38.6 square miles.

The US Wilderness Act minimum threshold is of 5,000 acres (2,023 hectares), equating to 7.8 square miles.

We have seen that Michael Hedges' analysis concluded that Dartmoor's northern wilderness occupies about 77 square miles and its southern wilderness about 49 square miles.

I have made my own rough analysis of potential wilderness area, using John Hayward's *Dartmoor 365* map, counting squares where there is no made up road, no large reservoirs, no conifer plantations and no significant building or intact enclosures. Tracks, including military, did not negate a square unless they are tarmacked, nor did ruined houses, huts, tinning or other industrial relics, prehistoric remains and crosses but intact buildings such as Nun's Cross Farm and Ditsworthy Warren barred a square from counting as wilderness. It is an arbitrary selection and could be argued that I have permitted too many signs of human activity but this is a starting point to determine the area that might be wilderness.

I came up with a total of 51 square miles in the north and 26 in the south.

A further estimate based on the centre of the square being at least a mile from one of these negating factors gave 30 and 15 square miles.

Obviously the potential wilderness area varies according to the criteria by which it is measured and by taking only whole mile squares my estimate was likely to be lower than Hedges'. He suggested a total of 126 square miles, whilst my estimate was 77 square miles, or 45 working on a mile from any of the negating factors.

My walks determined that the 'Northern Wilderness' could stretch from Great Mis Tor to East Mill Tor. That's a distance of 8½ miles. East to west it might be from Watern Tor to Brat Tor – 5½ miles. This rather rough approximation would give an area of 47 square miles. The south could perhaps be Ter Hill to Three Barrows (5 miles) and Eylesbarrow to Ryder's Hill (4 miles), giving an area of 20 square miles, a total of 67 by this very rough method.

With four estimates by different methods varying from 45 to 126 square miles (average 79), it would seem reasonable to conclude that the wild central areas of Dartmoor are large enough to be designated as wilderness.

- Remote
Martin Hawes in the *International Journal of Wilderness* writes:

> '*But remoteness is not an explicit requirement of the US Wilderness Act, and it is not clearly implied by the definitions of wilderness adopted by the IUCN and the European Commission (EC). Each of these definitions characterizes wilderness areas as large, natural, and free of permanent settlements.*'

Incidentally, the magazine's own publicity raises an interesting question – '*The International Journal of Wilderness is the tool of choice for wilderness managers and advocates*', but if somewhere is managed can it be wilderness?

In an article headed, '*Why Wilderness Should be Remote*', Hawes makes some interesting points. He notes that wilderness has often been defined as remote or in terms that imply remoteness but that it is not a criteria included in the definitions from wilderness related originations. It wasn't mentioned in my dictionary definitions but '*remote / isolated / far from civilisation*' were amongst the most common words put forward by my fifty-one respondents. We must therefore give it consideration in relation to Dartmoor.

Hawes' article generally concerns larger areas of wilderness, Tasmania in particular and considers the impact on remoteness of building tourist lodges, overnight huts and helipads, all of which he says reduce wilderness value. The huts, which would be staffed and serviced by helicopter, he says would affect two components of wilderness character:

> '*Apparent Naturalness, which is a measure of remoteness from artifacts such as roads, dams, and buildings; and Remoteness from Settlement. The development would rank as a "settlement" because it would be continuously occupied for much of the year.*'

Equivalents on Dartmoor might be military installations, dams and communication masts. Each instance reduces the remoteness and wilderness value of the surrounding moor. I have already commented that the military roads on Dartmoor significantly impact on the wilderness characteristic of a large area of the northern moor. Each reservoir has had a similar effect and had Swincombe been built it may have negated the whole moor's claim to be a wilderness. These are however not settlements so according to Hawes would impact on *'apparent naturalness'* but not *'remoteness from settlement'*. Others though may consider that such intrusions, even if not occupied by people, do impact on remoteness.

Most dictionary definitions of remote are quite simple; *'far away'* or *'distant'*. Dictionary.com helpfully adds a second definition; *'far from any centre of population, society, or civilisation; out-of-the-way'*. This would seem adequate for our purposes except for one crucial omission – how far is far? Dartmoor as a whole is not remote but our question needs to be, are parts of it remote?

Some years ago my brother took a geography field trip to a farm near Two Bridges. A small charge for such visits was one way the farmer supplemented his income. Sheep paid the rent, mending neighbours' fences covered food and essentials, while presents and 'luxuries' came from student groups and campers. My brother suggested he was, *'out of the way up there'*. The farmer was dismissive – *'Tavistock is just down the road'*. It's nine miles but his perception was that the farm wasn't remote.

Cut Hill is often quoted as the most remote point in Southern England and remote is frequently used in descriptions of central Dartmoor. It is relative. Four miles from a road is considered remote in England but not necessarily in the Amazon Rainforest or Australian Outback. Fur Tor is well known as being Dartmoor's remotest tor. It is not remote from all human activity but in terms of England it's a long way from a road or house.

With no clear definition we cannot say for certain whether parts of

Dartmoor qualify as remote, but in terms of common usage of the word, certainly in reference to England, it would seem reasonable to say that the central areas of the moor are remote.

- Wild

  There is a difference between 'wild' and 'wilderness'. In simple terms, a wilderness has to be wild but a wild place is not necessarily a wilderness. Wilderness can be a place and hence a noun but it is also descriptive. Wild is more often used as an adjective. It is employed in many contexts and refers to something that is untamed or uncontrolled, including animals, plants, weather, fire and even people.

  In relation to place dictionary definitions tend to be similar to those for wilderness: *'uncultivated, uninhabited, desolate, natural'*.

  There is little doubt that Dartmoor is somewhere that people come to experience wild country. The adventure guide company *calltoadventure.co* lists thirteen *'truly wild'* places to visit in the UK and starts with Ducks' Pool (although illustrated with a photo of a Dartmoor tor that is clearly some way from the 'pool'). The travel blog *findingouradventure.com* calls Dartmoor, *'a wild and rugged environment'*. The National Parks UK website heads its Dartmoor section:

  > *'A Land of Contrasts : Wild, open moorlands and deep river valleys, with a rich history and rare wildlife, striking tors and swathes of heather, Dartmoor will touch your soul.'*

  Although definitions are similar the bar to qualify as wild seems lower than for wilderness. Whilst the purist may argue that Dartmoor has been modified by humans to an extent that it is not wild, the description is used so commonly that most people would consider parts of Dartmoor to be wild.

- Uncultivated

  Whilst there are places within the National Park that are cultivated, the central 'wilderness areas' are not. Historically there was some cultivation on the moor, for example at the Hound Tor Medieval Village, but changes

in climate made this prohibitively difficult. More recent attempts to cultivate significant areas were generally unsuccessful, due to the climate and soil quality. The closest to cultivation in potential wilderness areas is probably enclosures around former farms and warrens, where potatoes in particular were grown, although this was never easy. However, as can be seen for example at Huntington Warren, cultivation has altered these small areas of moor. It is probably safe to say that with the exception of very small areas, most of which are outside the central cores, the 'wilderness' is uncultivated and that any cultivation that did take place in a limited way was historic.

- Undeveloped

  A *Ministry of Housing Communities & Local Government* report in 2018 stated that 91.5% of land in England was *'non-developed'*. The Government's *'Land Use Statistics'* in 2022 stated that 91.1% was non-developed and that, *'the top 3 land use groups were 'Agriculture' (63.1%), 'Forestry, open land and water' (20.1%), and 'Residential gardens' (4.9%)'*. Developed land was considered to be only that which had been built on.

Other definitions vary slightly but generally undeveloped land is considered to be land on which there are no buildings or roads. At first sight it would therefore seem that Dartmoor's 'wilderness areas' are undeveloped but what about the houses that used to be here? Did the likes of Brown's House, Grimspound, Huntingdon Warren, thousands of Bronze Age hut circles, quarrying and tinning activity mean that Dartmoor was once developed? If it was developed even to a limited extent but the historic buildings have been long abandoned can it be wilderness? Do the military roads prevent much of Northern Dartmoor from being a wilderness?

No buildings have ever been constructed on a very large percentage of the land in central Dartmoor but we cannot say that it has never been developed at all. It is a question of degree and of history.

When visiting the remote Indonesian wilderness of Raja Ampat, Simon Reeve looked at a project to breed and release zebra sharks, rebuilding the population decimated by fishing. The *'re-sharking'* he told viewers showed that *'wilderness can be restored'*. Does this mean that as nature takes back Dartmoor's old mine workings and settlements wilderness is returning?

- Untamed
Collins dictionary defines untamed as:

> *'An untamed area or place is in its original or natural state and has not been changed or affected by people.'*

Cambridge dictionary offers:

> *'Left in a natural or wild state.'*

The simple answer would therefore seem to be that Dartmoor is not untamed. The land has been altered by people, although the main changes are historic. Once again however we need to consider the relevance of removing trees thousands of years ago and digging for minerals a hundred plus years ago.

It however could be argued that whilst the central 'wilderness' areas of the moor have been altered by people, they are still rugged and wild. Like a 'wild' animal in a zoo, they have been affected by humans but are not tame. It could also be said that whilst humans have altered the moor it is still wild, so not untamed.

- Little Used or Modified by Human Activity
Dartmoor has not been left to nature. It is used by humans. The question is therefore can the degree of usage and modification be described as 'little'?

Looking only at the 'wilderness areas', there are probably three main categories of use:

1. Farming – Grazing of sheep, cattle and ponies.
2. Military – Training and exercises, including live firing.

3. Recreation – Walking, running, cycling, camping (wild / backpack camping), rock climbing, swimming, photography, fishing, bird watching, observing nature and organised events such as the Ten Tors. The list cannot be exclusive as the moor is used for many other activities – by artists, poets, writers, archaeologists, letterboxers, picnickers, geocachers, hunters (trail or illegal?) and kayakers to name a few more.

To help gauge the degree of use encountered on a typical walk I shall consider my visit to Cut Hill. I met a farmer with his dogs, saw sheep, cattle and ponies, two groups of campers (one of whom had been fishing) and a group of five walkers. I climbed stiles over walls and crossed bridges over a stream and leat. I walked through a peat pass cut for fox hunters and beside military range posts. Afterwards I read of archaeological investigations that have been undertaken on Cut Hill, of letterboxes on the summit and a geocache hidden by Cut Hill Stream.

Even this remotest part of Dartmoor is, or has been used but whether it is merely 'little used' is a matter for conjecture. It may be a matter of comparison. Compared to most of England (other possible wildernesses excluded) the central areas of Dartmoor are little used but there is still significant and varied use.

In some ways 'modified by human activity' is clearer. Much of the land has been modified by felling of trees, mainly in the Bronze Age era. Swaling, the use of fire to control vegetation, took place on Dartmoor 8,000 years ago and continues to this day. Numerous structures of various sizes have been built over thousands of years, although most are ruins, extensive earthworks of tinning and china clay extraction remain, signs of peat extraction can be seen, ancient tracks, tramways, leats, stone walls and tramways cross the moor. The course of rivers have been altered and huge amounts of stone worked, moved or taken from the moor. Human actions have directly caused the loss of wild creatures such as wolves, bears and wildcats, and indirectly through our use and changes to the land, of others including fish and insects.

Grazing of livestock continues, preventing the growth of trees. Modern rewilding and peat restoration projects can still be classed as modification by human activity, even if the aim is to get back to an environment as it was before people altered it. On a wider scale, man-made climate change is impacting on the moor, and will increasingly do so, as bogs and rivers dry and the frequency and intensity of storms increase.

As with 'undeveloped' it is a matter for debate whether activity that took place centuries ago is relevant in determining an area's wilderness characteristic but it is clear that human activity had and continues to have, considerable influence on the moor.

Several email respondents gave the word 'untouched'. It could be said that for somewhere to be untouched by humans no one has ever set foot on it. Clearly this is not the case for Dartmoor, or indeed almost anywhere in the world, so I assume they did not mean it literally. Unaltered or unmodified would probably be better words. It is however a word I found in notes written during one my walks:

'What from afar looks to be untouched wilderness shows many signs of human activity when viewed close up.'

- Natural

Finally natural. A first glance at most of Dartmoor suggests that it is natural. It is uncultivated, largely undeveloped and nature seems to prevail.

It is a word with many uses and definitions. In this context *dictionary. com* gives us:

'Existing in or formed by nature (opposed to artificial).'

Collins dictionary offers:

'Natural things exist or occur in nature and are not made or caused by people.'

Once again it is arguable. Whilst Dartmoor's landscape has been influenced by people it still consists of natural entities – grasses, flowers, trees and is inhabited by a host of insects, birds and other animals.

Having considered the criteria perhaps it will help make a decision if we turn it round the other way and ask what is it, if anything, that stops Dartmoor being a wilderness? Various factors could be considered marginal or arguable but the one that stands out is 'little used or modified by human activity'. There is no doubt that the moor has been and is still used and that it has been modified by human activity. Modification to the central 'wilderness' core has however been mostly historic – notably felling of trees, disturbance of the ground through mineral extraction and the construction, albeit in a limited way, of homes and monuments. Its use now for farming, military and recreation has on the whole maintained a longstanding status quo. Once again we come back to the key questions - does historical activity negate wilderness characteristics and can the activity and human modification of Dartmoor be classed as 'little'?

As we have seen, perception of wilderness varies considerably. Not only do our definitions vary but our understanding and experiences have huge influence. To someone who has never seen such country much of Dartmoor may seem to be wilderness but an Amazon explorer might find it tame. Many who visit Cut Hill and such remote parts of the moor consider them to be wilderness but to an expert archaeologist they are landscape heavily influenced by humans.

Black Elk (1863 – 1950), a holy man of the Oglala Lakota Native American people, who looked at it from the perspective of those brought up in what many consider to be wilderness, wrote:

> 'Only to the white man was nature a wilderness and only to him was the land 'infested' with 'wild' animals and 'savage' people. To us it was tame, Earth was bountiful and we were surrounded with the blessings of the Great Mystery.'

Maybe the same applies on Dartmoor. Do the people who live and work on the moor consider it less wild than those who merely visit?

Having looked at each aspect of the wilderness we can say that Dartmoor probably qualifies in terms of size, lack of cultivation and population. Natural, wild and untamed have similar but not identical meanings and are questionable, whilst there is little doubt that Dartmoor has been influenced by human activity, although the degree and historical nature may not preclude it from being wilderness. To complicate matters even more, is it necessary for something to meet all aspects of a definition in order to qualify?

Chapter Forty-Six

ENGLAND'S LAST WILDERNESS?

If Dartmoor, or at least parts of it, are a wilderness, we need to consider whether it is England's last. If only Dartmoor is to qualify as wilderness it would need to stand apart from the moors and mountains of our other National Parks and from other landscapes that may not be considered traditional 'wilderness' but may meet the criteria we have unearthed. These I shall consider first.

The grass and heather-covered heathlands of Dorset, Hampshire, Norfolk and Suffolk may not be traditional wilderness but meet most of the criteria. Dunwich Health on the Suffolk coast is a good example but perhaps too small to qualify. Breckland, in Norfolk and Suffolk is a much larger area of heath but much of it is grazed. The medieval word Breck however meant an area of heathland broken up for cultivation before being allowed to retreat back into wilderness.

Wilderness is not a word generally associated with coasts but the wildest cliffs of Northumberland or Cornwall could be considered, as could the salt marshes and mud flats of Essex, the shingle of Suffolk and the remote expanses of Lincolnshire sand. I have twice walked on The Broomway, an ancient and highly dangerous route across Maplin Sands to Foulness Island, and out on the mud a mile from land certainly has the feel of wilderness but once the tide comes in this is under the sea. If we are to count the seabed there must be countless areas of wilderness.

The remote sea walls of East Anglia have wilderness feel but they are managed and bounded by land that is cultivated or grazed. The National Trust describes Northey Island, a tidal island in the Blackwater Estuary, which is farmed and managed and on which there is just one house, as, *'The closest you'll get to true wilderness in Essex'*. I shall take this as confirmation that the county's salt marshes, whilst often remote and perhaps wild, are not wilderness.

Orford Ness, a remote ten-mile-long shingle spit in Suffolk, has strong wilderness claims but was used extensively for various top secret military activities, with many relics remaining. Only part of it is accessible to the public and this solely on paths that have been cleared of ordnance. As on Dartmoor, one is instructed not to touch anything that might be of military origin and blow you up. Part of the southern end of the spit is farmed but the northern end, closest to Aldeburgh, has fewer obvious signs of human activity. The fact it is considered unsafe for people to visit suggests that military relics, and potentially dangerous ones at that, remain on the shingle. Other than maybe size, the northern end of the shingle spit meets most of the definition's criteria but maybe not the requirement for little used, although much of the usage is historic.

Like Dartmoor, the Lake District, Peak District, North York Moors and the Cheviots are grazed, although there are wild places out of reach of all but the most adventurous sheep. The mountains of the Lake District are higher than Dartmoor but highly managed for farming and in order to accommodate the large numbers of people who wish to visit and climb them. They are less remote than central Dartmoor and generally considered to be less wild. The moors of North Yorkshire and particularly Northumberland are the areas of England most like Dartmoor but does Dartmoor stand apart?

The terrain on Edale Moor and Kinder Scout in the Peak District is similar to parts of Dartmoor, with bogs and peat hags. The contrast with the beautiful but gentler valleys was quite a surprise the first time I walked there, suddenly discovering this wild landscape after climbing a waterfall on what was then the route of the Pennine Way. It was an environment that reminded me very much of the centre of Northern Dartmoor and if Dartmoor is wilderness this wild landscape is too. The Pennine Way has since been diverted around the summit plateau of Kinder Scout, mainly to reduce peat erosion but also to encourage walkers to avoid this desolate environment, where there was no path and a compass was required to navigate through the peat hags.

William Atkins' book *The Moor – A Journey into the English Wilderness*, confirms Dartmoor as a wilderness, along with nine other areas of England, including Kinder Scout and the Northumberland moors. He explores the moor north of Otterburn Camp, which like parts of Northern Dartmoor is criss-crossed with military tracks and where the public are frequently barred from access.

Visit Northumberland describe the 400 square miles of Northumberland National Park as:

'one of England's finest landscapes.'

'steeped in culture and heritage spanning thousands of years.'

'remote and rugged beauty.'

'England's last great wilderness, populated by less than 2,000 people however, this living, working landscape has a vibrant community, with picture-perfect hamlets and villages to explore as well as the bustling gateway market towns of Wooler, Rothbury, Bellingham and Haltwhistle just outside the National Park's boundary.'

Few would disagree with the first three statements but the last is contentious. Have they walked to Cut Hill, Aune Head or Crane Hill to dismiss Dartmoor before claiming that Northumberland has England's last great wilderness? Does the *'living, working landscape'* not negate its wilderness characteristics?

I am quite willing to accept that parts of Northumberland's National Park are wilderness but if the same criteria are used, then so is Dartmoor. Neither are therefore 'England's Last Wilderness'.

The addition of *'great'* to Visit Northumberland's claim could mean that they accept there are other wildernesses in England but that theirs is the best. Carter and Skilton called Dartmoor *'England's last great wilderness'*. Let's call it a draw.

Finally to consider, is Dartmoor the last wilderness in Southern England? It is the only really wild moorland in the south but in order to accommodate

Dartmoor as a wilderness we may have to stretch the definition, so it is probably unfair not to do the same for other areas. I visited Orford Ness when writing *Suffolk Coast Walk* and considered it a wilderness then, so it would seem unfair to change my mind now.

It may not be England's last but a decision is going to have to be made - is Dartmoor a wilderness at all?

Chapter Forty-Seven

REFLECTIONS

My seemingly miscellaneous Dartmoor walks have ended up with three underlying themes; access, threats and wilderness. To these controversies I could perhaps add the differences of opinion as to aspects of the moor's history and the varying versions of some of its stories. Maybe I should also add to the themes, cows, safety and last of all, cakes!

One would think that access should not be an issue in a National Park. People should be able to walk anywhere but as we have seen, this is far from the case. Whilst one can walk freely on CRoW 'Access Land', in other parts of Dartmoor access is restricted by landowners or military usage. No one can visit Vixen Tor, the moor's highest granite stack unless they choose to trespass and large swathes of the northern moor are frequently closed for live firing. Even if one can walk on the moor, actually reaching it is often difficult. Public transport is limited, and car parking restricted, particularly on the southern moor where two key parking areas have been closed by landowners.

Access however goes beyond simply whether one can get to, or walk on Dartmoor. A balance has to be found between maintaining intrusive stone paths, hard tracks and military roads, that facilitate use of the moor for walkers and cyclists, and their impact on the moor's wildness. Dartmoor should not be wholly inaccessible to those less able to walk, or who use wheelchairs or trampers, and the Miles Without Stiles scheme is helping to open up the moor to all. It is hard to find ways to accommodate everyone but it is right that the centre of Dartmoor is allowed to remain wild and the moor does not become a 'theme park'.

Had it not been for the dedicated efforts of campaigners more of Dartmoor would have been lost to china clay extraction, conifer plantations, reservoirs and other developments. Each incursion into the moor reduces its size, wildness and hence the value of what remains, making it easier to justify further developments. There is no doubt that the DPA, led for many years by the indomitable Sylvia Sayer, along with other organisations and individuals, have saved Dartmoor. We would not be debating whether the moor is a wilderness but whether the remnants of this wonderful oasis could be a National Park at all.

Hopefully we have seen the last of threats to decimate the moor. Attitudes have changed and any attempt to flood or extract minerals from key areas of the National Park is likely to be rejected. There are however still threats, some on a smaller scale and others a result of mankind's activities worldwide.

To some rewilding is a threat, with reduced grazing changing generations of farming practice, increased vegetation covering prehistoric remains and new trees and shrubs altering the moor's appearance. To others however it represents humans putting right some of the damage they have caused, increasing biodiversity and helping to combat climate change.

As I wrote this book it became apparent that views as to whether Dartmoor is a wilderness are sharply divided.

I have already used quite a few quotes with opposing views. Hugh Farrer in *Wild and Free – Fifty Years of the National Park*, gives another example of how people see Dartmoor differently, writing of his first visit when he and a friend walked across the moor from Tavistock to Gidleigh. Asking his friend whether he would go again the response was, 'No. *It was just a barren desolate waste, a wilderness with nothing to see*'. Hugh disagreed:

> 'That land was unique. I had never seen anything like it before.' 'Beyond else I sensed an atmosphere, the strange alluring atmosphere of a place with a deep sense of history. I did not know it at the time but I had been hooked, and Dartmoor was calling me to return.'

E.J. Beer, writing in the *Torquay Natural History Society Transactions & Proceedings for the year 1949-50* gives us yet another word: '*Dartmoor is a jungle*', which he says means '*a wild. i.e. uncultivated place*'.

I have put off making up my mind on the wilderness question to the very last chapter but now I must come to a decision.

My forty-five walks took me to the remains of homes where people have lived on the open moor from prehistoric times to the 20th century. I saw a plethora of prehistoric sites, medieval crosses, relics of industrial activity and the railways and leats that supported them. I walked on footpaths, tracks and roads, crossed stiles, bridges and walls. Cows, sheep or ponies were seen on most walks and only once did I fail to see any people. Signs of land management by grazing, swaling and fencing were often visible. Military paraphernalia litters the northern moor. Only in Dartmoor's central cores was the result of human activity less obvious, but if one looked it was always present. When I walked searching for wilderness I often felt I'd discovered it but also found that even in the wildest, most remote places, humans have left their mark on the moor.

As Annabel Crowley wrote in *The Dartmoor Society Newsletter*:

> 'The moor has been occupied and worked by humans for thousands of years, in multiple ways;'

So how can it be wilderness?

It feels like wilderness and looks like wilderness. Many people who know the moor describe it as wilderness. How can I disagree with William Crossing, arguably the greatest writer, chronicler and authority on Dartmoor? But how can I disagree with the archaeologist and cultural environmentalist Tom Greeves, often considered to be the leading modern authority on Dartmoor, who is adamant that it is not wilderness? For every respected commentator who considers Dartmoor to be a wilderness there seems to be another who gives good reasons why it is not. Is it significant that only those who say it is not a wilderness tend to give justifications?

I could conclude that there is no right or wrong answer. The definition is not sufficiently clear to say yes or no. 'Little used or modified by human activity' is open to too much interpretation. Does historic or prehistoric activity count? Nowhere have I found a definition that says yes or no.

So how do I decide?

I considered Orford Ness to be a wilderness when writing *Suffolk Coast Walk* and have said that it would seem unfair to change my mind now. Is this significant? Before embarking on this book I had never considered exactly what comprises a wilderness but would have had my own subconscious perception of what I thought it was. Orford Ness seemed to me to be a wilderness, as did Kinder Scout, Rannoch Moor and the Flow Country in Scotland. All quite different but all wildernesses. I would have sat on Fox Tor and looked to Whiteworks, not doubting that it was wilderness in front of me, or on Fur Tor without a second thought as to whether it really was wilderness all around.

It is this perception that leads many to describe Dartmoor as wilderness. They are not looking for signs of human activity that may preclude it from meeting the definition – they just feel that to them it is a wilderness. The definition of a word is not only what the dictionary tells us, it is also in its usage. Dartmoor may struggle to meet all the criteria set down by dictionaries and others who have defined wilderness, including my own effort, but can it still be wilderness if that is what many people think it is?

I could end with a quote from Lady Syliva Sayer, a remarkable lady who did more than anyone to preserve the wildness of Dartmoor. These words were reproduced in *DPA News* shortly after her death in January 2000:

WILD COUNTRY OR WILDERNESS?

'I have noticed that very often when speaks of wild and natural landscape it is the signal for someone to get up and say there is no truly natural or virgin landscape left now in these islands, and that we preservationists must remember that even the remotest parts of Britain, even uncultivated Moorland, are in fact man-made, or the result of man's activities through the ages: and this is usually said in order to disarm opposition to some projected plan for exploitation or development of an upland area – usually, but not always, in a National Park. But I think we must get away from these arguments about whether our last remaining areas of uncultivated land do, or do not, look as they did before man evolved

from apes and started domesticating other animals and tilling the earth. For it simply does not matter now, and we should not waste time splitting verbal hairs.'

Lady Sayer is probably right that it doesn't really matter but I should not finish the book without reaching a conclusion.

Michelle Dibb in *Dartmoor into the Wilderness* gives possibly the best explanation that I've found:

'There is no true wilderness left in England any more. Man has left his footprint in most of our soils as he has settled and toiled over the centuries. Now most of England is covered by cities, roads or farmland – and even the stars are dulled by our lights.

A few places are left, however, where the formidable environment has prevented man from leaving such a significant imprint. Dartmoor is one of the places; a wilderness untamed harsh but beautiful and steeped in mystery and history.'

Technically Dartmoor is not a true wilderness. There has been and still is too much human interference. Even if we discount prehistoric and historic activity, the land is used, managed and the northern moor heavily impacted by the military. It is however as close as we have to wilderness in England and to many who walk on the moor, study, or write about it, the central areas of Dartmoor are a wilderness. If the likes of Crossing, Bainbridge, Ashbrook, Gill and of course my father agree that it is wilderness and this is a common usage of the word, who is to argue? Not me.

POSTSCRIPT

Just prior to publication I became aware of the following:

Vixen Tor
The conviction of Mary Alford, owner of Vixen Tor, for spreading farmyard manure and calcified seaweed to cultivate grass palatable for cattle, was quashed on appeal. Lord Justice Brooke and Mr Justice David Steel ruled that EU laws to protect flora and fauna were wrongly applied and that such activities to bring the land back into productivity are permissible and ordered her costs to be paid.

Grazing
In July 2024 the campaigning group Wild Justice announced that it was putting in process a legal challenge, *'calling for commoners (people who hold rights of grazing on common land) to be ordered to reduce stock on all Sites of Special Scientific Interest (SSSI) making up the SAC where grazing pressure is a problem (particularly from sheep in winter)', so that their habitats can recover.'*

Alan Endacott and Dr Tom Greeves wrote open letters to Wild Justice, urging them to reconsider:

As someone who regularly walks all over Dartmoor I am strongly inclined to agree with Endacott – *'Anybody who has known the Moor intimately over many decades will tell you that it is becoming overwhelmed with invasive molinia, western gorse and bracken, which are smothering all other species and making large areas virtually inaccessible'*.

And with Greeves – *'Indeed, there is absolutely no issue of current overgrazing on the Dartmoor commons. There was indeed historic grazing pressure on the Dartmoor Commons, especially in the 1970s and 1980s, but since the mid-1990s the demands of Natural England (formerly English Nature) for graziers to reduce stock numbers by up to 80% on certain commons has caused widespread* undergrazing, *leading to excessive growth of molinia (Purple Moorgrass) and gorse (both Western and European)'.*

One wonders whether those who glibly describe Dartmoor as 'sheep wrecked' have walked on the likes of Cut Hill, Crane Hill and Ter Hill.

Parking
It was announced in July 2024 that DNPA have secured a small parking area in a field near East Rook Gate, which will help facilitate access to the area of moor impacted by the closure of New Waste car park.

BIBLIOGRAPHY

The following books have all been helpful in providing or confirming information for this book:

A Book of Dartmoor	Sabine Baring-Gould
All the Tors	Emily Woodhouse
Along The Dart	Judy Chard
Crossing's Guide to Dartmoor	William Crossing
Dartmoor	Crispin Gill
Dartmoor (Collins rambler's guide)	Richard Sale
Dartmoor 365	John Hayward
Dartmoor Captured	Michael Hedges
Dartmoor Forest Farms	Elisabeth Stanbrook
Dartmoor into the Wilderness	Michelle Dibb
Dartmoor The Threatened Wilderness	Brian Carter & Brian Skilton
Dartmoor Themes – A Walkers Guide	J.H. Powell
Dartmoor Then and Now	F.H. Starkey
Dartmoor's Tors and Rocks	Ken Ringwood
Dartmoor Wilderness Walks	Simon Dell
Devon's Century of Change	Helen Harris
Eleven Minutes Late	Matthew Engel
Escape to Dartmoor	Michael Hedges
Follow the Leat	John Robins
Gems in a Granite Setting	William Crossing
Haytor Down	DNPA
High Dartmoor	Eric Hemery
Industrial Archaeology in Devon	W.E. Minchinton
Railways Round Dartmoor	Bernard Mills
Railway Tracks to Princetown	Colin Henry Bastin
St Leonard's Sheepstor	Church Guide
The Book of Trespass	Nick Hayes
The Compleat Trespasser	John Bainbridge
The Dartmoor Oak Copses : Observations and Speculations	I.G. Simmons

The Meldon Story	DPA
The Moor – A Journey into the English Wilderness	William Atkins
The Redlake Tramway and china clay works	E.A. Wade
The Romance of Dartmoor	Jeffrey W. Mallim
Thurlow's Dartmoor Companion	George Thurlow
Torquay Natural History Society Transactions & Proceedings for the year 1949-50	
Walking on Dartmoor	John Earle
Walking on Dartmoor's Ancient Tracks	Eric Hemery
Walking The Dartmoor Railroads	Eric Hemery
Walking The Dartmoor Waterways	Eric Hemery
Walks Around Haytor	DNPA
Walks Around Postbridge	DNPA
Walks on Dartmoor Paths and Trackways	Michael Caton
Wild and Free 50 Years of the Dartmoor National Park	DPA
When The Train Came to Town	Museum of Dartmoor Life

The following magazines have also been helpful:

Dartmoor News
Dartmoor Magazine
Dartmoor Matters (DPA)
Dartmoor Society Newsletter

Paul Rendell's *Dartmoor News*, with its mix of news snippets and more in-depth articles, has proved extremely useful and I have frequently quoted from it. I have subscribed to the magazine for some years but inherited from my father a full set of issues going back to 1993, which I much enjoyed reading from cover to cover.

I have also made use of various websites, most notably:

www.dartefacts.co.uk
www.dartmoorexplorations.co.uk
www.holidayindartmoor.co.uk
www.legendarydartmoor.co.uk
www.richkni.co.uk (Dartmoor Walks)
www.torsofdartmoor.co.uk

ALSO BY PETER CATON

Walks Discovering Lesser Known Dartmoor

A guide describing routes of 1½ to 10 miles, enabling walkers to discover the beauty, history and hidden places of Dartmoor, the wildest, most remote and arguably the most beautiful area in Southern England.

The walks will take you to antiquities dating from the Bronze Age and even earlier, to hidden waterfalls and gorges, abandoned remote dwellings, fascinating industrial archaeology, majestic tors and wonderful viewpoints.

For those who don't know Dartmoor they provide routes for interesting walks of varying length and difficulty. Whilst some of the points of interest will be familiar to those who know the moor well, the walks will take you to places that very few people visit, passing little-known artefacts with something new for almost everyone.

Produced in full colour with routes clearly marked on OS maps, the book includes comprehensive background information on the moor and the history, stories and legends of the many places visited on each walk.

Published by Matador (Troubador)

ALSO BY PETER CATON

50 WALKS ON THE ESSEX COAST
A walking guide covering the entire publicly accessible coast of Essex. Most of the walks have different options with lengths ranging from 2 – 15 miles, catering for both serious ramblers and those looking for just an afternoon stroll.

NO BOAT REQUIRED
EXPLORING TIDAL ISLANDS
Peter sets out to be the first person to visit all of the 43 tidal islands that can be walked to from the UK mainland. He explores islands that few know exist and even fewer have visited, and finds that our tidal islands are special places with many fascinating and amusing stories.

SUFFOLK COAST WALK
Peter explores all 162 miles of Suffolk's unique coastline, describing the route for fellow walkers, with an engaging narrative that tells of the beauty, history and wildlife of this mysterious and varied coast.

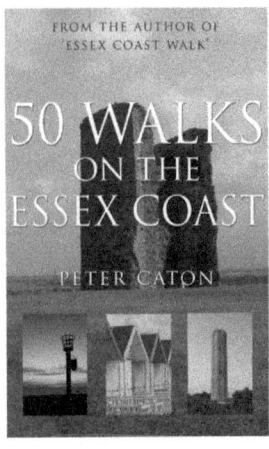

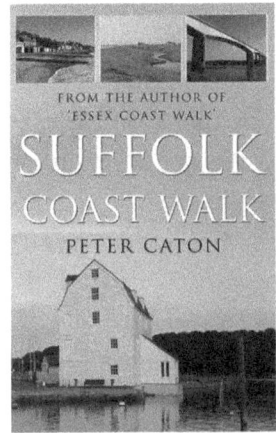

ESSEX COAST WALK

A narrative describing Peter's walk along arguably the longest coastline of any English county. With a wealth of information and gentle humour to match the coastline's gentle beauty, the book makes for easy reading.

REMOTE STATIONS

Combining a love of remote places and travelling on our more interesting trains, Peter visits forty of Britain's most lonely railway stations. Most are still in use but a few closed long ago, including two on the Princetown railway.

THE NEXT STATION STOP
FIFTY YEARS BY TRAIN

A 10,000 mile tour of Britain, discovering what it's like to travel on our modern railways and contemplating train journeys made over the last fifty years.

All published by Matador (Troubador).